Missiological Models in Ministry to Muslims

Sam Schlorff

Middle East Resources

Published by:

Middle East Resources
PO Box 96
Upper Darby, PA 19082

Telephone: (610) 352-2003

Rights for publishing this book in other languages belong to Middle East Resources. For further information please contact the publisher at the address above.

ISBN-10: 1-881085-04-X
ISBN-13: 978-1-881085-04-1

Cover Design: TJ Walsh

Edited and Produced by Perez Print Productions
Printed in the United States of America

Contents

Contents

Abbreviations

Journals, Publishers, Organizations, and Acronyms

BFBS: British and Foreign Bible Society

BT: Bible Translator

EMQ: Evangelical Missions Quarterly

IBMR: International Bulletin of Missionary Research

IMC: International Missionary Council

IRM: International Review of Missions

LCWE: Lausanne Committee for World Evangelization

MARC: Missions Advanced Research and Communication Center

MBB/MBBs: Muslim Background Believer(s)

MW: Moslem World/Muslim World

P & R.: Presbyterian & Reformed Publishing Co.

SCM: Student Christian Movement

SPCK: Society for the Promotion of Christian Knowledge

WEF: World Evangelical Fellowship

WCC: World Council of Churches

Languages and Other

Ar. Arabic

Eth. Ethiopic

Gr. Greek

Heb. Hebrew

Syr. Syriac

lit. literally

pl. plural

sg. singular

The Phonetic Transliteration of Arabic Letters/Sounds

(The same system is used for several Hebrew words cited, for sake of simplicity.)

We have used the simplified system of William Saal's *Reaching Muslims for Christ* (Chicago: Moody Press, 1991) for the transliteration of Arabic. It can be summarized as follows.

Sounds as in English: pronounce *b, d, f, j, h, k, l, m, n, s, t, w, y,* and *z,* and the short vowels *a, i,* and *u,* as in English.

Sounds represented by two English letters: pronounce *dh* as in *th*at, *th* as in *th*ink, *kh* as in A*ch*! (German), *sh* as in *sh*all, *gh* with a slight gargle sound as in the French *r,* and *DH* as will be explained next.

The Arabic Emphatics: *H, S, D, T,* and *DH* represent emphatic sounds for which there are no equivalents in English. *H* represents an aspirated *h.* For all practical purposes, the emphatics *S, D, T,* and *DH* may be pronounced like the normal *s, d, t,* and *dh*—with an emphasis if you can.

Various: The backward apostrophe ' (the semitic "ayn") represents a kind of gutteral grunt, the apostrophe ' (the "hamza") a simple glottal stop, and the *q*, for which again there is no English equivalent, a gutteral *k*. The Arabic *r* is rolled as in Spanish.

Long vowels: *aa*, *ii*, and **uu** represent long vowels that are stressed in pronunciation; *aa* is pronounced as in "h*a*t," *ee* as in "b*ee*t," and *uu* as in "h*oo*t."

Acknowledgments

Writing this work, *Missiological Models for Muslim Ministry*, has been much like taking a long journey; the process began forty years ago when my wife and I returned to the United States after our first term of service with North Africa Mission (now Arab World Ministries). Since we were to be here several years, I decided to begin graduate studies at Westminster Theological Seminary in Philadelphia. After breaking the "journey" to return to missionary service in 1967, and then resuming it eleven years later, the first leg of the journey was completed in 1984 with a Th.M. from Westminster and a thesis that became the main source of the present work. Two of my professors contributed greatly to the theoretical underpinnings of this work, the late Drs. Cornelius Van Til, who gave me a solid grounding in apologetics, and Harvie Conn, who guided my studies in missiology.

For their encouragement in those early years after completing the thesis, I am thankful for the late Warren Chastain of the Zwemer Institute (then in California). He saw the value of the thesis and encouraged me to have it published but advised that considerable rewriting and editing would be needed to make it publishable. Although I soon set to work on it, other responsibilities and later a period of ill health did not allow enough time in one stretch to complete the revision process—until recently. I especially want to thank my good friends, Dr. Warren Gaston, whose proofreading and editorial feedback helped to greatly improve the book, and Dr. Anees Zaka, with the Board of Church Without Walls, for their help in getting it published.

I also wish to acknowledge the contribution of those over me in North Africa Mission / AWM, especially Messrs. Harold Stalley and Robert Brown, early leaders who were encouragers and mentors in ministry to Muslims but are both now with the Lord. A number of my contemporaries in AWM have also contributed much to my thinking, through personal interaction, participation in study groups, or writing articles for a small quarterly for missionaries that I edited. I will not try to list names for fear of overlooking someone, except for the late Wendell Evans, who collaborated with me on one project and succeeded me as AWM missiologist when I retired. I especially want to thank several who kept prodding me to finish it; my colleague John Haines read an early manuscript and sent me his feedback.

While the following may sound strange, it is genuinely sincere; I also want to express my thanks and my indebtedness to several whose writings on the Christian approach to Islam and to contextualization in Islamic society I have critiqued; I'm thinking especially of men like Bishop Kenneth Cragg, anthropologist Charles Kraft, and missionary author Phil Parshall. I have really learned very much from studying their writings or interacting with them, and I want to acknowledge that indebtedness.

Finally, this would not be complete without also acknowledging the contribution of my good wife, Frederica. It was she who, long before computers facilitated the process, spent many hours typing my thesis and my course papers, and then retyping the final edition, not to mention typing the proofs of the above-mentioned quarterly. She also strongly encouraged me to get back to completing my work on the manuscript and put up with my long hours at the computer and the late nights. Thanks, Frederica.

Last of all, I want to thank God for making this work possible; all the credit for it goes to Him. I thank Him for His work of salvation through the Lord Jesus Christ, who died on the cross for my sin and the sin of the whole world. I thank Him for the work of the Holy Spirit in my life and for answering prayer for His help in writing and revising this work; so many times, finding myself at an impasse for the right words, I took the problem to Him, and He led to the solution. I also thank Him for friends in our home church in the Philadelphia area (Aldan Union Church), and others who receive our prayer letter, who were faithfully praying for God's help in the project on my behalf. I can truly say that whatever is of value in it is attributable to Him. To God be the glory!

Foreword

David Lundy

Out of a lifetime devoted to the study of Islam and interacting with Muslims, the author has written a pièce de resistance that every serious practitioner of faith sharing among our Muslim friends should read. For many years Sam Schlorff served as Arab World Ministries' (AWM) missiologist. His suitability for that job is never more apparent than in this scholarly survey of evangelistic strategies to use in effectively sharing Christ given a Muslim worldview.

In the first section of the book, Sam reviews and critiques the various theological emphases and evangelistic models used historically by Protestant Christians vis-à-vis Muslims in the nineteenth and twentieth centuries. He similarly interacts with the historical range of approaches used in the subject under discussion in each chapter, such as concerning the value of religious dialogue in witnessing to Muslims. Although they are not for the fainthearted, these surveys provided me with new insights and deeper appreciation for those who have gone before the current generation of missionaries. Sam's extensive bibliography is worth the price of admission.

Particularly noteworthy are the chapters in parts two and three that deal with a timely topic at the beginning of the twenty-first century in witness to over one-fifth of the world's population. That concerns how much contextualization is appropriate. Proponents of what have fashionably been called insider movements or C5 and C6 approaches to church planting may have taken the good thing of contextualizing the gospel too far. Sam makes it clear that indeed they have. In so doing, he has come to the same conclusion that AWM has, namely, that going beyond a C4 strategy in church planting leads one to adopt the methods of communicating Christ across cultures that compromise the unchangeable message (leading one into syncretism). To give two major examples of where C5 would be considered by AWM (and the author here) to have gone too far is allowing the follower of Jesus (no problem with him or her not referring to himself as Christian if not deliberately hiding faith in Christ) to continue to worship in the mosque going through the prayer forms of the *Salat*, or in reciting the *Shahada* publicly and audibly. Among Sam's persuasive arguments about thinking twice before "filling [such] non-Christian *cultural forms* with supracultural (that is, Christian) meanings" are the following:

- Quar'anic terms such as *Iisa* as found in Sura 3:45 rarely carry meanings that are more or less Christian (chapter 3 and chapter 11).
- We fail to see that the Christianity that the Qur'an dismisses is not authentic Christianity in the first place, and so when we use terms about our faith that they are familiar with, it is filtered through this false perception of Christianity which distorts what Muslims hear (chapter 11).
- To allow a fledgling national church to use the Qur'an apologetically to prove Christian doctrines is to signal to the Muslim the Christian's acceptance of the authority of the Qur'an (chapter 5 and chapter 11).

More than just delivering theory, Sam has given those on the ground day by day interfacing with Muslims some practical applications on how to contextualize without compromise in "The Church in Islamic Culture: A Biblical-Theological Model." I like his emphasis on churches being formed: given the *ummah* of Islam and the biblical mandate to gather individual believers into churches (e.g., Acts 20:28). He reassures those seeking to plant churches within Muslim societies that as they deal with the forces that tend to produce a form of extraction when they are faithful to the Word in their discipling and church formation that this in fact is not the chief stumbling block to Muslim resistance to the gospel. Rather he attributes this to the essentially ideological nature of Islamic society as evidenced, for instance, in the *dhimmi* system imposed on churches in the Muslim world and the imposition of the *ridda* (law of apostasy). Ultimately he wisely places the onus on the emerging national church to "corporately evaluate critically their own past customs in the light of their new biblical understandings, and to make decisions regarding their response of their newfound truths." His conclusion resonates with balance that recognizes the unique nature of the local culture and the universally valid Word of God: "We who are outsiders to the culture really have no business pontificating about how the young church should contextualize in word or worship. We simply do not have the intimate knowledge of the different cultural forms that is needed, or the meanings associated with them, to make such a call. Our role [as foreigners] is to ground the national Christians in the Word of God sufficiently that they will recognize what should be contextualized and how."

While some current missiological thinking might consider Schlorff to be too conservative by contending, in effect, that contextualization is not the key to unlocking the Muslim mind and heart, his profound grappling with the different models of contextualization means that he must be taken seriously by all those who seek to serve God faithfully among Muslims. Thanks for leaving us this legacy, Sam.

David Lundy
International Director
Arab World Ministries

Preface

It is now the twenty-first century. Islam is fast becoming a challenge not only to the missionary enterprise but to world civilization as well, and that in more ways than one. The events of 9/11/2001 have changed international relations forever, and terrorism, suicide bombings, and the like have become news items almost daily. The political and social power of Islam is also rapidly becoming a force to be reckoned with. Christianity is still the largest religious block in the world and is said to have greater growth in sheer numbers, but statistics show that on a percentage basis Islam is growing more rapidly. What brings this home in concrete terms is the demographic patterns that we see emerging in recent years. The ethnic European population of Western Europe is declining while the population of Muslim countries continues to increase; Islam is the fastest growing religious block in the world. For all Muslim countries, the overall fertility rate in 1988 was 6 live births per woman,[1] compared with 1.1 births per woman in Spain and 1.7 in Britain in 2000.[2] This demographic disparity has been going on for some time now, and there is no sign of any change on the horizon. "Italy now has the world's oldest population. For every 100 people under the age of 15, the country has 120 people over 65. The patterns are reflected across the continent. . . . The European Union expects its workforce to dwindle from about 200 million now to 160 million by

1. John R. Weeks, "The Demography of Islamic Nations," *Population Bulletin* 43/4 (December 1988), 12.
2. Jeffrey Fleishman, "The Changing Face of Italy," *The* [Philadelphia] *Inquirer Magazine*, January 23, 2000, 6–13.

2020. European leaders are wondering who will fill jobs, pay taxes and fund social and pension programs."[3]

While Europe's population is declining, across the Mediterranean the Muslim countries of North Africa, Turkey, and the Middle East have burgeoning populations and not enough jobs for those entering the work force. Is it any wonder then that those governments have come to view immigration as the option of choice for solving the demographic problem? The countries of Europe appear to be a ready-made solution to the need. The result is that we are now witnessing the Islamization of Western Europe by immigration at an unprecedented rate. France, Austria, Germany, Holland, Belgium, England, and the Scandinavian countries now have sizable Muslim populations that are growing and becoming politically active. As for North America, we are not lagging far behind.

The challenge faced by the churches of Europe and North America has never been greater. Opportunities to reach Muslims are not lacking, and the Lord is not slack in seeking them. Christians are answering the missionary call, and Muslims are responding to the gospel in significant numbers. As for missions to Muslims, the question of how best to contextualize the gospel in the Muslim world so as to improve church growth has now become one of the hottest topics of discussion. But is the picture improving? That is *the* question! The missionary enterprise urgently needs to take a long, hard look at the theoretical underpinnings of its Muslim ministry and ask some hard questions. In recent years, evangelicals seem to have relied more on the tools of the social sciences than on theological research and reflection to improve their efforts.

The time therefore seemed appropriate to make my own contribution to the discussion. The present volume grows out of graduate studies in apologetics and missions at Westminster Theological Seminary in Philadelphia, completed in 1984,[4] and the things learned in ministry, research, writing, and teaching during forty years of service in Arab World Ministries (formerly North Africa Mission). The present volume is not a book on Islam per se, although you will find a lot about Islam in it, nor is it about how Christians should witness to Muslims. There are many excellent works on those subjects already. Rather, it is a historical and theological study of the theology of mission that has motivated Protestant evangelical

---

3. Ibid., 9.

4. See Sam Schlorff, "The Missionary Use of the Qur'an: An Historical and Theological Study of the Contextualization of the Gospel" (unpublished Th.M. thesis, Westminster Theological Seminary, Philadelphia, 1984).

ministry to Muslims over the past two centuries. It's the most exhaustive study of this nature of which I'm aware.

To keep it manageable, this study will be limited almost exclusively to Protestant and evangelical approaches to Islam. It must be recognized, however, that Protestants and evangelicals are part of a wider context and have influenced, and been influenced by, that wider context. For one thing, the early Protestant missionaries drew heavily on older Roman Catholic studies of Islam. Their approach has therefore been influenced by those earlier approaches to some extent, as well as by Muslim responses. Later influences include the scientific study of religion, the debates on the theological evaluation of other faiths, and especially the social sciences. We shall refer to this wider context from time to time.

Note also that the Protestant approach to Muslims has evolved over the years. We can discern changes in the approach from time to time. Most of these did not represent major changes. When, however, problems seemed to call the then current approach into question, a period of groping ensued, and this was followed by a paradigm shift, the adoption of a new contextual model or of several different models. Before going on to the first chapter, let's take a quick look at what's ahead by section and by chapter.

Part one gives a historical overview of Protestant approaches to Muslims, from the time of Henry Martyn at the beginning of the nineteenth century to the present; in two chapters we look briefly at the principal contextual models that motivated missionary approaches during that time frame. Chapter 1 studies the imperial model of the nineteenth century, and chapter 2 looks at five models of the twentieth century. The focus of these chapters is on the principal writers associated with each model, their ideas, the rationale given for their approach, how it evolved, and the problem areas and consequent paradigm shifts.

Part two takes a closer look at how these writers approached Islam, cutting across the various models of approach through a study of the methodologies and tools employed. Thus, chapter 3 studies the problem of Christian-Muslim communication—its origin in the Qur'an's borrowing of biblical terms and its worldview differences, the semantic changes and distortions this has introduced, and the Arab Christian response to such changes, including the effect on Arabic Bible translations. There are many important issues discussed in this chapter that affect other aspects of the model.

Chapters 4, 5, and 6 examine how Christian workers have used Qur'anic phrases and Islamic forms to communicate the gospel to Muslims. We have classified approaches into two broad categories: those that approach the Qur'an negatively and those that approach it positively. The first, studied in chapter 4, quotes the Qur'an "against Islam," that is,. as a basis for an ethical and historical criticism of Islam aimed at refuting its claims. The second is treated in chapters 5 and 6. Chapter 5 examines the proof-text approach that quotes the Qur'an to try to support Christian positions attacked by Islam, while chapter 6 looks at what I call the "New Hermeneutic in Qur'anic Interpretation" that seeks to lay the foundation for a new interpretation of the Qur'an more or less compatible with Christianity. Finally, chapter 7 examines the "dynamic equivalence" (or translational) model that draws on the social sciences in proposing an Islamicizing approach to the church for Islamic culture.

In part three, we come to the key question toward which we have been moving: As servants of Christ committed to Him and to the extension of His kingdom, how should we approach the contextualization of the gospel and of the church in Islamic culture? It is a complicated question involving several issues, and the position taken on one issue inevitably affects the position one takes on others as well. We begin, therefore, by studying the four primary issues that are involved in any contextual model. Taken together, these comprise the contextual model. These issues are treated in chapters 8 through 11.

Chapter 8 considers the question of the object of mission to Islam. Opinions on this run the gamut, from the radical displacement of Islam sought by the polemicists of the nineteenth century to achieving a global "community of communities" characterized by justice and peace, as envisaged by the ecumenical movement today. Our focus is on gaining the biblical perspective on the subject. Next, chapter 9 examines the way the approach adopted evaluates other religions, Islam in this case. Here again, views run the gamut, but we focus on understanding the biblical approach to evaluation found in Romans 1 and 2, as expounded by J. H. Bavinck. Chapter 10 considers the question of the appropriate contextual or theological starting point for relating to the culture. Here we find two broad approaches. The one starts within Islam; a Christian will quote passages from the Qur'an or use Islamic cultural forms, seeking to give these "Christian meanings." The contrasting approach that will be recommended starts with the Scriptures, using the Qur'an and Islamic culture as a bridge for communicating the gospel but without trying to give them "Christian meanings."

Thus, the stage is set for examining the central component of the contextual model. Chapter 11 deals with the question of the most appropriate cross-cultural hermeneutic. By its nature, this is more demanding than the kind of monocultural hermeneutic to which we are accustomed in the West. Once again, we find two approaches to interpretation being used, a hermeneutic of synthesis and a hermeneutic of analysis. These correlate with the two approaches to contextual starting point just mentioned. Chapter 12, then, ties together these four subissues—objective, theological evaluation, contextual starting point, and hermeneutical method—into the model that I have called "the Betrothal model." Presented here, with well-defined parameters, is a genuinely biblical alternative to the dynamic equivalence model. Finally, an appendix presents an excellent example of an approach that fits within these parameters: the *Meetings for Better Understanding* model of Church Without Walls.

A Historical Overview:
Six Contextual Models

The Nineteenth-Century
Imperial Model

The Protestant missionary approach to Islam began with Henry Martyn (1781–1812). Martyn went to India in 1806 as a chaplain in the British East India Company. During a stay in Persia the year before his untimely death, he wrote three polemical tracts in debate with a Persian Muslim who wrote in defense of Islam (translated in Lee 1824:80–160). These are the first Protestant writings addressed to Muslims.

The Period of Polemics (1811–1900)

George Sale and Henry Martyn

Prior to Martyn, the few Protestants to write against Islam were non-missionaries who wrote for Westerners, not Muslims. They wrote at a distance from Islam, without the firsthand knowledge of Islam the later writers had. Except for the works of George Sale (1697–1736), what they wrote about Islam was often inaccurate. Sale's translation of the Qur'an with "Preliminary Discourse," first published in 1734 (Sale 1850:xi), is still valued by scholars today (Watt 1970:174). It is note-worthy that this work, which went through many reprints around the world, was widely used by the early Protestant polemicists. Sometime early in the twentieth century, the first four chapters of the "Preliminary Discourse" were translated into Arabic and published separately as a polemical work, with corrective explanations and appendices added by the translator (Sale 1925).[1]

This early approach is characterized by an aggressive polemic, known as "the Mohammedan Controversy," which used the Qur'an liberally to disprove Islam. Shaped largely by the colonial model of Western (especially British) imperialism, the polemicists' attitude toward Islam was basically negative. Even though most of them would have agreed that "of all non-Christian religions it contains the largest amount of truth" (Rouse n.d.:v), they felt that it also has fatal "weaknesses." As one of them put it:

> The amount of truth which is included in the Religion of Islam has . . . commended it to the acceptance of vast multitudes of our fellow-creatures. The errors, superstitions and falsehoods with which these doctrines are mingled have deceived the followers of the "Arabian Prophet" to their ruin. The evil results which have followed are everywhere patent. (Tisdall 1895:53)

When one analyzes the polemicists' evaluation of Islam, one is struck by the pervasiveness of belief in cultural and religious evolution. It is assumed that an evolutionary process is at work in the various cultures of the world. The differences that exist between societies, from the most primitive to the most advanced, are explained in evolutionary terms and are attributed to the differing degrees of truth each contains. In the evolutionary framework, Islam is classified as an inferior religion, somewhere between the primitive cultures of Africa and Asia and the advanced civilizations of the Christian West.

Sir William Muir and Gustav Weil

Like Martyn, Sir William Muir (1819–1905) was an administrator in the British East India Company. He wrote several important historical works on the life of Muhammad and on the Caliphate, as well as several polemical works addressed to Muslims, that give an evolutionary

1. It's ironic that it was translated for this purpose, because in his day Sale was charged with putting Islam on a par with Christianity; his "Preliminary Discourse" defends Muhammad against charges made by Humphrey Prideaux about him being an impostor (1697).

explanation for the "inferiority" of Islam.[2] His writings had considerable influence on the missionaries of his day. The following quotation sums up his view of Islam.

> As a Reformer, Mahomet did, indeed, advance his people to a certain point; but as a Prophet, he left them immovably fixed at that point for all time to come. As there can be no return, so neither can there be any progress. The tree is of artificial planting; instead of containing within itself the germ of growth, and adaptation to the various requirements of time and clime and circumstance, expanding with the genial sunshine and the rain from heaven, it remains the same forced and stunted thing as when first planted twelve centuries ago. (1878:64; see also 1883:56–57; 1887:266)

Muir's comment on what Gustav Weil wrote about the future of Islam is instructive. Weil had theorized (1878:132) that Islam would be able to save itself from oblivion by adapting to the modern world, much as did "reformed Judaism," that is, through dropping outmoded ideas and practices and retaining those eternal truths that are universally believed (cited in Muir 1878:63–65). Here is Muir's reply:

> But with Islam, how can this be possible? The whole stands upon the same ground of divine authority; pilgrimage, lustration, and fasting are as binding as the creed itself, and the Moslem may in vain seek to free himself from the obligation of the veil, to abolish the license of polygamy, divorce, and slavery, or to abate the command which reduces Jews and Christians to a position of inferiority and humiliation. In deference to the opinion of Christian nations, some amelioration and improvement in these things may be attempted, but it will be against the grain and contrary to the law that binds the Moslem conscience. (1878:64ff.)

Muir contrasted the backwardness of Islamic civilization with the advancement of the West, which he attributed to the spiritual principles of the gospel.

> It [Christianity] did not, indeed, neglect to guide the Christian life, but it did so by the enunciation of principles and rules of wide and far-reaching application. These, no less than the injunctions of the Coran, served amply for the exigencies of the day. But they have done a vast deal more. They have proved themselves capable of adaptation to the

2. For a variation on this theme, see Koelle 1889:457, 464.

most advanced stages of social development and intellectual elevation. And what is infinitely more, it may be claimed for the lessons embodied in the Gospel that they have been themselves promotive, if indeed they have not been the immediate cause, of all the most important reforms and philanthropies that now prevail in Christendom. (1883:51–52)

Muir was convinced that because of its fatal weaknesses, Islam was destined to fade away and be replaced by Christianity (1883:57–58). The political subjugation of the Muslim world to the colonial powers was to him sure evidence that Islam was slowly and surely fading away before his eyes. In an article originally published in *The Calcutta Review* in 1852 he states, "At every point of contact with Islam, Christianity has the temporal ascendancy. The political prestige of Mohammed is departed forever. The relation of France to Africa, and of Russia and Austria to the Turkish and Persian dynasties, evinces in a striking light the depression of Islam" (1897:100).

William St. Clair Tisdall, Samuel Zwemer, and Others

Many of the polemicists shared Muir's vision of the future of Islam, most notably William St. Clair Tisdall (1859–1928), an Anglican missionary to Persia and one of the leading Islamicists of the day (1895:230). Imad Ud-Din (c. 1830–1900), an Indian convert from Islam who became a well-known polemicist, went so far as to prophesy that India would "be Christian even as Great Britain now is," concluding that "however much our enemies, Hindoos, Mohammedans, Dayanandis, and others, may oppose and revile, the time is most assuredly coming when they will not be found even for the seeking" ([1893]:7). As late as 1916, Samuel Zwemer (1867–1952) devoted an entire book to *The Disintegration of Islam*.

What does this evaluation of Islam imply concerning the objective of Muslim evangelism? The polemicists generally described the objective in terms of the radical displacement of Islam by Christianity, or of "bringing Islam crashing to the ground" as Tisdall put it (1910:vi, 2). In a sense, this understanding of the objective is contradicted by one important element in the polemicists' approach to Islam, the positive uses of the "truths" of Islam in support of Christian teaching, which would seem to imply a more positive objective. Tisdall writes:

In dealing with all systems of religion, and especially those to which we are opposed, it will be our highest wisdom carefully to distinguish the truths which may exist in them from the falsehoods with which they are commingled or overlaid, and strive to cleanse the jewel from the mire into which it has fallen. If instead of doing this we vainly endeavor to overthrow the whole structure because the Enemy of Souls has entrenched himself therein, we are measuring our puny strength against the adamantine bases of the world, and our efforts can avail only to strengthen that which we would assail. (1895:8)

The inconsistency in such a procedure was not perceived for some time. Later on, however, this emphasis on the positive use of the Qur'an will have considerable influence on the development of a new approach to the Qur'an and to Islamic culture.

A Period of Doubt and Searching (1900–c. 1930)

Around the turn of the twentieth century, the Protestant missionary force began to have doubts about the validity of the polemicists' evaluation of Islam and their objective. They began to notice a number of problems and inconsistencies: if it is true that the Qur'an contains a large amount of "truth" that more or less upholds the truth of the gospel, then why a totally negative evaluation? Why must all be destroyed? If an evolutionary process is indeed at work within Islam, then why not build positively on the truth that it is acknowledged to have and thereby help it to advance toward the higher truth of Christianity? In any case, cannot one acknowledge that there is *some* good in Islamic culture?

Later on, other considerations will also be brought forward. Cultural anthropology, for example, has shown in recent years that the attempt to classify and evaluate cultures on an evolutionary scale is untenable. Today, it is also quite obvious that Islam, not to mention other religions, is far from dying out; it is experiencing a resurgence, which has brought it back to the center stage of the world. For years, however, Protestant missionaries were lulled into complacency by the illusion that Islam was dying out; they misinterpreted the reforms they saw being introduced as "frantic efforts . . . to save the ship" (Zwemer 1916:1).

Edinburgh 1910 and Jerusalem 1928

The question of the proper Christian attitude toward non-Christian religion now began to preoccupy the missionary enterprise. It figured prominently at the World Missionary Conference at Edinburgh in 1910.

In its "General Conclusions," the *Report of Commission IV* of the Conference noted an agreement on "two very notable points."

> The first of these is the practically universal testimony that the true attitude of the Christian missionary to the non-Christian religions should be one of true understanding and, as far as possible, of sympathy, . . . that the true method is that of knowledge and charity, that the missionary should seek for the nobler elements in the non-Christian religions and use them as steps to higher things, that in fact all these religions without exception disclose elemental needs of the human soul which Christianity alone can satisfy, and that in their higher forms they plainly manifest the working of the Spirit of God. . . .

> But, along with this generous recognition of all that is true and good in these religions, there goes also the universal and emphatic witness to the absoluteness of the Christian faith. (World Missionary Conference 1910:267–68)

The theme of a positive evaluation and approach became even more pronounced in later studies and discussions, particularly within the conciliar movement. At the Jerusalem Conference of the International Missionary Council in 1928, the question of the "values" to be found in the non-Christian religions was one of the main subjects of discussion. Ten years later, at the Tambaram Conference of 1938, the question of the "continuity" versus "discontinuity" of Christianity with non-Christian religions was at the center of the discussion.[3]

Articles in The Moslem World

What interests us here is not the debate on non-Christian religions in general. It is rather what missionaries to Muslims were saying in evaluation of the Qur'an and Islam in particular, as well as their view of the objective of Muslim evangelism. A survey of articles, which appeared during this period in *The Moslem World*, founded by Zwemer in 1911, is enlightening. One missionary, who favored "the simple, loving, full preaching of the Gospel of Jesus Christ" devoid of all polemic (Fairman 1926:272–74), describes the problem of the polemical approach in the following terms.

> There are no Moslem lands today where something is not being attempted to win Moslems to Christ. Yet relatively, and actually, very little has been

---

3. For an overview of this debate, see Anderson 1961:7–15. For the evolution of the debate since 1938, see Hallencreutz 1970.

accomplished. . . . The failure is on our part, and its secret must lie in the method we have hitherto adopted. . . .

The Controversial Method . . . has been, and is still, the most widely adopted and used for many years. When I first came to the field, I was practically told that this was the only possible way of approaching the Moslem. It involves having an expert knowledge of Islam and its books, so that a powerful attack may be made on the whole system. Its main motive is destructive attack, in the hope that when success has been attained, and Islam disintegrates beneath the force of our polemic, it may be possible to build upon the ruins the nobler edifice of Christianity. For many years I used this method, and many others have done the same and are still doing it. . . . But what has been gained? Our opponents have been beaten in argument, *but they have not been won for Christ*. . . . Destructive criticism never yet won a soul for Christ.

Others, however, influenced by the positive uses of the Qur'an that had been developed in the nineteenth century, went a step further. Building on the apostle Paul's statement that he had become all things to all men (1 Cor. 9:22), another writer suggested that the missionary to Muslims should ask, "Have I become *as* a Mohammedan to lead these Mohammedans to Christ?" (Purdon 1924:140). Taking his cue from Paul's use of pagan sources in his Areopagus address (Acts 17:23, 28), he declares: "To become then 'as a Mohammedan' means—to know and utilize divine truth in the Islamic faith, and from these seek to lead the devotees of Mohammed to seize the only truth that can really satisfy their soul" (141). He nevertheless felt that Qur'anic truth is insufficient in itself to lead a Muslim to Christ. "The Koran . . . *abounds* in 'points d'appui' for the Christian missionary. He cannot, of course, find in it sufficient truth to lead a soul into the glorious liberty of the sons of God, but he will find sufficient to establish or confirm that need for which alone the Saviour can provide" (142).

Still others sharply disagreed with the new approach. One writer registered his disagreement in these terms:

In the old days, from the time of Raymond Lull until quite recent times, the missionary to Mohammedans was utterly uncompromising in his attitude towards Islam. . . . Now the pendulum has swung far over to the other side, and the missionary is exhorted to spend his time searching for 'points of contact'. He is told that in order to convert the Mohammedan or even to win his friendship, he must be a diplomat; that he must never mention the prophet Mohammed, but merely preach Christ. . . . We are not to condemn what we know to be wrong in Islam, but we must seek out what good there is in Islam and give it our unstinted praise. . . . When you have brought out all your 'points of contact' between Christianity and Islam you have but emphasized the great gulf between the two rival religions. . . .

Islam is undoubtedly crumbling, and our best policy is to let it crumble instead of trying to find strong pieces in its walls upon which we may build Christianity. The whole miserable structure must come down and the foundation be relaid, and then, perhaps, in the rebuilding we can work in some of the old stones and the old beams. Islam was founded upon a man, and it cannot be permanent even though it endure a long time. (Mylrea 1913:402–4, 406)

Summary of the Imperial Model

It is now time to draw some conclusions about the imperial (polemical) model. We will summarize the model in terms of five of the more significant elements that together make up the model, and then evaluate the model in term of its strengths and weaknesses.

The Objective of Mission: to "demolish the old building"—Islam—and "build on its ruins a new edifice," namely, Christianity.

Theology of Non-Christian Religion: a negative evaluation coupled with the evolution of religion idea. On the "scale of civilization," idolaters and animists are at the bottom of the scale and Christianity is at the top, while Islam, held to be "defective, inferior, and dying out" is only part of the way up the scale (Doctrine of "Discontinuity").

Contextual Approach: mixed but mostly non-contextual. On the level of theology, Islam is attacked with aggressive polemics with a view to hastening its demise, "truths" are salvaged for building the new edifice, and certain Qur'anic passages are used as "points of contact" on which to build theologically in presenting the gospel. On the level of church strategy, apart from translating the Scriptures, hymnbooks, confessions and creeds, commentaries, and the like into the national language, there was little or no real contextualization.

Hermeneutic: mostly monocultural, but we also see a synthesizing tendency; Qur'anic proof-texts are used to "refute" the Qur'an and to support certain Christian teachings against Islamic attacks.

Church Strategy: In the Middle East, the early vision was to revive the ancient Eastern churches in the hope that these would then evangelize the Muslims. The result: schism in those churches and the creation of new evangelical denominations; converts from Islam are integrated into existing churches, triggering the "rejection mechanism"—persecution, recanting, or flight. In North Africa, the early vision was to "pluck a few brands from the burning" (an inadequate vision for church planting). Results: unstable churches or none at all.

Strengths: The model recognizes the discontinuity between Islam and Christianity, seeks to maintain the uniqueness of Christ and the gospel, and holds a high view of Scripture.

Weaknesses: discrepancies and contradictions—the theory of the evolution of religion, and the idea of building on the supposed "truths" of Islam to present the gospel.

The Model Today: seems to be defunct in its original form, although some polemic is still around (to be treated in a later chapter).

2

Five Models
of the Twentieth Century

From the works cited in chapter 1, it is clear that missionary views on Islam and on the approach to Islam were becoming polarized. As a result, two opposing attitudes to Islam emerged. These translate into two very different approaches that have been called the direct approach and the indirect approach respectively (Bavinck 1960:132); the latter is also known as the fulfillment method.

The Direct Approach Model

The direct approach model represents in some respects a continuation of that of the polemicists. Missionaries who were theologically conservative tended to evaluate Islam in negative terms and to think of the objective in terms of radical displacement. They did not formulate a clear-cut alternative to the approach of the polemicists.

They differed from the polemicists, however, in one important respect: they downplayed the value of polemic and used it only as a last resort. Not only did it seem to generate more heat than light, but also it aroused a bitter polemical counterattack. Many concluded that, as a practical rule, polemic should be avoided, except perhaps with a serious inquirer, and that one should "stick to the direct presentation of the gospel." The destruction of Islam did not begin in earnest until after one had become a Christian, or at least a serious inquirer.

Christy Wilson Sr.

J. Christy Wilson Sr. (1891–1973), a Presbyterian missionary to Persia, and later professor of missions at Princeton Seminary, is representative of the direct approach. Concerning the old polemical works he writes:

> These are monuments of a system that is past; they may still be of use today, after a man has come far along the Christian path and has the love of Christ in his heart. They may serve to drive out the vestiges of Islam, but they are no longer examples of the line of approach we should follow in presenting Christ to the Moslem heart. "The Great Moslem Controversy" has gone into the limbo of things that are past. . . . Today he who would present Christ to the Moslem heart should be an expert in avoiding argument. (1950:41–42)

Much like the author of the first *Moslem World* article quoted in chapter 1, Wilson held that "the foundation of our approach must be the *direct presentation of Christ.* We should concentrate upon this as the sum and substance of our work" (1950:46). This was the view of the majority of evangelical missionaries and faith missions at the time. They tended to concern themselves with pragmatic questions about methods that work but neglected critical reflection on the model that molded their approach to Islam.

One result of the change of approach is that the old polemical works were discontinued and gradually went out of print. In 1932, it was reported that "a few years ago a group of Christian workers in Egypt agreed to adopt certain guiding principles in respect of their literature for Muslims. These [included]: To withdraw from circulation all that kind of controversial literature which, in the end, proves a hindrance or gives unnecessary offense to Muslims" (Jones 1932:299). A similar decision is reported concerning a "Christian Literature for Moslems Committee" meeting in Lahore in 1935 (Zwemer 1941:232).

Summary of the Direct Approach Model

The Objective of Mission: essentially the same as that of the imperial model, that is, the radical displacement of Islam.

Theology of Non-Christian Religion: Again it is essentially negative, like the imperial model.

Contextual Approach: It is mostly non-contextual but avoids polemic, seeking to achieve the goal by the positive presentation of Christ and demonstrating God's love through one's life.

Hermeneutic: It is monocultural in that it presents the gospel without reference to Islam, but the synthesizing tendency of the imperial model is avoided.

Church Strategy: It is basically the same as that of the imperial model. In North Africa, missionaries are saying that worshiping groups must have "government recognition" to be considered churches.

Strengths: its stress on presenting Christ and the gospel; its high view of Scripture and of Christ; its correction of the excesses of the imperial approach.

Weaknesses: The question of the relation of the gospel to Islamic culture remains unanswered; Islamic culture is not taken seriously enough.

The Model Today: The goal of the positive presentation of Christ is still around in evangelical circles.

The Indirect, or Fulfillment, Model

Another sizable group of missionaries and Islamicists also saw problems and inconsistencies in the nineteenth-century polemic but came to very different conclusions. Picking up on certain of the polemicists' seed ideas, they developed from these a creative new approach. If Islam contains so much truth, they reasoned, then how can that truth be totally invalidated by its errors? Many felt the negative evaluation of Islam to be one-sided; it dwelt so exclusively upon the error and evil present in Islam that it lost sight of its good side.

In sum, the attitude toward "the truth of Islam" underwent a complete turnabout. Rather than being annulled by the error with which it is thought to be mixed, as the polemicists believed, Islam was now held to possess a latent power on which the missionary might rely in presenting the gospel. These considerations seemed to imply a different approach to Islam, an indirect or fulfillment method, which starts with positive elements within Islam and builds on them the truth of the gospel.

This new approach appears in numerous publications. An early example is the missionary training manual entitled *The Presentation of Christianity to Moslems*, published in 1916 by the Board of Missionary Preparation of the Foreign Missions Conference of North America (later called The Division of Overseas Ministries of the National Council of Churches in the U.S.). One chapter in the manual, written by Duncan Black MacDonald (1863–1943), then professor of Islamics at the Kennedy School of Missions of Hartford Theological Seminary, lists twelve things that "Christianity may add to Islam" (1916:77–89).

Bevan Jones

The changes that this new way of thinking introduced into the Protestant approach to Islam were nothing short of revolutionary. It suggested that Islam must be viewed as a work of the Holy Spirit. If Islam contains truth, then that truth must somehow be from God and attributable to the working of the Holy Spirit. This is the conclusion that Bevan Jones seems to have come to in *The People of the Mosque* (1932). Confessing his indebtedness to the ideas of Dr. J. N. Farquhar,[1] Jones asks,

> How else are we to account for the innumerable fragments of truth to be found in other religions except on the ground that God's Spirit is quietly at work in the hearts and minds of men, notwithstanding human opposition and imperfection? So then we require patience, understanding and sympathy in our study, and with these faith to believe that there is something of real worth to the Kingdom of God at the heart of Islam. . . .
>
> If it is conceded that . . . God's Spirit is even now at work within Islam, who are we that we should set limits to the developments that may yet take place among Muslims under the influence of that Almighty Agency. There is, the present writer ventures to think, a Power at work within Islam that shall yet put to confusion the calculations of its most rigidly orthodox leaders, and, at the same time, rebuke the little faith of many a preacher of the Gospel. (1932:245–46)

1. See Sharpe 1965 for his contribution to missionary thought.

This new way of thinking also suggested a new objective. If the truth found in Islam represents the work of the Holy Spirit, then it is no longer possible to think of Islam as being destined to destruction. One does not destroy the work of the Spirit, even if it is incomplete. Instead, one seeks to bring it to completion. Accordingly, Lootfy Levonian, dean of the School of Religion at Athens, argues that "Christ's end was fulfilment, not destruction. That should be the end, the goal, the motive principle in the relationship between the Moslem and the Christian also" (1931:123). The term "fulfillment" as used here expresses the belief that, as the whole truth, Christianity completes the partial and defective truth of Islam. Here, the nineteenth-century theory of a religious and cultural evolution reaches its culmination.

The polemicists had sought to lead the Muslim to leave behind the partial truths of Islam and embrace the full truth found only in Christianity. The proponents of fulfillment sought a broader basis from which to lead the Muslim to Christ; stress was placed on the continuity between Islam and Christianity. In this perspective, communicating the gospel meant using what was partial and defective in such a way as to bring to completion what until then had only been latent. It meant helping the bud to burst into full bloom.

In *Christianity Explained to Muslims*, Bevan Jones grounds the preaching of the gospel in the spiritual experience that we supposedly have in common with Muslims. Just as the apostles and early Jewish Christians had been led, despite their Jewish prejudices, to accept the deity of Christ and the Trinity because they experienced the ministry of Christ and the Holy Spirit in their lives, he argues, so spiritual experience must be the basis of our appeal to the Muslim (1937:61, 70–72, 108). "Let us, then, invite the devout Muslim to explore the phenomena of spiritual experience, his and ours. In his heart, as in ours, the Spirit of the Living God is assuredly at work" (72).

Summary of the Fulfillment Model

The Objective of Mission: to fulfill through the gospel the deepest needs and aspiration of Muslims that Islam itself cannot satisfy.

Theology of Non-Christian Religion: an essentially positive evaluation coupled with the evolution of religion idea. Islam is incomplete and deficient, in that it contains "moments" of truth and goodness; this is positive in that what is partial may be fulfilled by what is complete, that is, Christianity (doctrine of continuity).

Contextual Approach: to work for the fulfillment of Islam. In theology, build on the "partial truths" of Islam, causing them to open up and bloom into the full truth of the gospel. In the church, again there seems to be little real contextualization.

Hermeneutic: The Bible and the Qur'an are interpreted in such a way as to bring the biblical and Qur'anic perspectives more or less together (a hermeneutic of synthesis).

Church Strategy: As indicated, it seems to be much the same as in previous models.

Strengths: It tries to relate the gospel message to Muslim culture and abandons the totally negative evaluation of the imperial model.

Weaknesses: Its view of the evolution of religion is intrinsically relativistic and undercuts the gospel message and the authority of Scripture. It is intrinsically syncretistic.

The Model Today: The concept of fulfillment is still with us today, even among some evangelicals, but it is generally modified or combined with other ideas, such as the dialogical model of the WCC that will be covered later.

The Dialectical Model

Hendrik Kraemer

In 1938, at the Tambaram Conference of the International Missionary Council, the new approach described above, identified as the doctrine of continuity, was seriously challenged by Hendrik Kraemer (1888–1965) of the Dutch Bible Society. Influenced by the theology of Karl Barth, Kraemer vigorously opposed the doctrine of fulfillment: "To use it engenders inevitably the erroneous conception that the lines of the so-called highest developments [of non-Christian religions] point naturally to Christ, and would end in Him if produced further" (1956:123). He argued for a doctrine of discontinuity, insisting on the unique status of the "Christian revelation" which stands in judgment on all religions, including Christianity itself. Keep in mind, however, that Kraemer is not arguing for total discontinuity, as one might suppose from his strong language. What he is arguing for is a dialectical approach to non-Christian religion, which combines discontinuity and continuity.

> Biblical realism is fully aware of this fundamental and demonic disharmony [in mankind], and therefore has a dialectical attitude towards it, at the same time saying yes and no. It holds that God still works in this disharmony, shines dimly through it and performs His judgement over it and in it, for in the light of Biblical realism the disharmony in man is not only fundamental and demonic, but also and above all guilty. Above the dialectical unity of yes and no, however, there rises triumphantly an ultimate divine yes in God's saving Will toward mankind and the world. (1956:125–26; see also 1939; 1956:352–53)

Kraemer's critique of the idea of continuity has had a profound effect in many ways on Protestant approaches to Islam, especially within the conciliar movement. Except in continental Europe, however,[2] it appears that few missionaries to Muslims, who are predominantly Anglo-American, have followed his dialectical approach. It is noteworthy, however, that the concept of "interreligion" that appears especially in Kraemer's later writings (e.g. ,1960) has been worked over to become a major aspect of the WCC program of interreligious dialogue.

Summary of the Dialectical Model

The Objective of Mission: the transformation of both Christianity and Islam by the "Christian revelation."

Theology of Non-Christian Religion: It is dialectical in that it affirms both continuity and discontinuity, both synthesis and antithesis between Islam and Christianity, both divine judgment on all religions and their radical transformation.

Contextual Approach: It incorporates both continuity and discontinuity on the premise that Truth itself is dialectical; the theme of "interreligion" is introduced for the first time and is given considerable stress.

2. For examples, see Christensen 1952–1953 and Rudvin 1979.

Church Strategy: Interestingly, it appears to be much the same as the previous models.

Hermeneutic: a dialectical approach to interpretation, involving both the principles of analysis and synthesis (see chapter 11).

Strengths: its recognition of the discontinuity between Islam and Christianity, its critique of the doctrine of continuity, its insights into and critique of Islam and other religions.

Weaknesses: It views dialectic as a principle of Truth itself rather than as a manifestation of sin, as is the case in Scripture; it tends to be based more on pure dialecticism/existentialism rather than on the biblical evaluation of man.

The Model Today: It exists mainly among a few European dialectical theologians; it has, however, had considerable influence on the dialogical model of the ecumenical movement.

The Dialogical Model

To sum up so far, missionaries to Muslims became more and more polarized during the first half of the twentieth century. The indirect approach, more or less positive, became identified mainly with liberal theology and the ecumenical movement, whereas the direct approach, more or less negative, became identified mainly with evangelical theology and an independent position vis-à-vis the ecumenical movement. Neither side, however, was able satisfactorily to resolve the problems that led to the abandonment of the nineteenth-century polemic. On the one hand, those who sought the solution in a positive evaluation of Islam were led, on the basis of their presuppositions, to use methods that increasingly tended to cut them loose from biblical authority. On the other hand, those who held a negative attitude out of commitment to biblical authority failed seriously to come to grips with the question of the relationship of the gospel to Islamic culture.

In the 1950s, significant developments began to take place in both camps that marked the beginning of another phase in the evolution of the Protestant approach to Islam. While the new approaches are rooted in those just described, they are sufficiently different to be considered a new phase in the approach. Let us then examine these new developments.

Kenneth Cragg and Interreligion

The first development to be noted is the rise of the dialogical approach. Interreligious dialogue, as it now exists, is rooted in the positive evaluation of Islam and the doctrine of fulfillment. In Protestant circles, one who has played a leading role in laying the theological groundwork for dialogue with Islam is Bishop Kenneth Cragg (1913–), an Anglican. His views on the approach to Islam are set forth in a number of important books that must be reckoned with in any study of Christian witness to Muslims today.

Cragg's first work, *The Call of the Minaret*, charts the course that he will follow in all his books. His approach is based on "the conviction that there is a call in the call [of the muezzin] which the non-Muslim ought also to heed" (1956:173). He then elaborates what this means for the Christian. "There are tremendous questions inseparable from a glad acceptance of what Islam in measure portends, questions of the how and the whence within the good the minaret declares" (179). He later expands on what he means by this.

> To embrace and then fulfill the wide dimensions of these disturbing but tremendous relationships is the Christian answer to the summons of the Muezzin. . . . If we respond to him with his own seriousness we shall not silence or suppress the meanings we have learned in Christ to the very things for which he pleads or for which he speaks. The more fully we do him justice, the more inevitably we involve him, and so ourselves, in the significance of Christ. For us that involvement means expression. Who shall say all that it involves for him. (1956:184)

What "involvement in the significance of Christ" will mean for the Muslim is spelled out further in a chapter on the "Muslim unawareness of Christ." There, Cragg writes that for us as Christians "the objective is not, as the Crusaders believed, the repossession of what Christendom has lost, but the restoration to Muslims of the Christ Whom they have missed" (1956:246). Cragg calls this a "spiritual," as opposed to a "territorial retrieval," and declares that "to restore Christ transcends all else" (256–57). In his second book, *Sandals at the Mosque*, he explores further the idea of restoration, often in terms of fulfillment: "The nature of the gospel is such that the impact of Christ is not totally to displace, but paradoxically to fulfill what is there" (1959:92).

It seems that Cragg is moving beyond the idea of fulfillment in the unilateral sense it had earlier, to what might be called multilateral fulfillment. This involves the principle of open religion, a Christianity and an Islam both open not just to a clearer understanding of their own sources but also to truth from other sources and perspectives. Yet Christ represents, in some sense, the fulfillment of both. In later writings, the exploration of various avenues to this new dimension of fulfillment, which he calls "inter-religion," is his principal interest (1977).

The World Council of Churches' Program of Dialogue with Muslims

As it exists today, dialogue with Islam is a child of the ecumenical movement. From the beginning, its prime movers have been the World Council of Churches (WCC) and the Vatican. The Roman Catholic Church's program of dialogue originated in the Second Vatican Council (1962–1965), which issued a "Declaration on Non-Christian Religions" and paved the way for the creation of the Secretariat for Non-Christians (SNC) in 1964. The SNC has inspired or sponsored a number of high-level dialogues with Muslim government officials and academics (Boormans 1978:11–34; Schlorff 1983).

The acknowledged leader in Christian-Muslim dialogue, however, has been the WCC; after several preparatory consultations, it held a number of dialogues with Islam beginning in 1969. In 1971 the WCC Sub-Unit for Dialogue with People of Living Faiths and Ideologies (DFI) was created to carry on this program.

One significant result of these consultations has been the evolution of the WCC conception of the objective of dialogue. At the Kandy Consultation of 1967, in which Roman Catholics, Orthodox, and Protestants participated, the concluding statement on "Christians in Dialogue with Men of Other Faiths" indicates the direction of the thinking of those present.

> We are not agreed among ourselves whether or not it is part of God's redemptive purpose to bring about an increasing manifestation of the Saviour within other systems of belief as such. This very fact is one of the reasons which should make us leave it to the conscience and inner illumination of those who within other systems take up Christian discipleship, whether or not it is God's will for them that they should leave their own social and religious community. Normally conversion leads to baptism and incorporation into the Church. There may, however, be situations—personal or social, spiritual or practical—in which the Church may support the individual in his decision to postpone or abstain from baptism. (WCC 1977:19–20)

The condemnation of "proselytism" that recurs in the concluding statements of a number of WCC-sponsored dialogues (e.g. Broumana 1972, Colombo 1974, Legon 1974, Hong Kong 1975, Chambesy 1976) is also significant (1977:91, 105, 115, 123, 140). At Hong Kong and at Chambesy, proselytism was defined as "the compulsive, conscious, deliberate and tactical effort to draw people from one community of faith to another" (123) and "adding members to the Christian community for reasons other than spiritual" (140).

The problem with these statements is that they contradict the missionary nature of both Christianity and Islam. It is of the essence of Christian mission and Islamic "da'wah" to make converts. For its part, Islam has never renounced recruiting converts from the Christian community. What then can such statements mean? At the very least, they hide a host of ambiguities and leave many unanswered questions. Leaving aside the question as to the intent of the Muslim participants, what, we must ask, do they mean to the WCC?

Even when we grant that manipulation, using material inducements, or appealing to unspiritual motives in order to make converts is contrary to the New Testament, there is still a problem with such statements. Do they leave any room for evangelism, as traditionally understood, or disciple making? Do they leave any room for baptizing Muslims who have come to Christ? That is doubtful. They use vague, subjective, and emotionally laden terms, such as "taking advantage of a person's weakness" or "subtle coercion," which permit one to brand any disapproved conversion as "proselytism."

It seems quite clear that any evangelism that leads to disciple making and church planting as defined in the New Testament qualifies as "proselytism" and is therefore disapproved. There are, without a doubt, theologians and churches in the ecumenical movement for whom these are still legitimate objectives. It is also clear that the DFI and many WCC-related missions in the Muslim world no longer hold these objectives, as far as ministry to Muslims is concerned.

The WCC now defines its objective in terms of realizing a global community incorporating all religions and ideologies and characterized by justice and peace. The following extract from the WCC *Guidelines on Dialogue* speaks of its "vision" for a worldwide "community of communities" and for "dialogue in community."

> At the Colombo consultation of 1974 the vision of a worldwide "community of communities" was discussed. Such a vision may be helpful

in the search for community in a pluralistic world; it is not one of homogeneous unity or totalitarian uniformity, nor does it envisage self-contained communities, simply co-existing. Rather it emphasizes the positive part which existing communities may play in developing the community of humankind. . . . For Christians the thought of a community of communities is further related to the kingly rule of God over all human communities. . . . (1979:6)

The term "dialogue in community" is useful in that it . . . focuses attention on the reasons for being in dialogue. . . . Most Christians today live out their lives in actual community with people who may be committed to faiths and ideologies other than their own. . . . But there are concerns beyond the local which require Christians to engage in dialogue toward realization of a wider community in which peace and justice may be more fully realized. (1979:9–10)

Summary of the Dialogical Model

The Objective of Mission: to create a synthesis of spiritualities and bring all religions and ideologies together into a global "community of communities" characterized by justice, peace, and "dialogue in community."

Theology of Non-Christian Religion: Basically positive; Islam is seen as one of several religions imperiled by the destructive forces of the world.

Contextual Approach: interreligious dialogue leading to "interreligion"; hold dialogues with Islam that issue in common statements, such as the condemnation of "proselytism."

Hermeneutic: introduction of the "new hermeneutic" in Qur'an interpretation that views the Qur'an as a source of truth for interreligious dialogue and implies accepting the Qur'an as a word of God (a hermeneutic of synthesis).

Church Strategy: work for building up a sense of being a part of a one-world community and at the same time push for the acceptance of religious pluralism in Muslim society.

Strengths: the original concept of dialogue, which, in itself, is biblically valid.

Weaknesses: relativism, syncretism; the loss of the authority of Scripture and of the uniqueness of the gospel.

The Model Today: current in ecumenical circles; evangelicals reject the ecumenical model but still make some use of dialogue in the biblical sense.

Dynamic Equivalence or the Translational Model

The evangelical approach to Islam has been undergoing a period of flux and change in recent years. Increasingly impatient with the slow progress and meager results in Muslim countries and the fragility of churches of converts from Islam, many evangelicals have been rethinking their assumptions and approach, and especially their attitude to the Qur'an and Islamic culture, and have cast about for a new model of approach for ministry to Muslims.

Evangelical Ecumenical Structures and Consultations

What has brought about these changes? One factor has been the rise of what might be called evangelical ecumenical structures. These were created for the purpose of uniting evangelicals and harnessing their largely untapped resources for reaching the unreached. Two organizations that have been especially influential are the Lausanne Committee for World Evangelization (LCWE), formed following the International Congress on World Evangelization held in Lausanne, Switzerland, in 1974, and the World Evangelical Fellowship (WEF), successor to the Evangelical Alliance that was founded in 1846.

A number of international or regional consultations have been held, often with the close involvement of one or both of these bodies, that have significantly shaped the evangelical approach to Islam. These are the Conference on Media in Islamic Culture, sponsored by International Christian Broadcasters and Evangelical Literature Overseas and held in Marseille, France, in 1974 (Shumaker 1974); the Conference on the World of Islam Today, organized by the Evangelical Alliance and held at High Wycombe, England, in January 1976 (Evangelical Alliance 1976); the Consultation on Gospel and Culture, organized by the LCWE and held at Willowbank, Bermuda, in January 1978 (LCWE 1978); the North American Conference on Muslim Evangelization, sponsored jointly by the LCWE and World Vision, and held in Colorado Springs, Colorado, in October 1978

(McCurry 1979); the Mini-Consultation on Reaching Muslims, a part of the Consultation on World Evangelization of the LCWE, held in Pattaya, Thailand, in June 1980 (LCWE 1980); and the conference convened by the LCWE in Zeist, The Netherlands, in July 1987, to consider critical issues in Christian witness among Muslims (Woodberry 1989a).

The Influence of the Social Sciences

The most important influence behind these changes has been the social sciences, and especially the increasing number of missionary scholars trained in these disciplines. I include here cultural anthropology, sociology, linguistics, translation theory, and communication science. These have changed evangelical attitudes toward culture and non-Christian religions and have revolutionized the evangelical missionary enterprise through the infusion of new ideas. The explosion of missiological studies by evangelicals in recent years has been nothing short of phenomenal.

It was at the Marseille Conference on Media in Islamic Culture that missionary anthropology began significantly to affect the evangelical missionary enterprise in the Muslim world. The sponsors wanted the conference to wrestle seriously with the problem of the cross-cultural communication of the gospel to the Muslim mind, rather than be just another fair for exchanging information about methods that seem to work (Shumaker 1974:6). Charles Kraft, professor of anthropology at Fuller Theological Seminary, was chosen to address the cultural dimension of the task. His lectures introduce what will become the main themes of the translational model.

A Return to the Use of the Qur'an

Early in the twentieth century, as we saw, reacting against the excesses of the nineteenth-century polemicists, evangelical missionaries had decided to discontinue using the old polemical literature that made extensive use of the Qur'an. Today, however, we find evangelicals once again returning to the Qur'an as a basis for presenting the gospel to Muslims. And we are once again seeing some of the old polemical classics, long out of print, being reprinted, distributed, and used with Muslims, along with new titles of a similar nature.

In a paper presented at the High Wycombe conference and published in *Missiology*, Fu'ad 'Accad, former general secretary of the Bible Society of the Levant, argued that missionaries should return to using the Qur'an as a "bridge" over which to lead the Muslim to faith in Christ

(1976:332). He exemplified the approach in *Have You Ever Read the Seven Muslim-Christian Principles?* (1978). Written for Muslims, the book claims that these seven principles, fundamental to the gospel, may be found in the Qur'an as well as the Old and New Testaments. (For a more complete exposition of his approach, see his recent, posthumously published work, *Building Bridges: Christianity and Islam*, 1997). Michael Youssef, an Egyptian Christian associated with the Haggai Institute for Advanced Leadership Training, likewise claims that "just as the Apostle Paul found it legitimate to use the unknown god on Mars Hill to introduce the Athenians to the true and living God, I, too, through the pages of the Qur'aan, try to point my Muslim friends to the Savior of the World" (1980:4). Abdiyah Akbar 'Abdul-Haqq, an evangelist with the Billy Graham Association, also makes extensive use of the Qur'an in *Sharing Your Faith with a Muslim* (1980). As the Thailand report bears witness, however, many evangelicals do not agree that the Qur'an constitutes a valid bridge to faith.

Summary of the Translational Model

The Objective of Mission: It is viewed in terms of the emergence of "a people movement to Christ" that remains more or less within Islam.

Theology of Non-Christian Religion: Human cultures are considered neutral vehicles for the contextualization of the gospel and the church; that is, Islam and Islamic culture are viewed neither negatively nor positively but as neutral for purposes of contextualization.

Contextual Starting Point: On the assumption that Islamic culture is a neutral vehicle, Islam is considered a legitimate starting point for contextualization. This means that, in theology, Qur'anic passages may be used as a theological starting point or source of truth for the gospel (e.g., trying to prove the crucifixion on the basis of certain Qur'anic passages). As concerns the church, it means importing Muslim ritual forms, such as the ritual prayer, into the convert church and attempting to fill them with Christian meanings.

Cross-Cultural Hermeneutic: This model employs a hermeneutic of synthesis; it interprets the Bible and Christian forms along with the Qur'an and Muslim forms in such a way as to more or less bring the Christian and Muslim perspectives closer together toward a kind of dialectical unity.

Church Strategy: to raise up dynamic equivalence "Muslim" churches that remain within Islam. In the spectrum of possible church types that has been defined by one writer, this is the C–5 church (to be studied further in chapter 7).

Strengths: It takes Muslim culture seriously.

Weaknesses: I shall go into those in some detail as I outline my proposed model in chapter 12.

part two

A Closer Look: Methodologies and Tools

3

Qur'anic Language and the Protestant Arabic Bible

The Problem of Christian-Muslim Communication

Arab Christian and Muslim religious vocabularies overlap to a certain extent, but there are important differences. One could say that the two communities speak different religious languages. As a result, a vicious circle of misunderstanding has become endemic to Christian-Muslim relationships. Professor Ali Merad, a Muslim, describes the problem this way:

> It is a fact that the language of faith of Christians has not always had the same sound to Muslims. The result is misunderstandings and simplistic reductions of the order of: naSaara = kuffaar = mushrikuun, i.e., Christians = unbelievers = polytheists. . . . Our respective cultural traditions, elaborated separately and in mutual ignorance, have ended up raising between us barriers of concepts, of ideas, and of mental attitudes which are apparently insurmountable. Our theological language, with its increasing and complex technicality, with its heavy conceptual and emotional baggage, due to the accumulation of our cultural acquisitions and of our affective and religious experiences, is too often a source of ambiguity and of incomprehension. (Merad 1975:7, author's translation)

The problem goes back to the beginning of Islam. As the Qur'an and Islam came into being, vocabulary from the Bible and the Jewish and Christian communities of the Middle East was Arabized and Islamized, but often with significant differences in meaning. In addition, large numbers of the Aramaic-speaking and Syriac-speaking peoples embraced Islam over time and began speaking Arabic, and thus many who remained Christian were more or less obliged to adopt Arabic as well. Aramaic, Syriac, and Arabic are cognate languages, however, so the change was not great.

There were considerable consequences, however. The Aramaic/Syriac languages eventually died out for the most part, except for pockets of Christians of the eastern churches who continued using Syriac,[1] especially in their church liturgy. Where Christians adopted Arabic, they retained in their religious vocabulary some Syriac forms that Muslims do not use. And when the Bible was later translated and published in Arabic, these Syriac religious and liturgical forms were used in the translation instead of native Arabic forms. In sum, there is a language gap. Some of the terms used in the two communities are very different; often, however, they are identical or similar in form but used in such different ways that they have taken on very different meanings. And this language gap complicates Christian-Muslim communication.

In this chapter, we shall examine the linguistic dynamics of the situation and their impact on Christian-Muslim communication. Although a similar gap exists in other languages used by Muslims, we shall limit our study to the situation as it exists among speakers of Arabic. The reason for this limitation is simple; I am not familiar with the other languages of Muslim expression, such as Persian or Urdu, or with the history of the contextualization of the gospel in those languages. Nevertheless, since Arabic is the basis for the religious and theological terminology of all Muslims whatever their language, this study will have significance for those working in other languages as well.

Proper Names and Religious or Theological Terms of Biblical Origin in the Qur'an

When one opens the Qur'an, one cannot help but notice affinities with the Bible—most notably references to biblical personages, places, and objects, and to stories about them. With all due allowance for phonetic

---

1. Syriac is a dialect of Aramaic, with its own script, that has survived into modern times; many Syriac-speaking people were Christian before Islam came and had the Bible and Christian literature in Syriac.

changes that occur when words pass from one language into another, many of these names are still sufficiently close to the biblical forms to be recognizable. The list of proper names that have passed into the Qur'an with little or no phonetic change include[2] *aadam* (Adam) and *Hawwaa'* (Eve); *nuuH* (Noah), *ibrahiim* (Abraham), *luuT* (Lot), *isma'iil* (Ishmael), *isHaq* (Isaac), *ya'quub* (Jacob), *yuusef* (Joseph), *muusa* (Moses), *haaruun* (Aaron), *dauud* (David), *sulaimaan* (Solomon), *maryam* (Miriam, Mary), and *zakariya* (Zechariah). In most cases, these have come into the Qur'an not directly from Hebrew or Greek but indirectly through one of the other Semitic languages of the Near East, mainly Aramaic/Syriac (Jeffery 1977:12–13).[3]

A second group of proper names, much fewer in number, has undergone unusual phonetic change. These include *qaabiil* (Cain), thought to have been changed to rhyme with *haabiil* (Abel. *qayin* and *hebel* in Heb.), *yaHyaa* instead of *yuHanna* (John [the Baptist]), and above all *'iisa*, or *'iisa ibn maryam* (Jesus, son of Mary). The Qur'anic forms of these names cannot be explained by the usual patterns of phonetic transformation.

In addition to proper names, there are religious or theological terms of biblical origin that have become, or have inspired, the technical terms of Islam.[4] These include *allaah* (God; cf. Heb. = El, Eloah), *allaahumma* ("O God"; cf. Heb. = Elohim), *nabiy* (Prophet), *firdaus* (Paradise), *jahannam* (Gehenna/ Hell), *masiiH* (Messiah), *tauraah* (Torah), *injiil* (gospel, evangel), *shaiTaan* (Satan), and *naSaara* (Christians).[5]

Qur'anic Literary Style

Richard Bell, who has made a thorough literary study of the Qur'an, describes its various literary features in some detail in his *Introduction to the Qur'an* (Watt 1970). From among these, the only feature of Qur'anic style that to my knowledge has ever been mentioned as a potential vehicle for the gospel is the esthetically attractive Arabic rhymed prose (saja') form that gives the book its distinctive assonance. This feature can only be appre-

---

2. For an explanation of the transliteration used here, see "The Phonetic Transliteration of Arabic Letters/Sounds" after the table of contents.

3. Mingana (1927:80) estimates all foreign influences on the Qur'an to be Syriac (including Aramaic and Palestinian Syriac) 70%, Hebrew 10%, Greco-Roman 10%, Ethiopic 5%, Persian 5%.

4. Books on Islam often have a glossary of such terms; see Jeffery 1958:243–48.

5. For a complete listing of biblical names and terms used in the Qur'an consult Horowitz (1925:145–227), besides the studies of Mingana and Jeffery.

ciated, however, when read in the original Arabic (the only Qur'an Muslims accept). Bell describes Qur'anic assonance in the following terms.

> There is no attempt in the Qur'an to produce the strict rhyme of poetry. In an Arabic poem, each verse had to end in the same consonant or conso-nants surrounded by the same vowels. . . . Only in very exceptional cases is it possible to find this type of rhyme in the Qur'an. What one finds, rather, is assonance, in which short inflectional vowels at the end of a verse are disregarded, and for the rest, the vowels, particularly their length, and the fall of the accent, that is, the form of the end-word of the verse, are of more importance than the consonants. (Watt 1970:69–70)

The Qur'an has always exercised a powerful influence on the Muslim mind. Pickthall, a British Muslim who translated the Qur'an into English, describes the book as "that inimitable symphony, the very sounds of which move men to tears and ecstasy" (1953:v). Its influence on Arabic literary style is unique. For centuries, the Qur'an has been the single most important model for Arabic literature, not merely because of the Muslim doctrine of *i'jaaz*, which holds that it is "inimitable," but also because of its literary power.

Christian Attitudes to Biblical Forms in the Qur'an

In view of these linguistic affinities between Bible and Qur'an, one might think that Arabic-speaking Christians would make use of them in communicating the gospel to Muslims. What do we find, however? To answer this question, let's examine the phenomena of phonetic change, semantic change, and connotative change in these borrowed forms, and how Arab Christians have responded to them.

Phonetic, Semantic, and Connotative Change[6] in Biblical Names in the Qur'an

Looking at biblical proper names in the Qur'an, we note that those that are basically unchanged phonetically are in common use by Arabic-

---

6. These terms derive from linguist De Saussure's distinction between "signification" and "value" (1966:114ff.), which Bible translators call "referential meaning" and "con-notative meaning" (Nida and Taber 1969:56ff.). This distinction has suggested the terms "semantic change" and "connotative change" used here; the term "phonetic change" is self-explanatory.

speaking Christians and in the Protestant Arabic Bible. That is no doubt to be expected, since the Christian community had been using them long before Islam came on the scene.

Some biblical names, however, have undergone semantic change in the Qur'an but not phonetic change. To cite just a few examples, *haamaan* (Sura 28.5, etc.) is anachronistically placed in Pharaoh's court in the time of Moses, rather than in Ahasuerus's court in the time of Esther; *maryam*, the mother of Jesus, is confused with Miriam, "sister of Aaron" (19:28; 3:31) and "daughter of *'imraan*" (66:12, Amram in the Bible); and the "Holy Spirit" (*ruuH al-qudus*) is identified with Gabriel, the angel of revelation (2:87). Note that in most of these cases, only the identity of the person or thing referred to is affected; except for the last, the biblical worldview is not seriously affected. What is notable, however, is that despite these semantic changes, these names are still used in the Arabic Bible as if nothing had happened. Apparently, this kind of change is only an inconvenience.

As for names that have changed phonetically, the Arab Christian response has been quite different. Even where there has been no semantic change, Arab Christians and most Arabic Bibles have consistently avoided them. The Qur'anic forms *qaabiil* (Cain) and *yaHya* (John the Baptist), for example, have never become part of Christian vocabulary. Instead, we find the phonetic equivalents of the Hebrew forms *qaayiin* and *yuHanna* [*al-ma'madaan*], no doubt taken from the Syriac. Some Christians may use the Qur'anic forms in verbal witness and some written materials for Muslims, but many reject even this concession to Muslim usage.

'Iisa, THE QUR'ANIC NAME FOR JESUS

Probably no distinctive Qur'anic form has aroused more debate than the name *'iisa* (Jesus). This is no doubt natural since Christ is at the heart of the Christian message. It is important to note, however, that the Qur'anic form does NOT signal a semantic change; like the term used by Christians it refers to Jesus of Nazareth, "son of Mary." There has, however, been phonetic change and, most importantly, connotative change, as we shall see. Although the Qur'an says many things about Christ that agree with the New Testament, in the last analysis the Christologies of the two books are in conflict. Let's look at the debate about using the Qur'anic form.

We need not go into the Christology of the Qur'an in detail since it has been thoroughly treated by others (e.g., Parrinder 1965). Suffice it to say that the Qur'anic Christ is not a divine being, nor did he die on the cross for the sins of the world; at any rate, this is the unanimous opinion of Muslim exegetes. In an article on the Qur'anic view of Christ, Ali Merad acknowledges more than most Muslims when he concludes:

> There is certainly no question here of a share in the sovereign freedom of God or of participation in the Omniscience of the Creator. There is no question even of God associating Christ in His work in the world, but simply an indication that a mission has been confided (*taklīf*) to him. An extraordinary mission, without precedence in the history of mankind. (1980:12)

Christians have differed sharply over whether we should use the form *'iisa*, and positions have changed little over the years. Some argue that we cannot use it because it communicates the Qur'anic view of Christ; others that we should use it since it is the form the Muslim knows; and still others that it matters little whether we use the one or the other (see, e.g., Madany 1981:7; Dretke 1979:34–35, 207–8; Marsh 1975:41). In any case, Arab Christians reject the form, preferring to use *yasuu'*, the Syriac transliteration of *Iésous*, the name used in the Greek New Testament (or *yasuu' al-masiiH*, i.e., Jesus Christ). Some may use *'iisa* in verbal witness to Muslims, while others prefer simply *al-masiiH* (the Messiah), also found in the Qur'an.

A look at Bible translation practices is instructive. Wilfred J. Bradnock, editor of *The Bible Translator*, did a survey of seventy versions of the New Testament or portions thereof in use in Muslim areas. He found that only thirteen (mostly recent) versions use *'iisa*, while seventeen use some form of "Yesu Almasih" and forty-two use a transliteration of "*Iésous Christos*" (1953:103–6). Arabic versions, including the standard Smith-Van Dyck Version of 1865, have generally used the form *yasuu'*.[7] The most important version to use *'iisa* is the Persian translation of Henry Martyn, published in 1814. According to Bradnock:

> Possibly because Henry Martyn's version was of such outstanding quality, it remained for many years the standard Bible and though subsequent editions underwent correction, the use of *'Îsa* has never been challenged. . . . It is in Persia only that a claim can be made for the consistent use of *'Îsa* in a full Christian context for over more than a century. (1953:102–3)

---

7. Zwemer reports that "in earlier Arabic translations, for example that printed by Richard Watson, London, 1820, the name is uniformly given as 'Isa'." (*MW* 1 [July 1911]:265).

OBJECTIONS TO USING *'Iisa* IN WITNESS TO MUSLIMS

There are two objections to using *'iisa* in witness to Muslims. First, the *'iisa* of the Qur'an is NOT the Jesus of the Bible; that is, that the Qur'anic term has a different meaning. One writer argues that those who use *'iisa* "overlook the fact that in so doing they are giving the Moslems quite a different set of ideas from what they intend." After summarizing the Qur'anic view of Christ, he exclaims, "One wonders . . . how any sane Christian missionary could even mention the name *'Îsa*, for fear of appearing to endorse such fabrications" (Fisk n.d.:3).

The problem with this objection is that it misunderstands the nature of language. It assumes that the term alone communicates the Islamic view of Christ, and that to communicate the truth that Jesus "will save His people from their sins" (Matt 1:21) one must use *yasuu'* or the like. Research in semantics has shown that this assumption is erroneous (Thiselton 1977a:76). It is only when used in a proper sentence (e.g., one that affirms that "Jesus is the Savior of the World") that the name communicates this truth.

It is true that in the Qur'an the connotative meaning of the name *'iisa* differs significantly from New Testament Christology, as we have seen. "Connotative meaning" refers to the total Qur'anic teaching about Christ. But that's a different matter. Here we are talking about the form's referential meaning, the person referred to by the name (see Thiselton 1977a:79). In sum, both *'iisa* in the Qur'an and *Iésous* in the Greek New Testament refer to the same person, Jesus "son of Mary," so the two forms have the same referential meaning.

This distinction is important; to fail to differentiate the two meanings only creates confusion. In any case, to use *yasuu'* or *Jesus* instead of *'iisa* does not necessarily bridge the gap because, as James Dretke has well pointed out, "what the Muslim reads into the name *'iisa*, he will as well read into the name Jesus when it is introduced to him" (Dretke 1979:35). In either case, then, one must explain the term. I conclude that if Christians can safely refer to Christ as "Jesus," even though Unitarians, Mormons, and Jehovah's Witnesses, who each have differing Christologies, also do so, then it is certainly possible to communicate the Christian view of Christ using the name *'iisa*. Has it not been used for two hundred years in the Persian Bible without detriment to the cause of Christ? However, there are other issues involved in the use of the name, so we will not draw any conclusions yet.

The second and principal objection to the form *'iisa* is that it is a corruption of the name God gave Jesus, meaning "Yahweh saves" (Matt 1:21). This objection assumes—again incorrectly—that the form *Iésous* in the Greek New Testament is the original name God gave Jesus and that it has the meaning "Yahweh saves." But *Iésous* can hardly be the original name, nor does it carry this meaning intrinsically. Bible scholars agree that the original name would have been the Aramaic short form *yeshuua'* (Joshua or Jeshua in our English Bible). *Iésous* is its inexact transliteration, borrowed from the Septuagint; since Greek has no "sh" sound and no "ayn" (the Arabic guttural vowel), the name was modified to fit Greek phonetics. Only the full form *yehoshuua'* carries the meaning "Yahweh saves" (Foerster 1964:284, 289). So on the assumption that one should use only the original name and that it must carry the meaning "Yahweh saves," one would have to rule out not only *'iisa* but also *Iésous*, and even *Jesus* and *yasuu'*. Does not the fact that God has sanctioned the use of *Iésous* in the New Testament tell us something?

Various explanations of the "corruption" of the term have been given; some say it was accidental, others that it was intentional. The larger question of the origin of *'iisa* has been much debated for years, but still remains an open question (see Loewenthal 1911:267–82; Hayek 1962:223–54). One theory that must immediately be laid to rest, however, claims that *'iisa* originated with Jews who referred to Jesus disparagingly as *Esau*. Not only is there no historical evidence for such a practice (Hayek 1962:241–47), but what evidence there is suggests that in Jewish society from the second century onward "the name Jesus is avoided" (Foerster 1964:286–87). In any case, to knowingly use a derogatory name would have been out of character for one who venerated Jesus and thought he was defending His honor by denying that the Jews had killed Him (Sura 4:157).

Changes to Religious and Theological Terms of Biblical Origin in the Qur'an

Let's now turn to the Qur'an's religious and theological terms. Here once again we find that, in general, terms of biblical origin that are phonetically unchanged are used by Arab Christians and in Arabic Bible translations, whether or not they have undergone semantic or connotative change. By contrast, those that have been phonetically changed are consistently avoided.

The Qur'anic terms for the concepts of scripture and divine revelation offer a revealing case study in the dynamics of phonetic, semantic, and connotative change and the Christian reaction to such changes. In *The Qur'an as Scripture*, Arthur Jeffery shows how these concepts underwent a radical transformation in postexilic Jewish tradition that was later adapted in the Qur'an. The result was that the Qur'anic terms associated with the concepts mean something quite different from what they originally meant in the Bible. Beside terms of biblical origin, such as *nabiy* (prophet) and *kitaab* (scripture), we find non-biblical terms such as *rasuul* (messenger), *tanziil* (sending down), and *waHy* (inspiration/revelation), all giving expression to the distinctive Qur'anic concepts of scripture and revelation (Jeffery 1952:3–68).

Some terms have undergone several kinds of change with significant consequences. The terms *tauraah*, *zabuur*, and *injiil* (Torah, Psalms, and Gospel) are a case in point. The first two can be said to correspond to parts one and three of the Hebrew Old Testament: the Law and the Writings (Heb. *ketubiim*). To refer to the latter, a collection of thirteen books, as the Psalms might seem strange, but we find the same usage in Luke 24:44. This could be explained by the position of the Psalms as the first and longest of the Writings. As for *injiil*, it could refer to the four canonical Gospels or to the entire New Testament considered as the repository of the Good News. These three terms might seem to correspond sufficiently to biblical usage as to be usable among Muslims. Still, there are significant semantic differences requiring explanation. In addition, there is the change from the Hebrew *mizmuur* ("psalm"—*mazmuur* in the Arabic Bible, pl. *mazaamiir*) to the Qur'anic *zabuur*, and the fact that the Qur'an knows nothing of the second division of the Hebrew Bible, the Prophets (Heb. *nebi'iim*).

Distortions of Biblical Concepts and Their Consequences for Christian Witness to Muslims

Such changes are symptomatic of the conceptual distortions Scripture has suffered under the impact of the Qur'anic worldview.[8] These derive from unbiblical presuppositions about the nature of scripture rather than from linguistic issues. In the Qur'an, the *tauraah* is no longer the Law that God revealed through Moses in raising up a people to His name, nor is the *zabuur* a collection of Hebrew poetry, or the *injiil* the "good news" of salvation through Jesus Christ. In the Qur'an, these three terms signify heavenly books successively "sent down," or dictated from the celestial archetype, "the Mother of the Book," to the prophets Moses, David, and

---

8. Note that here we are only considering conceptual distortions to the doctrine of Scripture; the Qur'anic worldview has distorted other biblical doctrines as well.

Jesus, just as the Qur'an was "sent down" to Muhammad. To Muslims, then, this implies that they should be in the form of direct address from God, just like the Qur'an. As an Islamic catechism puts it:

> It is to be believed that Allah . . . has books which He sends down to His prophets, and in which He makes clear His commands, His prohibitions, His promises and His threats, and that they are truly the speech of Allah. (quoted in Jeffery 1958:126)

Clearly, here is a major conceptual distortion of the biblical idea of scripture that profoundly affects how Muslims understand and respond to the Bible's revelatory claim and message. Since little in our present Bible fits this presupposition, Muslim scholars conclude that it cannot be identified with the *tauraah*, the *zabuur*, and the *injiil* mentioned in the Qur'an. They further conclude that the biblical texts that we have are corrupted, and their originals lost (see, e.g., Jeffery 1958:127; 'Ali 1977:282–87). Is it not interesting, then, that the Christian community continues to use the phonetically unchanged terms *tauraah* and *injiil*, even though they have undergone such substantial connotative change in the Islamic context, while avoiding the form *zabuur* that is unique to the Qur'an? In this case the consequences may not be serious, but at the least it would be helpful if one made a clear distinction between the Christian and Islamic concepts of divine revelation and Scripture.

Sometimes, however, the consequences of using Islamic language are serious. For example, Tisdall, in his revised edition of Pfander's *Mizânu l-Haqq*, instructs translators to use the expression *kalaam-ullaah* when referring to the Bible as the Word of God. "In English, the expression 'The Word of God' may mean (1) the Bible, or (2) Christ. In Arabic these are carefully distinguished, . . . the former being *kalâmu'llâh*, the latter, *kalimatu'llâh*" (1910:5). Later, he also writes about the Scriptures using the Qur'anic framework of "sending down" revelation (*tanziil*) (52ff.).[9]

Although the intent is laudable, the reality is that to refer to Scripture in this way is to squeeze it into an Islamic mold that conflicts with the biblical concept of Scripture. The forms *kalaam* and *tanziil* are concrete verbal nouns (masdars) signifying respectively "the act of speaking" (or simply "speech") and "sending down" (or "that which is sent down"). Such language applied to Scripture implies to Muslims that it

---

9. Tisdall recognizes that the Qur'anic expression "does not express the matter from the Christian point of view," but he still uses the term as if it does (1904:31 n. 2).

was "revealed" in the same way as the Qur'an and thus reinforces their tendency to interpret it within a Qur'anic framework and evaluate it by Qur'anic criteria. Whatever the circumstances, when Muslims read the Bible, they find that it does not fit their idea of a "heavenly book." And when Muslims hear the Christian explanation of biblical inspiration (i.e., that it was not dictated to the biblical authors but they were sovereignly led by the Holy Spirit to choose words that would infallibly communicate the Word of God), on Islamic assumptions, this implies to them that it is not from God. Within their presuppositional framework, they can only conclude that the Bible's inspiration is inferior to that of the Qur'an. The biblical concept of Scripture is thus distorted beyond recognition and its uniquely historical nature lost. Note the following quote:

> Muslims are aware that human imperfections seem to be included in the Bible. For example, the personalities of the Biblical prophets form part of the content of Biblical Scriptures. Moreover, the Biblical Scriptures include both history and the Word of God. The Bible seems to be a mixture of history and revelation. Therefore, it is extremely difficult to separate the true revelation in the Bible from the history and the human personality which the Bible also contains. Therefore, the Qur'an, as the final revelation, is the perfection and culmination of all the truth contained in the earlier Scriptures (revelations). (Kateregga, in Kateregga and Shenk 1980:27)

Before we go on, let me affirm that the Arab Christian community is certainly correct, and squarely within a Christian theological framework, when it refers to both Christ and the Bible as *kalimat-ullâh*—"Word of God." "*Kalimah*" is a feminine singular noun that, like *logos* in the Greek New Testament, signifies an abstract concept—a "word" in the sense of a "message." Thus, in the Scriptures the term *kalimat-ullâh* signifies both God's message to man, that is, the gospel, and Christ as the sum and substance of that message.

Continuing our study of the issues associated with Christian-Muslim communication, let us now take a look at the history of Protestant and evangelical efforts at translating the Bible into Arabic. It provides an excellent case study into the various forces that have shaped Christian-Muslim communication. The Roman Catholic Church and various early scholars also have been active in translation from a very early date, but to include them here would take us beyond the scope of this study.[10]

10. For an overview of Arabic Bible translation efforts, including the pre-Protestant translations, see Bailey and Staal 1982.

Nineteenth-Century Protestant Arabic Bible Translations

The Henry Martyn and SPCK Versions

It is noteworthy that from the start, Protestant Bible translation efforts began to display a bias against language distinctive of the Qur'an. The Bible Society's *Historical Catalogue* reports the publication in 1816 of an Arabic New Testament, translated by Nathaniel Sabat under the supervision of Henry Martyn. It adds, however, "The style adopted was intended to attract Eastern Moslems, who disliked the Newcastle Bible of 1811; but its resemblance to the phraseology of the Koran rendered it unacceptable to Arabic-speaking Christians" (Darlow and Moule 1963:2/69). *YaHya* is used for John the Baptist, but the traditional name for Jesus (*yasuu'*) is retained" (Bailey and Staal 1982:7). In any case, the translation did not receive wide acceptance.

In 1848, the Society for Promoting Christian Knowledge (SPCK) launched a Bible translation project under the supervision of Dr. Samuel Lee (1783–1852)[11] that was published in 1857 (Darlow and Moule 1963:2/71). The Arab translator engaged for the task was Faris al-Shidyaq (1804–1887), a Syrian Christian who also figures in the revival of Arab literature (Gibb 1962:248).[12] Because it was "very literal" and "stilted," the SPCK Version was abandoned for the Smith-Van Dyck Version when it appeared (Thompson 1956:5; Van Dyck 1891:92). Shidyaq describes Lee's translation style in one of his books, expressing annoyance at his pedantic avoidance of "rhymed prose and literary constructions" (i.e., Qur'anic assonance) and especially his insistence on using exactly "the same terms and constructions" as the original ('Abboud 1950).

The Standard Smith-Van Dyck (S-VD) Version of 1865

The Arabic Bible that has enjoyed universal acceptance among Arab Protestants, and has been in use for well over a century, is known as the Smith-Van Dyck (S-VD) Version. It was begun by Eli Smith (1801–1857) and, after his death, completed by Cornelius Van Dyck (1818–1895), both missionaries of the American Board in Syria; this version was published in 1865. Smith and Van Dyck were assisted by several Arab scholars who were also leaders in the renaissance of Arab literature in Syria, Butrus

---

11. Lee translated Henry Martyn's three polemical tracts; see chapter 1, n. 1.

12. According to Gibb, Shidyaq "was converted to Islam in the [eighteen] fifties, while in the service of the Bey of Tunis"; this would have been after his Bible translation work.

al-Bustani and Nasif al-Yaziji, both Christians, and Yusuf al-Asir, a Muslim sheikh (Thompson 1956:20–27; Saliba 1975:254–363).

Here also, according to H. H. Jessup, author of the early history of the American Board, "some would have preferred the style 'Koranic', i.e. Islamic, adopting idioms and expressions peculiar to Mohammedans. *All native Christian scholars* decidedly objected to this" (Jessup 1910:1/75). In other words, the unusual Qur'anic forms of biblical names, such as *qaabiil* (Cain), *yaHya ibn zakariya* (John the Baptist), *zabuur* (Psalms) and *'iisa* (Jesus), were avoided, as well as anything resembling the Qur'an's esthetically attractive literary style. Instead, they used the Syriac forms of biblical personal names and Syriac religious and theological terms, some of which also exist in Arabic but with very different meanings.[13]

Following are two of the more unfortunate examples. For the Greek term *nomos* (law), borrowed from the Septuagint (LXX) to render *torah*, the S-VD translators used the Syriac transliteration *naamuus* instead of translating the term. In classical Arabic literature, *naamuus* is an obscure term that the Arabs clearly did not understand in the sense intended,[14] but in modern Arabic usage it signifies *mosquitoes*! One can imagine the confusion of the average Muslim on reading this in the Bible or hearing it read.

Another common Syrianism in the Arabic Bible is the verb *'amada* and its derived and related forms, used in the sense of "to baptize," "be baptized," or "baptism." Much as the Greek forms *baptizo* and *baptisma* were transliterated instead of translated into English, the Syrian Church transliterated these Syriac terms into Arabic when it was Arabized. The form does exist in Arabic, but its use for baptism would not be clear unless one is familiar with Christian language.

In addition to the problem of its terminology, the S-VD version follows the Greek language structure too woodenly in the New Testament and is based on the Textus Receptus rather than on the critical Greek text. The

13. Complaints have been reported that the Smith-Van Dyck version contains "Syrian-isms which are not acceptable in Egypt" (Thompson 1956:26) or of "Syrian Arabic" that a sheikh in Oman said was "so strange that I understand nothing" (Harrison 1934:269). Both references are undoubtedly to Syriac; the term *suryaani* in Arabic signifies both Syrian, especially the East Syrian Church, and its liturgical language, Syriac.

14. Jeffery (1958:16) quotes a *Hadith* where Khadija's cousin, Waraqa b. Naufal, was to have said when told of Muhammad's encounter with the angel, "This is the *naamuus* which was sent down upon Moses the son of Amram" (see n. 6). Interpreters understand *naamuus* here to refer to the angel Gabriel, but even if it refers to the "sending down" of the Torah, the intended meaning is still terribly skewed.

net result of all this is that some important theological passages, especially in the Johannine and Pauline writings, are rendered difficult for the average non-Christian reader to understand. The cumulative effect is that it exacerbates the problem of Christian-Muslim communication.

Twentieth-Century Protestant Arabic Bible Translations

The Revised Smith-Van Dyck Version

The need for revising and updating the S-VD version had been proposed from time to time (Bishop 1936:153–60; Eerdman 1937:218–36). Finally, in 1954, the Bible societies set up a committee to undertake a complete revision. The Revised S-VD New Testament was published in 1972 but did not seem to have been widely accepted or circulated. In any case, the project to revise the S-VD Old Testament was abandoned because, by the time the New Testament was published, the Bible societies were already heavily involved in a new translation project.

The Good News Arabic (or Today's Arabic) Version

In 1967, the Bible societies launched an ecumenical Arabic Bible translation project with the involvement of Catholic, Coptic, and Protestant scholars. The goal was a translation that would be acceptable to all Arabic-speaking Christian communions and would be suitable for work among Muslims. The S-VD version was not considered suitable to this twofold purpose for various reasons. The *Today's Arabic Version* (TAV) New Testament was published in 1978.[15] To achieve the twofold purpose, this version used a newspaper-style Arabic familiar to Muslims and Christians and included some Qur'anic terms or constructions. This, however, aroused such sharp criticism from the evangelical Arab churches that it was revised a number of times to eliminate the most objectionable elements. When the entire Bible was published in 1993, it was called the *Good News Arabic* (GNA) *Bible.*

The Living Arabic Version, or Kitaab ul-Hayaat (also called the New Arabic Bible)

In 1973, Middle East Publications, an offshoot of Operation Mobilization in the Middle East, launched the Living Arabic Bible translation

---

15. Letters from United Bible Societies officials to the author, July 1984. See also Bailey and Staal 1982:9; B.T. 1967:153.

project, known as *Kitaab ul-Hayaat,* under the direction of Georges Houssney. The project was originally sponsored by Living Bibles International, which later merged with the International Bible Society. The *Living Arabic New Testament* (LANT) was published in Egypt in 1982 under the title *Al-Injiil: Kitaab ul-Hayaat (The Gospel: The Book of Life).* The complete *New Arabic Bible* (NAB) was published in 1988 under the title *Al-Kitaab Al-Muqaddas: Kitaab ul-Hayaat (The Bible: The Book of Life).* The key translators for the project who worked with Houssney were Saeed Baz for the New Testament and Samuel Shahid for the Old Testament. This translation uses a literary yet simple style intended for Christian and Muslim readers. It avoids uniquely Qur'anic language, which Christian Arabs tend to find offensive.

Siirat-ul-MasiiH

Both of the translations above represent a considerable improvement over the S-VD Version in terms of readability and simplicity. They avoid the obscure language of the S-VD but still use much of the old Christian religious language. About the time they were being prepared, a very different approach to Bible translation entered the picture. In 1987, a highly contextualized "scripture" in Qur'anic form was published under the title *siirat-ul-masiiH bi-lisaan 'araby fasiiH (The Life of the Messiah in a Classical Arabic Tongue)* (Owen 1987:50–59). It translated select portions of the Gospels using Qur'anic language and phraseology in the rhymed prose (*saja‘*) style of the Qur'an. Inspired by the positive impact of Tatian's *Diatesseron* (Gospel harmony) in the early Syriac-speaking church, the publisher cast it in the form of a Gospel harmony that he called *siira* (biography) to head off the usual Muslim charge that Christians are "corrupting" the Scripture. The *siira* form is well-known in Islamic literature from the early *siiraat-un-nabiy (Lives of the Prophet).*

However, besides using Qur'anic language and phraseology, the publisher also tried to imitate the Qur'an. In typical Qur'anic style, each chapter begins with the usual Qur'anic basmala (repetition of the phrase "in the name of God"), is given a title (e.g., "The Sycamore Tree"), and is labeled "revealed in Jerusalem" (*maqdisi*) or "revealed in Galilee" (*jaliili*). To top it all off, a short chapter reminiscent of the opening Surah of the Qur'an (*al-faatiha*) is added at the beginning, all with the idea that a contextualized translation of "Semitic interpretation" and Islamic theological terminology would facilitate a "Messianic Muslim" movement to Christ within Islam (Owen 1987:51–52).

As one might have predicted, however, because the *siirah* tries to "imitate the inimitable," the Qur'an, within two years after its publication the Muslim World League had issued a warning against it. Further, the Islamic Research Academy in Egypt asked the Sheikh of al-Azhar to have it banned (reported in the newspaper, *al-'alam*, published in Morocco, 2 April 1989). Today it appears to be shut out from distribution in the Arab world. At the least, one can say that, had the publisher been content to make it readable, understandable, and in good literary style without trying to imitate the Qur'an, the *siira* could well still be in circulation in the Arab world today.

Al-Kitaab al-Shariif

The year 1991 witnessed the publication of yet another translation of the New Testament, under the title *al-injil al-sharif* (*The Honorable Gospel*). An initial trial edition of the complete Bible was published in 2000 under the title *al-kitab al-sharif* (*The Honorable Scripture*). After revisions were made in the light of feedback, a second edition was published in 2003 for wide distribution (I'm told that a study edition is nearing completion). Originally developed under the auspices of the Assemblies of God, publication and distribution rights were recently turned over to a non-profit, interdenominational organization called the Sharif Bible Society. This is the first complete Arabic Bible intended strictly for a Muslim audience; all previous versions were intended for Christians or Christians and Muslims. *Al-kitab al-sharif* uses Qur'anic forms of biblical names, such as *'iisa* and *yaHya*, and goes to considerable lengths to find phraseology that Muslims understand and accept but that the translators hope will not be offensive to Christians.

Some Concluding Observations and Further Questions

The subject of bible translation is exceedingly complex, so let me begin by summarizing briefly the main facts discussed so far. Christian-Muslim communication problems, reflecting a tortuous history of Christian-Muslim relations, include the following:

- Islam absorbed much of its conceptual framework and vocabulary from Christianity, mainly Aramaic/Syriac-speaking Christianity.

46

- A majority of Middle Easterners embraced Islam, eventually switching to speaking Arabic.
- Under the impact of the Islamic worldview, the borrowed Aramaic/Syriac concepts and terminology were changed phonetically as well as conceptually.
- Most Middle Eastern Christians who had not embraced Islam also switched to speaking Arabic.
- Middle Eastern Christians imported many Syriac biblical terms into their religious Arabic and liturgy, rejecting the use of Islamic language because it was so different in meaning.
- Arabic Bible translations have followed the same practice of rejecting Islamic language until very recently.

The result of all this has been a tremendous communication gap between the two communities, and each side has seriously misunderstood the other.

These facts raise serious questions needing answers. But the issues are exceedingly complex. It is recognized that the total picture transcends the linguistic and communicational factors looked at so far; other factors will be looked at later. Let us consider where this might be taking us, in a provisional manner.

The first question that comes to mind relates to the Arab Christian pattern of avoiding religious language unique to the Qur'an and substituting Syriac-based biblical names and terms. Might a first step in overcoming the communication gap be to produce Bible translations for Muslims that use Islamic Arabic to communicate Christian truth? When I first began to study this issue, I was thinking more or less along those lines. More recently, it has become clear that the problem is too complex to be solved by linguistic solutions alone.

Since the 1990s the *Siira* and the *Shariif* Bible, both using Islamic Arabic to varying degrees, have entered the picture, not to mention the TAV/GNA and LANT/NAB, both of which have made important improvements in terms of intelligibility and simplicity. Therefore, I sought feedback from Christians in a variety of mostly Arab countries who are familiar with the above-mentioned versions, including a few Bible society personnel and other publishers. Some interesting facts have come to light that help put some things in perspective. It is noteworthy that the feedback received is all over the map. As one distributor perceptively noted, "I believe there are a variety of tastes and perceptions that constitute the very wide number of

47

people we try to reach." The comment can apply both to those distributing the Scriptures and to those who receive them. Clearly, the differences of opinion expressed on the different translations reflect many factors, not least of which is the subjective personal preference of the one judging. As expected, I found that there are still those who swear by the old *S-VD* translation of 1865 as the most precise and accurate. One respondent comments: "As far as I know the *Van Dyck* is used almost exclusively by Christians" but then goes on to report that in his country "the MBBs [Muslim Background Believers] enjoy using both the Van Dyck and the *Kitaab al-Hayaat*"[i.e., NAB]. Judging from the replies, it appears that the GNA and NAB have received near equal preference, depending on the country, but the NAB may have a slight edge in distribution because, as one noted, it was published first. Besides readability, preferences often turned on such factors as marketing, lower price, intended audience, or availability in-country, notably of a certain inexpensive bilingual New Testament. Then there's the *Shariif* Bible, the only one that targets the majority population. One respondent seems to express the opinion of most when he calls it "a rising star," adding, "but there are still very few convinced distributors." As for the *Siira*, most were aware of it, but their feedback confirms that it is no longer available in the Arab world.

On reflection, all this seems to indicate that the Christian-Muslim communication gap goes beyond the linguistic and communicational issues discussed so far. Clearly, we're up against a conflict of worldviews and ideologies as well. Is it not clear that Arab Christian resistance to the use of Qur'anic language represents a defensive reaction against the overbearing pressure of Islam? To counteract Islam's social pressures, the Christian community has understandably responded by raising social barriers to protect itself against the injustices of the Islamic social system. Its Christian religious language is one such barrier. There is a problem, however, in that barriers not only protect but also hinder social relations and evangelism.

We also noted that Muslims look with a critical eye at translations that cast Scripture in Qur'anic language. As we saw from our look at the *Siira*, Muslims tend to view it as an attempt to produce a scripture equal to the Qur'an that they consider "inimitable." One respondent reports that "similar attempts to make the Bible look like the Qur'an have been used as a justification for deporting foreigners and imprisoning Muslim converts. The accusation is 'tahriif' " [i.e., corrupting the scripture]. One respondent also reports hearing negative MBB comments about the *Shariif* Bible, that "it is deceptive, trying to be like the Qur'an."

48

All this points to the need to be sensitive to worldview and ideological issues, along with the linguistic and communicational issues, in our approach. The question of whether Christians can use the form *'iisa* is a case in point. There is no question but that *'iisa* has the same referential meaning as *Jesus*. But we dare not lose sight of the fact that it is so distasteful to the indigenous Christian community precisely because of the worldview factor, and I have the impression (although I didn't think to research the question) that many MBBs also find the form distasteful. One cannot therefore afford to be doctrinaire about using *'iisa*.

A second important issue that arises out of this study concerns the semantics of Qur'anic language. We noted that terms of biblical origin used in the Qur'an have often undergone significant semantic or connotative changes that affect how Muslims understand the Scripture and its message. But to my knowledge, little has been done to clarify the semantics of Qur'anic language comparable to what has been done for the semantics of New Testament language, or to compile what may already have been done for the benefit of Bible translators and others. Such a study would be a big help in overcoming the semantic gap.

A third important issue concerns the need for an approach that fosters good relationships between the churches of Muslim-background believers and the existing churches of the Middle East. This is critical. They need each other. For one thing, we need to encourage Muslim-background believers to become familiar with the language of the traditional churches so as to be able to use the Bible study tools that exist in Arabic—concordances, Bible dictionaries, and commentaries.

Clearly a number of important issues have come to light in this chapter, issues that need careful examination and reflection. It is recognized that we may not be able to reach complete agreement on all matters, but at the least we should have a clear understanding of the pitfalls to avoid.

4

Negative Uses of Qur'anic Phrases

The earliest and most extensive ways Christians have made use of Qur'anic phraseology in their approach to Islam were basically negative. As we saw in chapter 1, in the nineteenth and early twentieth centuries Christian workers typically viewed Islam in terms of a building condemned to destruction, and the negative uses came out of this approach for the most part. This involved polemical debates with Muslims, most notably those of Henry Martyn in Persia and Karl Gottlieb Pfander in India, and a wide variety of polemical writings by a number of authors (see Muir 1897:1–52, 89–101). The polemic focused on the criticism of Islamic ethics, and most notably the historical criticism of aspects of Islamic history.

The Criticism of Islamic Ethics

While many of the Qur'an's commands parallel those of the Scriptures, there are significant differences as well. It was these differences, real or perceived, that were the focus of the polemicists' criticism. The ethical teachings and practice of Muhammad were the focus of much of the criticism. As the Arab Prophet, he represents not only the Lawgiver for the Muslim but also the exemplar after which one must pattern his life. The polemic therefore aimed at removing the Prophet from his pedestal.

The Main Lines of Ethical Criticism

There are three main lines of criticism brought against the ethics of the Qur'an. These are that

1. Certain of the Qur'an's teachings are "immoral," namely, the "sensual" concept of paradise; the teaching that God leads astray whom He will and guides aright whom He will; and the sanctioning of polygyny, easy divorce, child marriage, concubinage, the male domination of women, female seclusion, the veil, slavery, the sexual use of female slaves, and the use of the sword to induce conversion.
2. Muhammad was "sensual" and "vindictive"; for example, he had as many as thirteen wives while limiting Muslims to four; he married the wife of his adopted son and sanctioned it by a revelation. And those who opposed him he had killed.
3. Islamic ethics are legalistic and focus on externals.

What stands out is that the polemicists' criticism of Islamic ethics was based mostly on their subjective evaluation of Islamic ethical practice contrasted with the higher ethical teachings of Christ, His sinlessness, and the inwardness of New Testament ethics.

By way of illustration, let us look at three representative writers: Karl Gottlieb Pfander, Sir William Muir, and G. H. Rouse. Pfander's first book, *The Mizanu'l Haqq (Balance of Truth)*, is representative of much that has been written. First published in Persian in 1835, the book was later translated into English (1867) and other languages of Muslim expression. It became the most widely used Protestant polemical work against Islam of the nineteenth century. The revised and considerably enlarged *Mîzân* of 1910 is largely the work of William St. Clair Tisdall.

Part three of the *Mîzân* is devoted mainly to the ethical criticism of the Qur'an. Pfander argues that certain of its teachings, such as its sensual view of paradise and the command to use force to make converts, are "at variance with the mercy, love, holiness, and righteousness of God" and are thus "proof against the divine inspiration of the Koran" (1867:97–98). In a chapter on how Islam spread at the beginning, Pfander attributes its success to "indulgences" such as these and concludes: "It must be conceded that a religion in which compulsion and war are lawful cannot be of the truth" (130). Pfander also devotes a chapter to the personal character of Muhammad in which he rehearses details of his many marriages, his recourse to revelation to "cover the disgrace" of taking his adopted son's wife, and his vengeful treatment of his enemies. All this is cited to show that Muhammad does not satisfy the "marks of a true Prophet" (117, 118, 77).

As for Sir William Muir, we have already seen some of his ethical criticisms of Islam in chapter 1. In *The Rise and Decline of Islam*, he rehearses many of the details already mentioned, stressing the fact that the objectionable practices are commanded by the Qur'an.

> What I desire to make clear is the fact that such things may be practiced *with the sanction* of the Scripture which the Moslem holds to be divine, and that these same indulgences have from the first existed as inducements which helped materially to forward the spread of the faith. ([1883]:34–35)

He concludes by arguing that although people in "Christian nations" may have done such things "it is in the teeth of their Divine law" ([1883]:35).

For his part, Rouse, in his *Tracts for Muhammadans*, contrasts the externalism of Islamic ethics with the inwardness of the gospel. He characterizes Islam as "outside religion" and argues that "true religion is not merely an external matter. It is internal" (n.d.:81). Circumcision and sacrifices are not what God requires, but rather circumcision of the heart, and the sacrifices of a contrite heart (81–82). The ritual prayer of Islam (Salaat) is defective and external in comparison with the spiritual nature of prayer in Christianity (168–81). The theme of externalism is prominent in Rouse's treatment of all the "acts of worship" (182–86, 208–11).

Problems with Ethical Criticism

There are many issues of an ethical nature that cannot be ignored in Christian witness to Muslims. The ethico-critical approach of the polemicists, however, presents serious problems. For one thing, much of it is based on an evolutionary view of religion and on the ethnocentrism that is so characteristic of the nineteenth century, rather than on Scripture. Moreover, it often merely assumes what it claims to prove. One of the most telling arguments against it is that it fails to do justice to the ethical seriousness of Islam. Arne Rudvin has argued, and I believe correctly, that Islamic ethics lay great stress on the inward man, and that to characterize Islamic ethics as external is "nonsensical" (1979:90). Tragically, about all the approach accomplished was to stir up a heated defense of Muhammad, thereby distracting the Muslim's attention from the gospel. In sum, it tends to harm the cause of Christ. The ethical criticism of the Qur'an was abandoned when the old polemical works were taken out of circulation in the 1930s. However, some of the old polemical works have been reprinted and are in use again, although not nearly as extensively as before.

The Historical Criticism of Islam

The Muslim Attitude toward Historical Criticism

Historical criticism is a more complicated issue. Muslims have always had an ambivalent attitude toward historico-critical studies. Interestingly, they generally have no quarrel with the method in the study of secular, that is, non-Islamic, history. It was in fact a Muslim, Ibn Khaldun (1332–1406), who is generally credited with having pioneered the critical study of history. When it comes to Islamic history, however, especially the historical facts about Muhammad and the textual history of the Qur'an, Muslims reject the validity of critical methodology.

The reason for their ambivalence lies in the Islamic view of history. Islam does not, like Christianity, view history as the medium through which God reveals Himself. To the Muslim, history is the arena in which God placed the *Ummah* (the Islamic community), to which He gave His eternal Word and the task of fulfilling, preserving, and propagating His message to the ends of time and space. Viewed as the verbatim reproduction of the eternal Divine Word (*tanziil*), the Qur'an is held to transcend history, and the Prophet and the early *Ummah* have assumed a quasi-suprahistorical status as well (Booth 1970:109–22; Smith 1957:11–47).

Accordingly, Muslims have been most reluctant to use historico-critical methods in the study of Islamic history. Ibn Khaldun exempted the "traditional sciences" (i.e., those based on Islamic law, as opposed to the "philosophical sciences") from his critical method (1958:2/436; Booth 1970:118). Muslims especially object to the use of critical methodology in Qur'anic study; to even entertain the idea is tantamount to *kufr* ("blasphemy"). It should be noted, however, that they have not been able completely to ignore the historical dimension of the Qur'an. They have been obliged, for example, to call upon historical circumstances in the Prophet's life, the so-called *asbaab an-nuzuul* ("causes of the descent"), to interpret many passages. Historically, Islam has allowed only for the criticism of *Hadith* literature (literature that reports the sayings and customs of the Prophet and his companions). Even there, however, Muslims scrutinize only the character and reliability of the *isnaad* ("chain of transmitters") of the *Hadiths*, not the text.

It is only in modern times that a few Muslim scholars have dared to use historico-critical methods in the study of Islam, especially modern Islamic history. It would seem that the main reason for this is the painful circumstances in which the Muslim community has found itself in the twentieth century, and its seeming inability to get control of its political destiny. Muslims have revised and adapted historical methodology to make it Islamic, but those who go that far are very few.[1] The historico-critical study of the Qur'an itself is still anathema, and the few who have ventured moderate attempts at it have seen their work suppressed.[2]

The Missionary Use of the Historical Criticism of Islam

In the West, the historico-critical study of Islamic history and the Qur'an began in the nineteenth century and continues today. We shall not, however, go into the methodology; our main interest is to examine how Christians have used historical criticism against Islam. In the beginning, a number of those who contributed significantly to the scientific study of Islam were missionaries and other Christians. Some of these have encouraged or used historical criticism for missionary purposes.

We want to look at how the two questions referred to, to which Muslims are extremely sensitive, have been treated: the question of the historical Muhammad and that of the historical sources of the Qur'an. As to the first, as we saw earlier, Muhammad represents the exemplar after which every Muslim should pattern his life. In some respects, Muhammad's role as an example for Muslims to follow is similar to that of Christ in the church.

It has been noted that Muslims "quite early, driven by their disputations with Christians, wove around the person and life of the Prophet a network of superhuman features" (Gibb and Kramers 1953:405). To the devout Christian, this legendary material seemed unjustly to put Muhammad on a level with Christ, or even above Him. In this situation, the historico-critical method seemed like a tool ready-made for removing the myths that were hiding the only too human features of the Prophet and for presenting him in his true light, divested of his undeserved halo.

1. For an excellent survey of modern Islamic approaches to history, see Haddad 1982.
2. For two cases, see Jeffery, "Higher Criticism of the Koran," *MW* 22 (January 1932):78–83, and Haddad 1982:46–53.

At this point, the ethical criticism and historical criticism of Islam merge somewhat.

Sir William Muir was one of the pioneers in the historico-critical study of Islam. He wrote several important historical studies on the life of Muhammad and early Islamic history. He was also one of the first to encourage the missionary use of the critical method. In an early work, Muir complained of the poor use of historical criticism by missionaries, and especially of the "utter want of the faculty of historical criticism" among educated Muslims (1897:87). He stressed the importance of "disentangling truth from falsehood" in the great mass of traditions about Muhammad.

> If we can, *from their own best sources*, prove to them that they are deceived and superstitious in many important points, and can thus establish the untenableness of some of their positions; while at the same time admit all statements that are grounded in fact;—we shall have gone a great way to excite honest inquiry and induce the sincere investigator to follow our lead. (88)

Later writers focused on what we might call the question of the Muhammad of history versus the Muhammad of faith. A typical example is S. W. Koelle, who sought to distinguish the "historical" from the "mythical" Muhammad in *Mohammed and Mohammedanism, Critically Considered* (1889:vii, 447). The first 241 pages look at "Mohammed viewed in the daylight of history," and the remaining 205 pages at "Muhammad viewed in the moonshine of tradition."

Another writer in this tradition is William H. T. Gairdner. He wrote several articles on the problem of the historical Muhammad in the *Moslem World* (1915; 1919). One of these is a reply to an article in a Muslim journal, written on the occasion of the Prophet's birthday, which, in his opinion, exceeded the bounds of truth in the way it claimed for Muhammad every virtue and disclaimed every fault, and in the process tried to besmirch the name of Jesus. "In short," he wrote, "*Ecce Homo* is to be transferred from the Nazarene to the Arabian" (1919:27). Vander Werff's appraisal of Gairdner is to the point.

> Gairdner sought to help the Muslim community to separate fact from fiction, myth from history. Because the system of Islam is largely structured on traditions, he encouraged Muslims to use historical criticism to get at the truth about Mohammed and his teachings. His purpose was not to

produce a reformed Islam, but to help Muslims to see their real dilemma and to become receptive to God's news in Christ. (1977:212)

As to the second question, that of the historical sources of the Qur'an, we note that Western scholars have long been fascinated with this question (Sidersky 1933; Watt 1970:184–86). Historians think historically and so try to trace the historical origins of ideas. Such an endeavor, however, is extremely upsetting to Muslims, who think transcendentally. They bitterly resent any suggestion that historical sources, whatever their nature, might have gone into the composition of the Qur'an.

There are of course serious problems with the Islamic view of the Qur'an. Some polemicists, therefore, felt that the historico-critical method represents a unique tool for refuting Muslim claims for it. They felt that if they could demonstrate that historical sources were used in the Qur'an, and could show which ones were used and where, the Muslim claim that the Qur'an is a revelation from God would be destroyed.

The principal author to attempt this was William St. Clair Tisdall. Tisdall has written a scholarly work for the scientist of religion, entitled *The Original Sources of the Qur'an* (1905). In this work, he traces various Qur'anic ideas to pre-Islamic Arabian, Sabian, Jewish, Zoroastrian, Christian, and heretical Christian sources. In addition, he has written a polemical work against Islam, *The Sources of Islam*, in which he uses the same data to try to disprove the revelatory claims of the Qur'an. After summarizing the Islamic view of the Qur'an, Tisdall lays down the following challenge: "Now, if we can trace the teaching of any part of it to an earthly Source, or to human systems existing previous to the Prophet's age, then Islam at once falls to the ground" (1910:2).

Tisdall's work, which was originally published in Persian around 1900, created quite a stir among Muslims at the time. It was translated into all the major languages used by Muslims, but it too was taken out of circulation when the polemical approach was abandoned in the 1930s. It has been recently reprinted in English and Arabic.

Recent Debate over the Validity of Public Debate and Historical Criticism in Muslim Ministry

As we saw in part one, by the twentieth century, missionaries were beginning to have doubts about the value of polemic as a means of winning Muslims to Christ. Most eventually concluded that it should be avoided. In the 1930s, they even pulled from the market all the old polemical works. It is all the more significant, then, that by the 1990s there has been a return to public debate and historical criticism in ministry to Muslims.

The impetus for this has come mainly from the Muslim side; for the most part, Christians are responding to Muslim attack. Since early in the twentieth century, there has been an increasing influx of Muslim immigrants to Europe and North America as a result of problems in the Muslim world—drought, political and social upheavals, widespread unemployment and lack of jobs, and the like. With the immigrants have come mosques and imams. Later, there came Islamic organizations dedicated to the indoctrination of Muslims in the West and the propagation of Islam. Financed largely by petro-dollars from the Arabian gulf, these have become increasingly sophisticated and aggressive in their attacks on Christianity. They like to challenge Christian leaders to debate and arrange for polemicists like Ahmed Deedat, Jamal Badawi, or Shabir Ali to debate them in a public setting, preferably in university lecture halls. A handful of Christian apologists, such as Josh McDowell, Jay Smith, and Anis Shorrosh, have risen to the challenge, but not all have been up to the task, and one or two have fared poorly.

As might be expected, the return of the debate format has precipitated a discussion of the validity of the approach. Many, still influenced by the writings of earlier missionaries, are convinced that public debate with Muslims is to be avoided. The January 1998 issue of the *Evangelical Missions Quarterly* carried three articles debating the question. Jay Smith, a missionary of the Brethren in Christ World Missions, ably defends the debate approach and the use of historico-critical studies of Islam in this context (1998a:28–35; 1998b:37–46). He has been heavily involved in responding to the challenges of Muslims in England—notably in Hyde Park, London, and the universities. Two respondents oppose the approach (36–42). The first, writing anonymously, argues that "the history of Christian mission to Islam teaches that . . . in the long term polemic evangelism does not work"; he cites the Agra debate of Pfander with Rahmat-Ullah al-Hindi in 1854, and the testimony of Thomas Valpy French and Temple Gairdner as evidence (36). Phil Parshall agrees, calling it "a rehash of that which has been tried, tested, and found wanting"; he cites the experience of Anis Shorrosh in his 1988 debate with Ahmed Dedaat as further evidence that the "harsh criticism of their revered holy book" only incites "a wildly antagonistic and even violent response from the local Muslims" (38–39). He then goes on to suggest five "alternative methodologies."

Some Conclusions

In response, we must acknowledge that debate and the historical criticism of Islam have limited value in Muslim evangelization. Muslim societies tend to be quite volatile at the slightest criticism of their prophet or the Qur'an. The above anonymous author is therefore surely correct when he writes that Jay's method would not work well in many parts of the world and that it is "suited only to the pluralistic, democratic, open kind of society in which we live" (Smith 1998b:37). However, I would agree with Jay when he argues that a response like his is necessary when it is the Muslim community in Europe and America that has thrown down the gauntlet by their attacks on Christianity and that they are winning converts to Islam with few responding to their attacks.

I cannot agree with those who argue categorically that history has proved that the debate approach does not work. For one thing, the argument assumes—incorrectly—that all debate is polemic. I have studied the early polemic writings extensively and would maintain that there were a number of problems with the Christian polemics that had little to do with the debate format. The word "polemic" often implies aggressive attack or harsh criticism. This was certainly characteristic of the approach in the nineteenth century, which sought to bring Islam crashing to the ground, but it is unfair to tag Jay's debates with such a label. I would agree that the early polemic was harsh and excessive, but surely one cannot assume that all who debate Muslims are like that. As we saw in chapter 1, those early missionaries were taught that polemic was the only approach worth using. That was a major factor behind the failure.

Along with that was the problem of the polemicists' highly rationalistic approach. It was assumed that unaided reason is able to distinguish the true revelation and prophet from the false. At the beginning of his *Mizan*, Pfander posited five criteria whereby "the truth of a written revelation may be demonstrated," and in a later chapter, he adds four marks of the "true prophet" (1867:vi, 77). The problem is that rational criteria for the true revelation that are universal and objective, and recognized by both sides, do not exist. At bottom his criteria were subjective and were merely assumed to be true. And this sort of thing occurred over and over in the polemic, both in their ethical criticism of Islam and in their historical criticism.

We shall return to this later in our discussion of the hermeneutical method. Nevertheless, several remarks are in order here concerning the way historico-critical studies of Islam are used. Probably most Christian scholars would agree on the positive value of the methodology for the study of both the Bible and the Qur'an. In any case, I am not questioning the legitimacy of the methodology in general or of its use to investigate questions about the Prophet or the Qur'an in particular. There is a problem, however, in the way the methodology has sometimes been used.

The problem is that interpreters have not always acknowledged the role of their presuppositions in their interpretation of the data, and, consequently, on the results obtained. Critical studies are not carried out in a presuppositional vacuum. Has not the so-called quest for the historical Jesus made that abundantly clear? Whatever one may say about the necessity for *Hadith* criticism and for separating fact from fiction in the traditions about Muhammad—an enterprise that some Muslim scholars also favor—it is nevertheless clear that one's presuppositions do influence how one interprets those facts.

The problem, for example, with Gairdner's approach to the question of the historical Muhammad is that there is no recognition of the influence of Gairdner's own presuppositions on the interpretation of the data. It is true that Muslims' transcendentalist presuppositions involve them in interpreting the facts about Muhammad in almost superhuman terms. But it is also true that Gairdner's presuppositions have involved him in interpreting those same facts in such a way as to preclude Muhammad's being a prophet. The critical results are simply presented as fact.

The same criticism applies to the attempt to disprove the revelatory claims of the Qur'an through a demonstration of its historical sources. Here again, I do not question the validity of using critical methods for investigating possible literary sources behind the Qur'an. Nor do I doubt that such sources exist. What is problematic is the claim that if the theory of sources can be proven, then Islam falls to the ground. Even if the existence of sources is proved beyond a shadow of a doubt, that is all that is proved. There can be no doubt, of course, that, given the Muslim's presuppositions, the proven existence of such sources would constitute a grave theological problem. The evidence may, therefore, properly be used to call those presuppositions into question. To claim, however, to have disproved the revelatory status of the Qur'an is to go beyond the evidence.

In recent years, Muslim scholars have charged that some "Orientalists" have abused the historical method by parading their biases against Islam as fact (Tibawi 1963; Said 1978). It must be acknowledged that there could well be some validity to their complaint. Is this so very different from evangelical complaints that extreme form critics have often been controlled by anti-supernatural presuppositions in Gospel criticism?

I maintain, however, that the historico-critical study of the Qur'an is valid and that Christians may legitimately use such studies to call into question Muslim claims for the Qur'an. As far as I can see, this is all that Jay Smith is doing in his debates with Muslims. I would add, however, in deference to the critics, that Christians should be careful not to go beyond the evidence when appealing to such studies in their witness.

I conclude, then, that the use of the debate format and historico-critical studies in outreach to the Muslim community in the West is valid and necessary, provided that they do not descend into bitter polemic or go beyond the evidence, but that these methods had better be avoided in Muslim countries.

5

Positive Uses of Qur'anic Phrases

In addition to the wealth of affinities with biblical names and terms mentioned in chapter 3, there are a number of Qur'anic passages with phrases that seem much like biblical and Christian language. Over the years, many Christians have attempted to use these in response to Muslim attacks. Two approaches are discernible: the use of select proof-texts interpreted as supporting a Christian position, which is the subject of this chapter, and what I call a "New Hermeneutic" of the Qur'an, which is the subject of the next chapter.

Proof-Texts Interpreted to Support Christianity

The Divine Authority of Scripture

In the Qur'an, a great many passages unequivocally affirm that the *tauraah*, the *zabuur*, and the *injiil* (i.e., essentially the Old and New Testaments) are from God. There are passages that speak of God "revealing/ sending down" these Scriptures to the prophets Moses, David, and Christ (e.g., Qur'an 3:3; 4:163; 5:43, 47; 17:55; 32:23). Others refer to these with the highest respect as the "Book of God" (e.g., 5:44), and a "sign," a "light," "guidance," an "admonition," or a "mercy" from God (e.g., 5:44, 46; 6:91, 154). Still others speak of the Qur'an as "confirming" and "preserving" these Scriptures (e.g., 3:3; 5:48; 6:92; 10:37; 15:19) and assert that "His word cannot be changed" (6:115). The Qur'an not only exhorts Jews and Christians to read and live by these books and "all the revelation that has come to you from your Lord" (5:68), but it exhorts Muslims to do so as well (e.g., 2:136; 3:84; 4:136; 29:46; 42:15) (see Hughes 1979:440–48).

The early missionaries, therefore, used the Qur'anic testimony to try to prove that the Bible as we know it is authoritative for Muslims as well as for Christians. Their argument went something like this: according to the Qur'an, Muslims are obliged to read the Old and New Testaments, which are in the hands of the Jews and Christians, and to accept them as the Word of God (e.g., Muir 1899). The unstated implication was that the Qur'an requires Muslims to become Christians.

This approach runs up against a problem, however. According to Muslims, the Qur'an also declares the Scriptures to be "corrupted" or tampered with (e.g., 2:75, 79; 3:78; 4:46), and, therefore, inauthentic and "abrogated" or superseded by the Qur'an (2:106; 16:101). These are the well-known doctrines of *taHriif* (corruption) and *naskh* (abrogation) over which a good deal of polemical ink has flowed on both sides.[1]

To counter these arguments, the polemicists once again sought help from the Qur'an, advancing the following three arguments (see, e.g., Tisdall 1904:32–40, 89–90).

1. The text of the Bible could not have been corrupted in Muhammad's day or before, since the Qur'an obviously considers the *tauraah*, the *zabuur*, and the *injiil* then existing to be authentic and authoritative. Likewise, the Bible cannot have been tampered with since that time, inasmuch as the Qur'an claims to "preserve" the former books and declares that "His word cannot be changed" (6:115). Moreover, there are so many ancient biblical manuscripts from widely scattered places, dating from before Muhammad's time to centuries after, that it would have been impossible to change all of them. The fact that all of these manuscripts have the same text proves that they have not been corrupted as claimed. This has been called "the exhaustive argument" (Rice 1910:177ff.).

---

1. See, e.g., Jones 1964:1-27, for an excellent survey of these questions.

2. Nowhere does the Qur'an charge Christians with having corrupted the Scriptures textually. It does say that some Jews changed or distorted the words when reading aloud (2:75; 3:78), but this only involves what Muslim scholars call "semantic corruption" (*taHriif ma'nawi*), not textual or "verbal" corruption (*taHriif lafDHi*).

3. Finally, the Qur'an *NEVER* claims to abrogate the earlier Scriptures. The verses on abrogation (2:106, etc.) are about certain verses (*ayaat*) in the Qur'an itself abrogating others. Furthermore, the idea that the Torah is abrogated by the Psalms, which in turn is abrogated by the Gospel, runs counter to everything in the Old and New Testaments.

The Deity of Christ

Other passages that Christians have used extensively are those that some Christians think can be given a Christian interpretation. To be brief, I have singled out passages most frequently used touching on three key theological issues separating Christians and Muslims: the divine nature of Christ, the Trinity, the historicity of the crucifixion, and the doctrines of sin and salvation.

The Qur'an has many things to say about Christ, some of which parallel what the New Testament teaches. But also one must say that the Qur'an radically misinterprets and distorts the biblical view of Christ. It misunderstands the expression "Son of God" to mean physical paternity (19:35, 88–92; 112:1–4) and "Trinity" to signify a triad of gods: a father, a mother, and a son (6:100–101; cf. 72:3; 5:116). Accordingly, the Qur'an vehemently denies that Christ is the "Son of God" or divine (5:17, 72, 75; 9:30–31) and rejects the Trinity (4:171; 5:73, 116).

There are, however, a number of passages that Christians have taken to teach otherwise. As we have seen, the Qur'an calls Christ "the Word of God" and "a Spirit from Him" (4:171; 3:45). It has Him born of a virgin (19:16–35) and calls Him "illustrious (*wajiih*) in this world and the next, and among those nearest to God" (3:45). He is the only prophet who is said to have created, and to have raised the dead (3:49). And of all the prophets, including Muhammad, Christ is never said to have sinned (see 3:36; 20:121; 71:29; 14:41; 28:15–16; 4:106; 40:55; 48:2). Finally, in a usage that is reminiscent somewhat of some Old Testament language, in many a Sura we find the pronoun "we" or other plural forms used in reference to God (e.g., 2:35; 3:25, etc., et passim).

Traditionally, Muslims have interpreted these passages in line with the totality of the Qur'anic teaching about God and about Christ. They view the "we" passages to be the Semitic "plural of majesty," found also in the Bible. As for the Qur'anic view of Christ, Ali Merad, quoted in chapter 3, is no doubt correct when he says that the most that can be said from the Qur'anic teaching is that Christ has been confided "an extraordinary mission, without precedence in the history of mankind" (1980:12). At several points in his study, he indicates that there is a certain mystery about this Christ. He ends with the remark that "alongside the denials and disputes, the Qur'an makes an appeal for a united search for truth (3:54) and for the bearing of witness (3:64)" and concludes that "basically what it seeks to do in this domain seems to be to provoke reflection rather than to furnish final answers" (1980:16).

Christians often have appealed, nevertheless, to the "we" passages as supporting the Christian position. For the most part, the approach has been to cite these passages as pointers to the divine nature of Christ and to the triune nature of God. However, some have gone further, arguing that the "we" passages can be understood and explained only if one accepts the deity of Christ and the Trinity (e.g., Tisdall 1904:104–67).

The Crucifixion of Christ

As concerns the crucifixion, four passages in the Qur'an touch on the death of Christ (19:33; 3:54–55; 5:117; 4:157–58). Only the last categorically denies that the Jews crucified Christ.

> And for their saying "We slew the Messiah, Jesus son of Mary, the Messenger of God"—yet they did not slay him, neither crucified him, only a likeness of that was shown to them. . . . They slew him not of a certainty—no indeed; God raised him up to Him.

The other three passages mention Christ's death (interpreting the verb *tawaffaa* used in two of them [3:55; 5:117] in its usual sense of God "taking someone to Himself," that is, causing him to die), but do not mention the crucifixion per se. Two passages mention two or three key events of His life in the sequence: His birth, His death, His resurrection, and His being "raised up" (*raafi'uka*), that is, His ascension (19:33; 3:55).

Putting these verses together and interpreting them in the total Qur'anic context, most Muslims have understood Sura 4:157 to mean that Christ was not really crucified. God only made it "seem so to them" (*shubbiha lahum*) by causing someone else to look like Christ and take his place, while raising Christ bodily into heaven. In the Muslim perspective, God would not allow His prophet to suffer such an ignoble death. As Merad concludes, "the death of Christ would have been a contradiction of the constant doctrine of the Qur'an" (1980:14). As for the other three passages, Muslims interpret them to refer to Christ's dying after his second coming at the end of the age (cf. 43:61).

Be that as it may, some Christians have attempted to prove that the Qur'an agrees with the biblical testimony to Christ's crucifixion. The usual approach has been to point to the three passages that speak of His death along with passages that say that the Jews slew God's messengers (2:87; 3:183) as Qur'anic evidence for the crucifixion. Surah 4:157–58 is interpreted to deny only that it was the Jews who crucified Him, not the fact of His death and crucifixion (e.g., 'Accad 1976:340; Youssef 1980:8–9).

The Truths of Sin and Salvation

When we examine how Christians have used the Qur'an in support of the doctrines of sin and salvation, we find much the same pattern. But here again, the Islamic view is radically different from that of Christianity. While the Qur'an acknowledges that man is weak and frequently does sin, nowhere does it intimate that he is a "slave of sin." Adam and Eve "fell" from the Garden, but they could nevertheless still save themselves: "We said, 'Get you down out of it, all together; yet there shall come to you guidance from Me, and whosoever follows My guidance, no fear shall be on them, neither shall they sorrow' " (2:38). In the Qur'anic view, God sent prophets to communicate to man His "guidance." And obedience to this prophetically mediated divine guidance is the key to man's eternal state (Scudder 1982:15–17).

In a word, man does not need salvation or redemption. In fact, the Qur'an explicitly rejects the idea of one person atoning for another's sins (17:13–15; 53:38–40). While it does contain the notions of ransom (*fidyah*, 2:184, 196) and of atonement (*kaffaarah*, 4:92; 5:89), it is always man who atones for his own sins by fasting, giving an offering, feeding the poor, or freeing a slave (see, e.g., Gibb and Kramers 1953:102, 205).

Accordingly, Muslims have unanimously rejected the biblical ideas of sin and of salvation as incompatible with Qur'anic teaching. One Muslim writer put it like this:

Thus the great and central idea of redemption through Jesus is de-nounced, and this stems from the basic concept that man is not born a sinner loaded with original sin so as to need a redeemer. Man is born of a neutral nature with a completely clean slate, and is capable of both good and evil. He is given both rational power and divine guidance through the prophets to induce him to choose the good and forsake the bad, but it is his duty to make the choice. He alone is responsible and answerable for his error if he errs. Every individual carries only his own burden of deeds and misdeeds and has himself to expiate his sins. (Nowaihi 1976:217)

Christians have not used the Qur'an as much for supporting the Christian doctrines of sin and of salvation as for other doctrines. No doubt this is because there is much less Qur'anic material that lends itself to this purpose. Nevertheless, there have been attempts to do so. The typical approach seeks to arouse first of all an awareness of personal sin by citing verses that denounce sin and reveal man's sinfulness. The idea of redemption is then introduced by citing one key verse as a pointer to the fact of redemption; in respect to Abraham's sacrifice of a ram in place of his son, this verse (37:107) declares: "And We ransomed him with a mighty sacrifice" (see, e.g., 'Abdul-Haqq 1980:148–49).

The Historical Development of the Proof-Text Approach

It will be instructive to examine the evolution of the proof-text method in the Protestant approach to Islam. It was used mainly from the second half of the nineteenth century onward. The earlier polemicists, such as Martyn and Pfander, relied mostly on philosophical and biblical arguments in their defense of Christianity.

Sir William Muir

Sir William Muir can be considered the father of the positive uses of the Qur'an among Protestants.[2] He made extensive use of the Qur'an to try to prove to Muslims that they should accept the Bible as revelation. His pioneering work, *The Testimony Borne by the Coran to the Jewish*

2. I recognize that writers had quoted the Qur'an in defense of Christianity long before Muir, and even Martyn. Where Muir pioneered was in developing his argument exclusively on the basis of the Qur'an. This marks the beginning of a trend that led to the modern positive approach.

and Christian Scriptures, first published in Agra in 1855, was influenced by the *Mîzân* of Pfander, but it made much greater use of the Qur'an. Using a procedure popular among Muslims, Muir quotes all the verses in the Qur'an relative to the Bible in their chronological order and comments on their implications for its inspiration and authority, citing the opinions of the most eminent Muslim authorities. He concludes that the Qur'anic evidence overwhelmingly shows that Muslims are obliged to read and believe in the present Old and New Testaments and accept their divine authority.

In a later edition of that work, to which he added a section summarizing the findings of Gustav Weil on the Qur'an's composition and teaching, Muir even attributes to the Qur'anic testimony to the Scriptures some kind of "saving" value. In response to Weil, who held that the missionary should focus his efforts in education, Muir replied:

> Not thus "can the Ethiopian change his skin or the leopard his spots." The evil lies deeper than that. We, on the contrary, hold the saving part of the Coran to be that which . . . so fully recognizes the authority of the Bible, and which warrants us therefore in pressing the acceptance of the Gospel upon the votaries of Islam. (1878:65)

Muir's work seems to have influenced later writers. One of these was a Syrian Christian, a Pastor 'Atiyah,[3] whose anonymously published Arabic polemical works were widely circulated and translated into other languages. Muir translated his books into English. In *The Beacon of Truth*, 'Atiyah uses the same hermeneutical method that Muir had used earlier, with a few additional twists of his own (1894:104–21). In the last chapter he uses the Qur'an to try to prove the deity of Christ, concluding:

> Now, my intelligent reader, do not all these distinctive epithets . . . point out Jesus to be of a marvelous origin and nature, far beyond that of any prophet or apostle? And, considering it all, can you blame the Christians for believing, in accord with the words of their Scripture, that He is the Son of the living God? (1894:143)

3. The author is identified as Pastor 'Atiyah in McCallum 1923:63. In the preface to his English translation of *Sweet First-Fruits* (London: Religious Tract Society, 1893), v-viii, Sir William Muir gives a brief biographical sketch of the author without naming him.

William St. Clair Tisdall

Another writer of importance in the development of the positive uses of the Qur'an was William St. Clair Tisdall. His revised and enlarged translations of Pfander's three polemical works are masterpieces. It is his version of the *Mîzân* that is usually quoted today. There are, however, significant differences between Pfander's original and the revised edition of Tisdall; although both have essentially the same structure, Tisdall makes more extensive use of the Qur'an both in the number of verses quoted and the variety of arguments. One cannot assume that the ideas expressed in the revised *Mîzân* are all those of Pfander.

Tisdall's most important work on the positive uses is his *Manual of the Leading Muhammedan Objections to Christianity*, which was first published in 1904. In it, he advises the Christian:

> Readily accept, *and make it plain that you heartily accept*, all the truth that is in any way common to Christianity and Islam. Then lead on from these points of agreement and show how much *truer* are some of their tenets than they have any idea of. You can show that the Bible teaches all that is true in such tenets of theirs, and that it goes very much further on such points than their theology does. (1904:19)

Tisdall then lists all the proof-text arguments that he feels can be used with Muslims (1904:21):

> (a) He is bound to admit the validity of arguments based on the assumption (for the sake of argument, as far as you are concerned) that the Qur'an is the Book of God, that every word and letter of it in the original is of Divine authorship.
>
> (b) He accepts the great doctrines of: (1) God's Unity, Almighty Power, Wisdom, Eternity, Unchangeableness, and that He is the union of all good attributes; (2) His creation of the universe, and His Divine government and Providence; (3) the Divine mission of all the Prophets (including Jesus); (4) the eternal distinction between the Creator and His creatures; (5) the existence of the world and of human personality, of the human spirit, of life after death, of future rewards and punishments, the Resurrection, the need of faith, the existence of good and evil spirits; (6) Christ's Divine Mission, His birth of a virgin, His sinlessness (all Prophets being by Muslims called sinless), His Ascension, His life in Heaven now, His future Advent, and that Christ is "the Word of God" (kalimatu'llaah) and "A Spirit from Him" (ruuHun minhu); that the Bible, *as originally given*, was a Divine revelation; and he believes

(8) that Idolatry is the one unpardonable sin. (Sura 4; An-Nisa' 51, 116)

Most of the book is concerned with showing how to answer specific Muslim objections. Like 'Atiyah, he devotes an entire chapter to the Trinity in which he cites a number of Qur'anic phenomena that, he says, "cannot be properly explained or understood except by accepting the doctrine" (1904:153; see 153–54, 164–65).

Toward the end of the *Manual*, there is a passage that underlines the inconsistency of attempting to use the Qur'an to support Christianity. Replying to the Muslim claim to find prophecies of Muhammad in the Bible, Tisdall argues that such a claim is inconsistent because it assumes the Bible to be authentic revelation while at the same time holding the present text to be corrupted and, therefore, not authentic. He insists, "You must really take one line of argument or the other" (1904:192; see also 4). However, as the following remark shows, he is unable (or unwilling) to see that he is doing the same thing.

> A Muslim may retort that by referring to the testimony of the Qur'an we are placing ourselves in the same position. But it should be pointed out that we appeal to the Qur'an not as if it had any real authority, but solely to show *him* that, *from his own standpoint*, many of his arguments against Christianity are untenable. (1904:192 n. 1)

Walter A. Rice

A few years later, Walter A. Rice published his comprehensive compendium on the Muslim controversy entitled *Crusaders of the Twentieth Century*. It is significant that Rice recognized the problem in Tisdall's argument and brought out its contradictory implications.

> The position, sometimes stated in words like these, "I bring forward these arguments for you because the Qur'an has weight with you," even with this qualification, can hardly fail to give some colour to the idea that the book possesses an independent value, and is therefore calculated to encourage the Muhammedan to rely upon it. . . .
>
> To attempt to prove essential Christian doctrine from the Qur'an is in effect to try and show that Muhammad was ignorant of the true meaning of his supposed revelation and uttered expressions containing ideas which no Musulman ever attributed to him. It is as though we are trying to cause the scales to fall from the eyes of the "true believer" in order that he might at last see clearly and find himself after all a

Christian! It is entirely against Muhammadan consciousness, and will provoke resistance to the uttermost, in the same way as we ourselves should fight strenuously against any attempt to prove to us that we had misread our Gospel, and that if only we understood it aright we should be Babis or Muhammadans. (1910:113–14)

In spite of this, Rice made some use of the Qur'an in support of Christianity, as others had done before him (see, e.g., 1910:114–16).

The Rejection and Later Return of Proof-Texting

As we saw earlier, by the 1930s, missionaries had begun to abandon the proof-text method along with the old polemic. Bevan Jones is typical. In an article published in the *Muslim World* in 1940, Jones rejects the idea that the Qur'an is somehow the Christian's ally. "Inasmuch as the Qur'an is the product of the seventh century A.D. and is markedly anti-Christian in places, we do not go to it for proofs of the Truth of Christianity or for evidence in favour of the claims of Christ" (1940:280; 291). In *Christianity Explained to Muslims*, Jones consistently avoids all appeal to the Qur'an, although the work is similar in some respects to earlier polemical works. He devotes a lengthy chapter, for example, to the Qur'anic testimony to the Bible, but concludes:

> The question . . . which we have been debating at length in this chapter, viz.: the integrity and authority of the Scriptures, can, and should, be determined on quite other grounds than those we have been obliged to examine. The intrinsic worth of the Bible will ever rest in its contents, and in the appeal which the Divine message therein, especially in the New Testament, makes to the mind and heart of man. (1964:27)

As we saw in chapter 2, Jones appealed to Muslims to explore the phenomena of spiritual experience in the conviction that this would lead them to accept Christ.

For many years thereafter, evangelical missionaries tended to frown on using the Qur'an as a basis for presenting the gospel. Christy Wilson Sr. probably expressed the sentiment of most when he wrote:

> The older apologists often used the Koran in their appeal to Moslems. Their explanation that they used it, not because they believed in it, but because it was accepted by the Moslem, was often not clearly understood, and, at best, was not very convincing. The more we know of the Koran,

and of Islam in general, the better; but we should rarely quote Koranic passages to induce Moslems to turn to Christ. (1950:46)

Since the 1970s, however, a number of Christians have returned to quoting the Qur'an to present the gospel. Among them is Fu'ad 'Accad, former general secretary of the Bible Society of the Levant, who advocates using the Qur'an as "a Bridge to Faith."

> The writings of ancient missionaries say that Christians should not make any use of the Qur'an lest the Muslims think that the Christians accept the Qur'an as a divinely inspired book. I would rather follow what God, Christ, Paul and others have done in using what is common to the people with whom they were talking. (1976:332; see also 1997, especially chaps. 2 and 3)

He goes on to quote a number of passages from the Qur'an as pointing to the deity of Christ, the historicity of His crucifixion, the authenticity and authority of the Scriptures, and the doctrines of sin and atonement. Many of these repeat what earlier writers had used. He has also written a brochure, *Have You Ever Read the Seven Muslim Christian Principles?* in which he gives seven principles said to "govern the fundamental relationship between God and men" ([1978]:2; also 1997:71ff.). He claims that these principles are "common to Judaism, Christianity and Islam," and with each quotes passages from "the Towrah (Old Testament), the Zabur (Psalms), the Injeel (the New Testament) and the Qur'an" that are said to teach that principle. They are, however, distinctly Christian principles.

Finally, one should mention Abdiyah Akbar 'Abdul-Haqq, an evangelist with the Billy Graham Association, whose book, *Sharing Your Faith with a Muslim*, uses background from the christological controversies in the early church to interpret Qur'anic passages concerning Christ and give them a Christian interpretation (1980:71–73, 138). Mention should be made also of the Markaz Ash-Shabiba ("Center for Young Adults") in Germany, which has reprinted many of the old polemical works in English and Arabic as well as a number of pamphlets and books by its own workers that quote the Qur'an extensively. One of the most notable of these is Iskander Jadid, a former Muslim (see the References Cited).

6

A "New Hermeneutic" in Qur'anic Interpretation

We now turn to that development in the positive approach that I have called a "New Hermeneutic" of the Qur'an. Why do I call it a "New Hermeneutic"? How is it new? To answer, we need to take a second look at the contradiction inherent in the proof-text arguments. Appeal has been made to the ambiguities in the Qur'an's testimony to Christ and the Scriptures to persuade Muslims to change their allegiance. Were Muslims to follow these arguments to their logical conclusion, they would have to reject the authority of the Qur'an and the prophethood of Muhammad and accept the Bible and the Christ of the Bible. Such a procedure, however, raises an important theological question: What kind of status are you according the Qur'an, whether explicitly or implicitly, when you quote it in support of a Christian position?

A Period of Transition

Polemicists such as Tisdall claimed that their use of the Qur'an did not imply that it has divine authority. This claim seems, however, to be contradicted by the facts. The very things the Qur'an is said to support—the divine authority of the Bible, the deity of Christ, and His atoning death—are distinctively Christian doctrines that, according to the Bible, are revealed only through the Holy Spirit. There is, moreover, something self-contradictory about the attempt to prove these things on the authority of the Qur'an. What it says, by implication, is that the Muslim's commitment to the divine authority of the Qur'an requires him to accept that of the Bible, and with it the Christian view of Christ and His work. In sum, the Qur'an is treated as if it both possesses divine authority and does *not* possess divine authority at one and the same time. No wonder the logic of the argument has not commended itself to many Muslims!

The ambivalence and contradiction inherent in the approach prepared the way for a new hermeneutic of the Qur'an based on the assumption that the book is in some vague sense a divine revelation. Christians began to sense these inconsistencies and felt that they should honestly face the implications of such a use of the Qur'an. Accordingly, we find over a period of years an increasing tendency to see in the Qur'an a work of the Holy Spirit and thus recognize it as being, in some limited, ill-defined sense, divinely inspired. This, with other developments to be examined later, set the stage for a new approach to the Qur'an.

A look at some of the writers of the transitional period highlights this ambivalence. A. T. Upson, founder of the Nile Mission Press in Egypt, has written a number of works for Muslims in Arabic under the pen name Abd Al-Fadi ("Servant of the Redeemer"). In many of these works, Upson quotes profusely from the Qur'an and Muslim authorities as a bridge for preaching the gospel (see References Cited). He wrote, for example, a series of Sermons, or "Khutbas,"[1] which he describes in these terms:

> Each one is based upon a Quranic verse and written in Quranic style, but the deduction is, of course, that the only prophet that can save is the Lord Jesus Christ Himself, and then there is generally an invitation to the Moslems to read the Christian Scriptures. (1913:419)

Although he sometimes used the Qur'an to support a Christian position (e.g. *Sin & Atonement*, 9), he was generally more cautious in his conclusions than 'Atiyah or Tisdall.

Two well-known missionary leaders whose writings helped prepare the new approach are William H. T. Gairdner (1873–1928) and Samuel M. Zwemer (1867–1952). In his important study of missions to Muslims,

---

1. *Majmuu'ah 'ashri khuTab: al-majmuu'atu l-'uula wal-thaaniyah* (*Collection of Ten Sermons: Collections 1 and 2*) (Cairo: Nile Mission Press, n.d.).

Lyle Vander Werff discerns two stages in their understanding and attitude vis-à-vis Islam and the Qur'an. Their earlier writings reflect the legacy of the nineteenth-century polemic with its negative attitude and objective of radical displacement. Vander Werff detects, however, a shift in the position of each around 1915, reflecting a somewhat more positive attitude toward Islam (1977:184–261, especially 215–16, 235). Neither, however, accepted the fulfillment model (see chap. 2), which was then becoming popular in missionary circles (1977:218–19). Likewise, neither spoke of the Qur'an as being in any sense inspired.

Whether or not Vander Werff is correct in seeing a change in their view of Islam, one thing is clear. Whereas both essentially shared in the negative approach to Islam of the polemicists, certain aspects of their thought were catalytic agents in effecting the changeover to the new hermeneutical approach. As far as Gairdner is concerned, one could single out, for example, his stress on using historico-critical methods to separate fact from fiction in the traditions about the life of Muhammad, and his recognition of "values" in Islam as representing a kind of "dim *preparatio evangelica* which will find its correction in the Christian faith" (1977:212–13, 217). As for Zwemer, one could mention his study on the Muslim view of Christ that foreshadows in some ways the new approach to the Qur'an (1977:240–41: Zwemer 1912).

By 1932, Bevan Jones was expressing the view that the Holy Spirit is at work in some way in Islam (1932:249–50). We do not, however, find Jones using a Christian hermeneutic of the Qur'an, as later writers do. This new attitude to the Qur'an, however, along with the influence of historical criticism in Islamic studies, the science of religion, and the dialectical approach to non-Christian religions, eventually gave rise to the new hermeneutic of the Qur'an among Christians.

The Development of a New Hermeneutic

Geoffrey Parrinder

Geoffrey Parrinder's book, *Jesus in the Qur'an*, is a good example of the new hermeneutic. The fact that he covers much the same ground invites comparison with the proof-text approach. In his study of the Qur'anic titles for Christ, Parrinder does not suggest that they point to His deity (1965:16–54). But when he comes to the crucifixion, he concludes that "the cumulative effect of the Qur'anic verses is strongly in favor of a real death and a complete self-surrender" (121). Parrinder's acknowledgement of "the undoubted revelation of God in Muhammad and in the Qur'an" (173) will no doubt be gratifying to Muslims, although most will not be happy with some of his presuppositions and conclusions or his use of historico-critical methods.

Kenneth Cragg

The foremost Protestant proponent of the new approach is Kenneth Cragg, an Anglican bishop. Since 1956, Cragg has written a number of books on various aspects of Islam (see References Cited). *The Event of the Qur'an* is particularly revealing as concerns his method. In it, Cragg proposes the main lines of a new hermeneutic that aims at the Christian recognition of the Qur'an as revelation. The traditional Islamic hermeneutic of the Qur'an has been one of the principal obstacles to such recognition. The task of Cragg's new hermeneutic, therefore, is to find a way to surmount this obstacle. How does he go about it?

Cragg's first step is to try to situate the Qur'an in its original socio-religious context, its *Sitz im Leben*. He argues that if we are to get at the real meaning of the Qur'an—that is, what it itself intended to convey to its original hearers—it must be interpreted against the background of Muhammad's struggle against idolatry in pre-Islamic Arab society. "It is the contra-pagan theme which is central to all else" (1971:15). Later controversies that resulted in other meanings being superimposed upon the text, must be disregarded.

> There is . . . a better hope of focus on the ruling terms and concepts of the book if exploring them can be relieved of the antagonisms incurred vis-a-vis the Biblical communities. These have too long monopolized attention or diverted it from the kindred objectives evident when the Qur'an is primarily seen as a mission to retrieve idolaters for a true worship. (1971:15)

This means that historical-critical methodology is at the heart of Cragg's hermeneutic. It involves looking at the Qur'an, as the book's title suggests, as a revelational "event," and treating it as something historical. This approach therefore brings him into conflict with the traditional Islamic view of the Qur'an. Islam views the Qur'an as a transcendental book transmitted verbatim from heavenly realms down to earth via the Prophet. To the Muslim, the Qur'an is independent of history, the very actualization of the Word of God. In this perspective, the study of its historical context is superfluous.

Cragg does not, however, try to use historical methodology to disprove the divine authority of the Qur'an or the prophethood of Muhammad.

He is nevertheless obliged to defend his approach at some length. He is not, he declares, trying in some subtle, underhanded way "to relegate the Qur'an to a sort of antiquarian realm of mere historical study," but rather to make it relevant to the present.

> The Qur'an could not have been revelatory had it not been also 'eventful'. As itself a total event within events, its study, like its quality, must live in history. . . . To be firmly in the seventh century is not to exclude the Qur'an from the twentieth. Rather it is to plant it there more intelligently. Historical and contextual study of the temper we intend in these chapters is calculated to have the book in its proper historical perspective *and* its abiding spiritual authority and to have it more powerfully so by refusing any separation however motivated, whether by academic historians or assertive dogmatists. (1971:17)

The conflict between the traditional hermeneutic of the Qur'an and Cragg's proposed new approach raises an important question: can the non-Muslim truly understand the Qur'an, or even rightly study it, without accepting the traditional view of the Qur'an and "submitting" to its authority as traditionally defined? Cragg feels he can. To try to justify this answer he makes a distinction between the "essence" of the Muslim's faith in the inspiration of the Qur'an and the "form" of his "security" in it.

> The *i'jaaz* of the Qur'an, its miraculous quality, is then the form by which Muslim conviction possesses its relevance. The outsider then can take it pragmatically in this way without holding it credally. In doing so he will differ from, and with, orthodoxy, but only about the form in which orthodoxy receives the significance he aims to share and, indeed, to revere. . . .
>
> The distinction serves to obviate both an impatient, external dismissal of the mystery of the Qur'an and a mutual alienation of sympathy and spiritual converse. A reverent religious study of the Qur'an becomes possible, which allows the Muslim still to safeguard the doctrinal formulation of what the book is to him and to his, and to do so as long as he wills. But it also allows the non-Muslim to come adequately to the same Scripture, in concern for what lies within that formulation, yet unimpeded by his embarrassment to its integrity. (1971:21–22)

A Comparison with the Proof-Text Method

In its approach to the text, the New Hermeneutic focuses more on the meaning of the Qur'an as a whole instead of appealing to isolated proof-texts. As concerns the historico-critical method, instead of using it to disprove the Qur'an, it uses it as a tool to aid the interpreter in correctly understanding its meaning. The main difference between the two approaches, however, is the starting point; instead of looking at the Qur'an from the outside and trying to use it to turn the Muslim from his faith, the Christian interpreter places himself by a kind of Copernican revolution on the inside and opens himself to its guidance. This involves taking the Qur'an to be in some sense a divine revelation and seeking to discern its message—for the Christian as well as for the Muslim.

A comparison of Cragg's approach and the proof-text approach might help us to better understand his method. How would he interpret the proof-texts mentioned above? Would he agree with those who interpret them as supporting distinctive Christian teaching? It may be that he does to some extent. In any event, he says that he has "deliberately excluded the themes of Muslim Christian polemic within the Qur'an in order to concentrate on what we have recognized to be the central thrust of Muhammad's *risaalah* [mission]" (1971:186). And elsewhere he encourages missionaries to use what he calls the "Christian potential of the Qur'an" (1979:197). In any case, it must be said that he approaches the Qur'an from a perspective quite different from the proof-text approach. His concern is not so much to prove Christian teaching as to lay the foundation for a new understanding of the Qur'an, more or less compatible with Christianity, which Muslims could accept and which would open the door to greater degree of Muslim and Christian unity.

> Non-Muslim reckoning with the Qur'an must have its due place and so also must an Islamic relation to such external bearings of their Scripture.
> . . .
> Surely this is the sort of religious openness we must be set to seek and to give. It is an openness where the themes of legitimate question and reserve of commitment . . . relate positively to the central issue of a recognized and, indeed, a shared objective. (1971:185, 187)

Before we close this chapter, a word needs to be said to explain why we have classed present-day evangelicals who use the Qur'an to present Christ to Muslims along with the proof-text approach rather than with the new hermeneutic just described. The reason is that there is no indication that they accept the Qur'an to be a revelation in any sense of the word, as Cragg has done. Despite some differences, they seem to be closer to the polemicists in their use of the Qur'an than to those who accept a revelatory status for the Qur'an. Some evangelicals, it is true, use a hermeneutic that borders on that advocated by Cragg and have been influenced by Cragg and others involved in the new hermeneutic. Nevertheless, since they do not accept the Qur'an as revelation, it seemed to be more appropriate to class them with the proof-text approach. Let history judge whether this is correct.

But what do we make of this New Hermeneutic in Qur'anic interpretation? Certainly, one must say that Bishop Cragg has embarked on an ambitious project. I note also that it definitely fits into the project of interreligion that the ecumenical movement embarked on some years ago (see chap. 2). But will it succeed? Will the Muslim community join him in this project? That is the question. There may be some who do, but it appears that the day when a majority of Muslims are involved in the project is still a long way off. But for us the main question is, Will a majority of evangelicals join in the project? I hope not.

7

An Islamicized Church
in Islamic Culture

In chapters 1 and 2, we examined in general terms six models for the contextualization of theology and of the church in Islamic culture. We shall now look more closely at one model's approach to church planting in Islamic culture. It is evident in retrospect that for some time this task had been undertaken without much theological reflection. As we saw, the imperial approach of the nineteenth century turned out to be most unrealistic as a vision for church planting. Along with demolishing Islam, proponents of this approach sought to revive the ancient Eastern churches in the vague hope that *these* would then evangelize the Muslim population. But things didn't turn out that way at all. The approach mainly resulted in schism in the ancient churches and the creation of new Protestant denominations mostly made up of those who converted from the ancient Eastern churches. There was a good bit of floundering and debate over how best to plant the church in Islamic culture.

In the first part of the twentieth century, as we saw, other models of approach were proposed, but without significant change in their vision of the church. But things began to happen. In 1938, for example, the Near East Christian Council held an *Inquiry on the Evangelization of Moslems* to wrestle with this issue, and it proposed the following approach:

It is [our] conviction . . . that the ultimate hope of bringing Christ to the Moslems is to be attained by the development of groups of followers of Jesus who are active in making Him known to others while remaining loyally a part of the social and political groups to which they belong in Islam. The ideal is that there should thus come into being a church whose only head is Christ, and which does not carry the stigma of being an alien institution, drawing men away from their natural social and political connections. (Riggs 1938:7)

What this means in concrete terms was not spelled out, except for these two recommendations: (1) converts should avoid identifying themselves as "Christians" because of the "exclusively . . . racial, political and social group-connotation" the term has with Muslims, and (2) "some spiritual equivalent of baptism, free from the false significance that has grown up in the thought of the Moslem, can and must be devised" (1938:7–8). It is unclear, however, if or how these recommendations were ever implemented.

The "Muslim Church"/"Dynamic Equivalence Church" Concept

In the evangelical camp, the quest for new Islamic church forms moved into high gear at the Marseille conference in 1974, where Charles Kraft made a strong plea "that we bend every effort toward stimulating a faith renewal movement *within* Islam" (1974c:143, emphasis added). Toward that end, he strongly suggested "that we encourage some Christians to become Christian Muslims in order to win Muslims to Muslim Christianity" (144). A reading of his four lectures makes it clear that he has in mind a movement that remains basically Muslim in ethos and culture; he refers to it as "a *Muslim church*, interpreting the term 'Muslim' as a cultural term primarily" (1974a:24).

These same ideas reappear again and again in later conferences and publications, using a variety of terms. Besides "Christian Muslims" and "Muslim churches," we read of "Followers of Isa," "Isa Muslims," "Muslim fellowships," "Jesus mosques," "New Creation Muslims," "House Masjids," and the list goes on. In the paragraphs that follow, we shall examine some of the main concepts and arguments involved in this proposal.

In 1977, veteran missionary John Wilder wrote "Some Reflections on Possibilities for People Movements Among Muslims" (1977:301–20). Drawing on his study of early Hebrew Christianity and the rise of Messianic Judaism in our day, Wilder theorized that "a people movement to

Christ might emerge" and outlined two possible scenarios: "A people movement to Christ which remains within Islam" or "A people movement constituting a new church of Muslim cultural orientation" (309–10). It was the first scenario, the vision of a movement that remains within Islam, that seems to have captured the imagination of evangelicals. On reflection, this could derive from the fact that no one has bothered to explain how a movement to Christ that remains within Islam (a Muslim church?) differs from a church of Muslim cultural orientation.

At the Colorado Springs conference of 1978, Kraft gave the concept a theoretical foundation in "Dynamic Equivalence Churches in Muslim Society" (1979a). Years earlier, Eugene Nida had introduced the concept of "dynamic equivalence" in Bible translation theory. The objective of dynamic equivalence was expressed in terms of bringing about an equivalence between the understanding response of the original receptors of Scripture and that of the receptors today for whom the translation is made; a number of procedural rules were then given to ensure faithfulness to the intent of the original text as well as equivalence in the new language (see Nida and Taber 1969). This approach has been followed in most modern translations, such as the New International Version. Kraft, however, took the model a step or two further and used it for church planting as well. On the basis of the premise that a Muslim's "faith-allegiance" can and should be distinguished from the "religious structures" of Islam, Kraft goes on to propose that a movement to Christ that remains attached to Islam could be considered a "dynamic equivalence" church.

> I would suggest that the goal be the bringing into existence of groupings of God's people within so-called "Muslim" cultures 1) that are committed in faith-allegiance to God in accordance to Biblical revelation and 2) that function within their own sociocultural matrix in ways equivalent in their dynamics to biblically recommended examples. (1979a:120–21).

Characteristics of a Dynamic Equivalence Muslim Church

What would a Muslim church look like? Already, at Marseille 1974, Kraft was laying his groundwork:

> I would press hard for a faith relationship with God and for faith renewal movement starting within Islam as a culture, based on the faith of Abraham (or Ibrahim), pointing to Qur'an, Old Testament and New Testament as the sources of our information concerning this faith, and issuing in a renewal and distinct people of God, who maintain their

Muslim cultural allegiance, worship forms and self respect. I would press further for this faith renewal movement to use all three books (Qur'an, Old and New Testaments) as its basis, and confidently expect and pray for them to discover both Jesus and the exciting relational aspects of the faith that Jesus characterized by referring to his relationship with God as a Father-Son relationship. (1974b:76)

Another writer has proposed that such a Jesus movement within Islam would need to "come to terms with the Arabian Prophet" (D.O. 1991:20–23); that is, they would recognize Muhammad as a prophet in some sense of the term. The prophethood of Muhammad would be understood in terms of "an Old Testament-style messenger" (22), whatever that means (see also Wilder 1977:311). He also writes: "I believe that a Muslim follower of Jesus could repeat the witness, 'there is no god but Allah and Muhammad is his messenger,' with conviction and integrity, without compromising or syncretizing his faith in Jesus" (21). He acknowledges, however, that one would have to hedge when it comes to accepting "the Qur'an as a book that verbally descended on Muhammad from heaven" and accepting the *Hadiths* (21).

Proponents usually assume that Christian Muslims would more or less continue to practice some of the five pillars of Islam, but the extent of the continuity is a question on which opinions differ. John D. C. Anderson seems to feel that they may continue to practice the ritual prayer and almsgiving and keep the fast of Ramadan. He suggests, however, that they would be wise "quietly to ignore" the Hajj and has problems with repeating the Shahadah (1976:296–97).

Phil Parshall seems to have mixed feelings; he seems to favor the model when he writes, "With certain key alterations or substitutions, the Muslim convert can continue the familiar pattern of prayer" (1980:202), but as for keeping the fast in the prescribed Muslim manner, he says "there can be no dogmatic answer" (210). Five years later, however, he discourages the "continued involvement in prayers at the mosque" (as opposed to praying at home). He writes, "The ritual is too closely connected to Islamic belief, theology and religious practice. I conclude that participation involves either compromise or deceit" (1985:184). He likewise draws the line at complete integration within Islam.

> I feel it will not be possible for such a total integration (as an Islamic sect) to occur and still allow mutual integrity. There are four reasons for this:

1. The unacceptable exaltation of Prophet Muhammad.
2. The centrality of the mosque to religious expression within Islam.
3. The denial by Muslims of the Christian view of Biblical authority as well as their rejection of our belief in the deity and atonement of Christ.
4. The desire of both Muslims and Christians to have an exclusive *ummah*. . . .
It is then possible that converts may be able to continue within the mainstream of life in a Muslim society yet distance themselves from things compromisingly Islamic (1985:194).

It is noteworthy that proponents assume that Muslim churches would probably be doctrinally unorthodox. Kraft speculated that they would be strongly monotheistic, would have "probably a more distant concept of God than we are familiar with in the West," would tend to be fatalistic and legalistic, and "would probably, like the Jews, be looking for a kingdom rather than a church" (1974c:142). John Wilder, for his part, envisages the following:

As to doctrine, the movement's Muslim orientation might lead it, among the more likely possibilities, to some form of retreat from the doctrine of the Trinity; a de-emphasizing or "explaining" of Christ's Sonship, perhaps through a device such as Adoptionism; a denial of Christ's true death; an acceptance of the inspiration of only those parts of Scripture they found most acceptable, such as the Pentateuch, the Psalms and the Gospels; and the discarding of one or both sacraments, retaining circumcision, possibly as a substitute for baptism. (1977:311–12)

Today, there is even a manual on how to start a Muslim church. Phil Goble, author of a work on how to start a Messianic synagogue, enlisted the collaboration of Palestinian theologian Salim Munayyer to produce the *New Creation Book for Muslims* (1989). They envision, in concrete terms, what a New Creation mosque would look like. Replete with Islamic language reinterpreted with Christian meanings, the book contains chapters on "The Straight Path of the New Creation" (the basic truths of sin and salvation in Islamic format), "The Prayer Life of the New Creation Muslim" (a Christianized Muslim ritual prayer), "The New Creation Confession" (the Eucharist, reinterpreted in terms of a Messianic *Id-ul-Adha*), and "The New Creation Pilgrimage" (baptism, reinterpreted in terms of the *Hajj* or Muslim pilgrimage). The book concludes with a chapter on "How to Start a House Masjid for New Creation Muslims." Keep in mind that everything in the book is purely and only theoretical; there is no indication that it comes from an actual church planting experience.

Three Theories behind The Model

It will be instructive at this point to examine several theories or assumptions, frequently expressed over the past thirty years, that lie at the heart of the dynamic equivalence or translational model.

MISSIONARY EXTRACTIONISM

The first theory attributes Muslim resistance to the church and the gospel exclusively to "missionary extractionism." According to Kraft, missionaries "have so often demanded that converts turn against their own culture and convert to a foreign culture" (1974a:27). Anderson, for his part, reproached missionaries to Islam for being "cultic" rather than Christian. He charged them with "the isolation of the convert from his culture" (1976:288) and even spoke in terms of missions to Muslims being a "failure" (289), a charge that others will later repeat (e.g., Owen 1987:51). According to Anderson, "we need to differentiate between the traditional concept of making a Muslim into a Christian, with all the transfer of his loyalties to an imported Christian sub-culture that this involves, and . . . that of making him into a disciple of Jesus Christ, with a primary loyalty to Him as Saviour and Lord from amidst his national ties" (1976:292).

By the time of the Colorado Springs conference in 1978, this theory was a basic assumption of a majority of speakers. In his keynote address, Don McCurry claims that "missions to Muslims have rejected the culture of the converts and imposed that of the missionary or evangelist" (1979:14). He describes this as "insistence on a double conversion, . . . first to Christ, and then to the culture of the missionary or evangelist," and claims that it "may well be the single most important reason for a greater lack of results in work among Muslims" (14). In *New Paths in Muslim Evangelism* (1980) and *Beyond the Mosque* (1985), Parshall assumes the theory to be true and calls it "erroneous methodology [that] should immediately cease" (1985:21; cf. 1980:230). There is no doubt that missionary extractionism has been a problem that has negatively influenced the Muslim response. But was it the sole, or even the main, cause of Muslim resistance? We shall revisit that question in a later chapter.

THE NEUTRALITY OF CULTURE

A second theory behind the model holds that the forms and functions of a culture are essentially "a neutral vehicle" for the communication of the gospel as far as the Christian is concerned (Kraft 1979b:113–15). We shall examine this theory in greater detail when we discuss the theological evaluation of religions in chapter 9.

MUSLIM FORMS WITH CHRISTIAN MEANINGS

On the assumption that culture is essentially neutral, proponents of the model go on to affirm that the Christian is free to take Muslim forms (e.g., Muslim religious language as well as religious practices such as the ritual prayer) and "fill them with Christian meanings." Kraft develops the theory in terms of several theological propositions, which I summarize as follows: (1) the difference between the Old and New Testaments is cultural rather than theological, the Old representing a "Semitic" cultural milieu, and the New a "Greek" milieu (1974a:23; 1979a:115ff.); (2) one may distinguish faith-allegiance from the religious structures that give it expression (117ff.); again, assuming that the religious structures of Islam are a "neutral vehicle." On this basis, he concludes (3) that God accepts Islam as a valid expression of Semitic churchness on the Old Testament model and (4) that one may therefore freely make use of Islamic forms in the new church and give them Christian meanings. Note how he develops the argument.

> God's Word develops in detail God's approach to a Semitic people. He starts where they are culturally and strongly influences the course of their culture from that point on. He accepts their cultural starting points with respect to everything except their basic allegiance. . . .

> The kinds of ritual, behavior patterns, places and times of meeting, music (if any), prayer times and postures, even doctrinal formulations are quite incidental to the allegiance that is being expressed through them. . . .

> I believe . . . that it would be thoroughly Biblical to work toward a recombination of Christian allegiance with so-called Muslim religious structures. . . . Indeed, . . . I believe that this is what Muhammad himself was trying to do: to combine an allegiance to the Judeo-Christian God with Arabic cultural structures. Abraham and Moses and Paul before him had performed similar recombinations between that allegiance and the cultures within which they worked. (1979a:117, 118)

The idea that one can fill Muslim forms with Christian meanings has become standard fare in seminars, conferences, and books on ministry to Muslims. In a chapter on "Form and Meaning" in *New Paths in Muslim Evangelism*, Parshall speaks in terms of "reinterpreting" Muslim practices.

> Of course, if we try to spread the gospel to Muslims by building on the similarities between Islamic practices and certain features of Christianity, these practices will all require a certain measure of reinterpretation. But it does seem that the closer we can relate to Muslim form, the more positive will be the response to our message, particularly in initial instances of evangelistic effort. . . .

> It should be pointed out that the Muslim performs all these obligations as a means of obtaining merit. This, of course, is incompatible with the Christian message of grace. But [he concludes] what the Muslim needs is a change of focus (i.e., meaning) rather than a mere change of form. (1980:59)

Here again, we shall revisit this whole question in a later chapter.

The *EMQ* Debate Over Islamicized Contextualization

Since the late 1990s, the *Evangelical Missions Quarterly* has become the arena of a debate over the pros and cons of what has been called "Islamicized Contextualization" (Eenigenburg 1997:310–15). The EMQ Debate (see References Cited) began with Parshall's lead article in the fall 1998 issue, entitled "Danger: New directions in contextualization" (404ff.). He sees a "dangerous slide" in some events—missionaries not only assuming a Muslim identity but becoming legally Muslim "in order to win Muslims to Christ," performing Salat alongside Muslims in the mosque, or affirming Muhammad to be a prophet of God—and these trends are making him "apprehensive." He cites a research project on what was called the "Islampur" case, where a convert community had resulted from an experiment in Islamicized contextualization somewhere in Asia. The most disturbing findings were these: 50% go to the mosque for the Salaat on Fridays, and 31% go more than once a day; 96% believe there are four "heavenly books," and 66% say the Qur'an is the greatest of the four; 45% do not affirm God as Father, Son, and Holy Spirit. So Parshall raises the question, "What do we have here? Contextualization or syncretism?" (406).

The other side in the debate was argued by a John Travis (*EMQ* 1998:407–8, 411–15). Travis proposes "The C1 to C6 Spectrum," which he calls "a practical tool for defining six types of Christ-centered Communities ('C') found in the Muslim context." C1 and C2 represent variants of the traditional churches found in the Muslim world, while C6 represents "small Christ-centered communities of secret/underground believers." In between are C3, "Contextualized Christ-centered communities using insider [i.e., Muslim] language and religiously neutral insider cultural forms" (self-identity: "Christians"), C4, "Contextualized Christ-centered communities using insider language and biblically permissible cultural and islamic forms" (self-identity: "followers of Isa the Messiah," or the like), and C5, "Christ-centered communities of 'Messianic Muslims' who have accepted Jesus as Lord and Savior" (self-identity: Muslims who follow Isa the Messiah) (407–8). Travis goes on to agree with Parshall that for Christians to legally become Muslims is probably going too far; he counsels expatriate co-workers to take on a C4 identity. He also acknowledges that Christians should not affirm Muhammad as Prophet or the Qur'an as the Word of God; he says "certain aspects of the role of Muhammad and the Qur'an must be reinterpreted" and cites the approach of Fu'ad 'Accad as "a tremendous starting point" (414–15). In the end, he acknowledges that "C5 may only be transitional" but concludes that if "the single greatest hindrance to seeing Muslims come to faith in Christ" is not theological but rather a matter of "culture and religious identity," then for the sake of God's kingdom, a way must be found to pursue the C5 path.

In that issue, the debate was concluded by Dean S. Gilliland, who teaches in the School of World Mission at Fuller Theological Seminary (*EMQ* 1998:415–17). As research director of the project that produced the report that was quoted, he felt a need to clarify a few aspects of the research that had been glossed over in the preceding articles. He concluded by stressing "the need for the passage of time because, like any other movement, this one [i.e., the Islampur case] is in process" (417).

The next year, the debate was continued in another article, "His Ways Are Not Our Ways" (*EMQ* 1999:188–97), by Joshua Massey, and in several letters to the editor (*EMQ* 1999:394–99). Then, in 2003, Scott Woods gave us "A Biblical Look at C5 Evangelism" (*EMQ* 2003:188–95).

Most recently, Parshall reopened the debate with another article, "Lifting the Fatwa" (*EMQ* 2004:288–93). The title, and perhaps even the article, was prompted by the shock of reading a statement by a C5 missionary who said, "I am praying Phil will lift his *Fatwa* against our ministry." Parshall reviews seven major "flash-points" behind his apprehensions about the method. After highlighting the problems, confusions, ambiguities, and still unresolved issues inherent in the C5 approach, he concludes, "And so, where do we end up? Consider the *Fatwa* (which was never decreed!) lifted. I do not want to end my life . . . known as a heresy hunter."

Parshall's article is followed by another by Massey, "Misunderstanding C5: His Ways Are Not Our Orthodoxy" (*EMQ* 2004:296–304). He argues that critics of C5 theory are really judging the "C5 Muslim follower of Jesus." He says they are guilty of judging C5 believers (1) from "Greco-Roman Gentile categories of orthodoxy instead of a Jewish understanding of Christ's mandate, (2) from a distance rather than in light of personal relationships with C5 Muslim believers, and (3) church-centered rather than Christ-centered missiology."

Remaining Questions

Despite Massey's effort to put the onus on those who doubt the model, questions remain. First, one must ask whether the C5 cases that have been cited demonstrate the viability of the model. Wilder cites two cases of which he has heard, the "Jesusists" of Turkey, and a group in Iran (1977:306, 308, 319–20 nn. 11, 12). Parshall acknowledges that "examples of contextualized witness to Muslims are rare" but nevertheless cites the case of two small groups in East Asia, begun about five years previously, that apparently were continuing within Islam (1980:21–27). At the Zeist conference in 1987, Rafique Uddin, a former Muslim living in East Asia, tells how he trained five couples of Muslim background in the approach and sent them out to carry on the work. He claimed that three imams had come to Christ, and that "in one area during two years, 1,200 to 1,500 have come to Christ" (1989:272). He describes his approach:

> In my current work I have suggested to many new and old believers in Christ (from Muslim background) that we practice both the five daily times of worship and the annual one month fast. I personally participate in these forms and recite Bible portions in five daily prayers. . . .

> To me and to many other first-generation believers in Christ it is a necessity that we continue the Islamic forms of worship but give Christian meanings to these forms. Growth in Christ is much easier if culture shocks can be mitigated through retaining as much as possible of the cultural forms of worship. (1989:269)

And there is the Islampur case already mentioned, which could possibly be identified with one of the above cases. It seems that the information given so far is too sketchy for one to be able to draw firm conclusions as to the authenticity or viability of these "churches" (giving sketchy details is of course a necessary security precaution). Moreover, we do not know whether or not all these groups still exist; convert churches in Muslim society have a way of disappearing after a few years. As Gilliland has well remarked, time is needed as well as independent investigations by objective third parties before one can with reasonable certainty consider these churches ongoing and viable. I can agree with Massey on much of what he says about relating to C5 believers, but I disagree sharply with him on one important point. If I question the C5 approach, it does not mean that I am "judging the C5 Muslim follower of Jesus," as he would have us believe. Only God is qualified to judge whether or not someone, myself included, is a true believer. But I *am* questioning the missiology of C5 operatives. And that brings us to the second question that remains: Is the C5 model (or the C4 model for that matter) biblically valid? We will examine that question in a later chapter.

part three

Toward a Biblical-Theological Contextual Model

8

The Object of
Christian Mission to Islam

As we saw in part one, the Protestant approach to Islam has evolved considerably over the years. To some extent, this reflects an evolution in the conception of the objective. But there were other factors as well. How one defines the objective is influenced by one's theology of religions, one's contextual or theological starting point, and the cross-cultural hermeneutic one uses in communicating the biblical message. And the contrary is also true; these constituent elements of the contextual model influence one's definition of the objective. They are part of a whole. We begin, therefore, by briefly examining the evolution of the conception of the objective in the history of the Protestant approach to Islam. This will lead to the question: How ought the objective to be defined?

Earlier Views

In the nineteenth century, as we have seen, the objective was defined in terms of the destruction of Islam and its radical displacement by Christianity. Displacement, however, is a purely negative concept, whereas Christ's Great Commission is positive. Kenneth Cragg has termed the approach "territorial retrieval" (1956:256). It may be that the polemicists had spiritual goals in mind as well, involving a change of allegiance from Muhammad, the Qur'an, and the Islamic community to Christ, the Bible, and the church. Nevertheless, they viewed displacement as primary, despite the incongruities already highlighted. But when displacement was coupled with the growing positive use of the Qur'an, the incongruities became more and more evident.

By the turn of the twentieth century, more and more missionaries began to sense the problems in the displacement model. Some began to try to redefine the objective in other terms. Although the idea of displacement was not absent, some began to think in terms of fulfilling the Muslim's deepest needs and aspirations. In its general conclusions, the World Missionary Conference (Edinburgh 1910) expressed it this way: "Jesus Christ fulfils *and* supersedes all other religions" (1910:4/268). Thus, the objective came to be defined in terms of the fulfillment of non-Christian religions. This paradigm shift turned out to be equally problematic, however; not only did it fail satisfactorily to correct the problem, but also it was vague and unrealistic.

Many missionaries were uneasy with the direction fulfillment was going. They agreed that the displacement model was inadequate and rejected its negative approach to Islam. As we saw, some focused on the direct presentation of Christ, aimed at winning Muslims to Him and planting His church. However, apart from the rejection of negative polemics, most do not seem to have formulated an understanding of the objective different from the displacement model.

The Ecumenical and Evangelical Views

Conceptions of the objective underwent still further change. Starting around the 1950s, two opposing models for mission began to emerge. One model that emerged within the ecumenical movement builds on the fulfillment idea with its positive evaluation of Islam and incorporates the dialectical approach to non-Christian peoples. As we saw in chapter 2, the WCC, through its Sub-Unit for Dialogue with Living Faiths and Ideologies (DFI), began to define the objective in terms of achieving a global "community of communities," characterized by peace and justice, where each religion and ideology plays a part. This vision of "dialogue in community" is generally accompanied by the abandonment of any thought of winning Muslims to faith-allegiance to Christ, usually referred to as "proselytism."

Meanwhile, a model for mission to Islam, distinct from that of the ecumenical movement, emerged in evangelical circles. The evangelical approach to the question of objective is a part of the renewal of evangelical interest in world evangelization since the 1960s and the emergence of a distinctly evangelical theology of mission (Johnston 1978).

To examine the views on both sides in detail would take us beyond the scope of this study. Suffice it to say that the difference between the evangelical and ecumenical theologies of mission can be expressed in terms of a disagreement over whether the Bible limits the mission of the church strictly to evangelism, discipling, and church planting or defines it more broadly in terms of changing the structures of society and achieving social justice. Evangelicals also disagree among themselves over whether mission includes social action along with winning people to Christ.

As concerns Islam, the evangelical model aims at winning Muslims to allegiance to Christ and to Christian discipleship and gathering them into churches rooted in some way in Islamic society. It is this stress on winning and discipling Muslims and planting Muslim convert churches that especially distinguishes the evangelical model from the ecumenical model with its focus on "dialogue in community." Evangelicals have given special emphasis in recent years to understanding the socio-cultural dimension of this task and the disparities between Muslim and Western cultures (McCurry 1979).[1] As we saw in the last chapter, this emphasis has led some to propose that the objective should be the emergence of "a people movement to Christ that remains within Islam." Many evangelicals are not agreed on this, however.

This brings us back to the questions raised at the beginning of the chapter: How ought the object of mission to be defined? Which of the above conceptions of the objective appears to be closer to that of the Bible?

Bosch's Critique of the Ecumenical and Evangelical Models

In his study of the ecumenical and evangelical models, South African missiologist David Bosch characterized the evangelical model as "an emaciated gospel" because evangelicals have tended to exclude social involvement from their idea of mission, or at least to relegate it to a

---

1. Note the similarities between the ideas expressed in McCurry and those of the Near East Christian Council Inquiry on the Evangelization of Moslems in 1938, which were rejected at Tambaram, according to Vander Werff (1977:263).

secondary place after evangelism (1980:202–11). According to Bosch, "there is a tendency among evangelicals to regard Christ as Lord only of the Church and not of the cosmos as well" (202). Bosch characterizes the ecumenical model as "a diluted gospel," in other words, "a reduction of the gospel" (212–20). He charges that ecumenical missionary theology lacks a sense of the reality of sin and consequently lacks a "resolute summons to repentance and conversion" (217). It redefines the kingdom of God in terms that lose sight of its eschatological nature, puts the stress on man building his own future, and ultimately erases the distinction between the church and the world (see also Clowney 1976:4–7).

Although he does not address the particular questions of the present study, Bosch's evaluation of the two theologies of mission is very much to the point. Take his critique of the ecumenical movement. No doubt, some churches, missionaries, and missiologists within the WCC accept the Bible as normative for their message and their approach to mission. However, the model set forth in recent years by the WCC Sub-Unit on Dialogue (DFI) is clearly an abandonment of the biblical objective for mission and a betrayal of the gospel. To bring about better understanding between the various religions and lessen the conflict between them through dialogue is doubtless, on the human level, a noble undertaking. It can hardly, however, be identified with the mission that Christ gave the church.

There is likewise much truth in Bosch's critique of the evangelical model of mission. It is true that we evangelicals tend to exclude socio-political "involvement" from our idea of mission, as Bosch has said. Evangelicals do get involved in the relief of human misery and the social betterment of mankind through extensive relief and development efforts of all kinds, but these activities are often separated from evangelism and in any case viewed as secondary to it, as Bosch noted. In missions and evangelism, we tend to steer clear of anything that borders on the political, because politics is viewed as evil.

Evangelicals tend to have an ambivalent, contradictory attitude toward Christian involvement in political action. We can't totally avoid politics, because we are "in this world" even if we are "not of it." We are involved in the political realm one way or another, but we are ambivalent about our involvement. So we major in the spiritual side of the ministry and emphasize the spiritual aspect of the biblical message. And in communications with Muslims, we deny having a political agenda of any kind in our ministry and downplay its political implications.

The Muslim Misunderstanding of Christian Mission

It's noteworthy that Muslims tend to have an entirely different view of Christian mission, and especially Christian humanitarian efforts. They assume that such activities are funded by Western governments, with a view to extending Western political control over the Muslim world. They typically charge Christian missions with being "imperialistic" and "immoral and despicable," and that we "take advantage of" the poor and needy in Muslim countries by "inducements to change religions" (Schlorff 1993:180). In a word, Muslims assume that Christianity is at bottom political in nature, and even territorial. Why would they assume such things and make such charges? For one thing, it is because that is precisely the way Muslim missionary efforts operate! It is noteworthy that the Qur'an includes "those whose hearts are to be won" (Surah 9:60) among the legitimate recipients of *zakaat* funds. In other words, *zakaat* may be used to induce people to embrace Islam. This practice has been well documented all the way back to the time of the Prophet (see Zwemer 1941:89–100).

The fundamental fact to keep in mind about Islam, then, is that it is not just a religion but is also, and above all, a political ideology. Muslim ideology is centered on the *Ummah*, the idealized Muslim community. The ideal is (1) that there be a one world community, the *Ummah*, (2) that it be governed by an Islamic state apparatus (the *Khilafa*), and (3) that it be under Islamic law (the *Shari'ah*), following the model of Muhammad at Medina. They view the *Ummah* as a "divine social order" that they identify with the kingdom of God, and they intend to extend Muslim rule over all the earth. As Abul A'la Maududi, a leading Pakistani Muslim thinker, has put it, Muslims "have a command from Allah to rule the entire world and to be over every nation in the world" (quoted in Gabriel 2002:81–82). Most Muslims are quite agreed on that point even though they may not agree on the means of achieving it. This ideology may not equally motivate all Muslims, but one thing is certain: while variations in commitment do exist, this is *the* ideology of Islam as a community. So come what may, unless they are able somehow to escape Islam, as part of the community all Muslims are *ipso facto* committed to this ideology. In a word, as already intimated, Islam is intrinsically both political and territorial in nature.

To return to the Muslim idea that Christianity is also territorial and political in nature, this assumption appears quite plausible when one considers the Crusades, and especially the history of missions to Islam. For many years, Protestant missions to Muslims were heavily implicated in colonialism and thus, quite naturally, expressed their objective in terms of radical displacement. Since that time, there has been precious little to lead Muslims to believe that modern missions are any different. It's only natural that they identify the West with Christianity, much as they identify the Arab world with Islam. They know, for example, that Western support for Israel comes mostly from a strong evangelical influence mainly in Britain and America. Couple that with their increasing frustration that for well over three hundred years, the Muslim world, which they believe should be at the head of world civilization, has been humiliated by Western dominance. All this helps explain the increasing anger Muslims have toward Christianity and the West. More and more, Muslims view the West—and Christianity—as the main obstacle to achieving what they believe to be their rightful place promised by God, and they are becoming angry. Christian missions may not have a political agenda as we see it. However, as Muslims see it, we do have such an agenda. In any case, our missionary efforts stand in the way of Islam achieving its goal, and that in itself puts us among the enemy.

Rethinking the Objective in the Light of Muslim Distortions

In the light of all this, I would argue that we evangelicals need seriously to rethink our conception of the objective of mission to Islam. This is going to mean some adjustments in the way we formulate the objective, which will affect our apologetic approach as well. Does this sound radical? Perhaps it is, but when our message and our ministries are so consistently distorted and misunderstood by Muslims, does this not suggest that we urgently need to go back to the drawing board? In any case, I am suggesting that missions to Muslims would do well to make the kingdom of God a central theme in their formulation of the objective of mission, as well as in their apologetic approach and their proclamation of the gospel to Muslims. We may not have a political agenda or territorial aspirations for the Muslim world, but our missionary work does have political implications that we would do well to discuss frankly as we proclaim the gospel of the kingdom for Islam.

Studies in the biblical theology of mission in the past thirty years point to the fact that the biblical doctrine of the kingdom of God is central to the Bible's view of mission (see, e.g., Jeremias 1967; Ridderbos 1962). According to Johannes Verkuyl, "the kingdom of God is that new order of affairs begun in Christ which, when finally completed by him, will involve a proper restoration not only of man's relationship to God but also of those between sexes, generations, races, and even between man and nature" (1978:198; see 197–204). He would seem to agree with J. H. Bavinck, who states that winning the nations to obedience to Christ, planting His church among them, and the final glory of God are not distinct and separate goals but rather "three aspects of a single purpose of God: the coming and extension of the kingdom of God" (1960:155).

Besides the need to address Muslim misunderstandings and distortions of what we are about, there are also important biblical reasons for making this change. It is surely significant that, according to the Gospel writers, from the beginning both John the Baptist and Jesus were proclaiming "the good news (gospel) of the kingdom" (Matt 4:23). Matthew records the beginning of Jesus' ministry in these terms, "From that time on Jesus began to preach 'Repent, for the kingdom of heaven is near' " (Matt 4:17). It is noteworthy that the phrase "the kingdom of heaven" occurs more than fifty times in Matthew's Gospel alone.[2] In other words, Jesus' message was that the kingdom of God had "come near" in His person and ministry.

There were important reasons why Jesus proclaimed His message to the Jewish people in the kingdom framework. They were looking for a political Messiah who would come and defeat the Romans and "restore the kingdom to Israel" (Acts 1:6); they were thinking only of a political kingdom, as the Hebrew kingdom had been. The kingdom Jesus was proclaiming, however, was something much greater. To launch into a thorough study of Jesus' teaching on the kingdom of God would be too massive an undertaking and beyond the scope of this chapter (I recommend Ridderbos 1962 as an excellent place to start). Suffice it to say that Bible scholars point out that whereas the kingdom Jesus established may have a political dimension in its present provisional phase ("the present evil age"), in its ultimate phase it exists on a fundamentally different level and is cosmic, universal, and eternal.

In sum, the kingdom of God in its present provisional form is not an intrinsically political entity, as the Jews envisioned it, nor yet is it an entirely future eschatological entity, as some people have thought; it is both present and future, both political and eschatalogical. During this life one may "enter the kingdom" by making Christ King over one's life. People may

---

2. Note that the other Gospel writers report Jesus' preaching in terms of "the kingdom of God." Bible scholars point out that Matthew's Gospel was written for Jews, whose reluctance to pronounce the divine name out of reverence for God is well known.

thus experience the "abundant life" of the kingdom in the here and now, even though they are not yet perfect, free from sin. This is the provisional phase of the kingdom. But, as we come to understand Jesus' teaching better, we learn that there will also be a fulfillment phase at the end of the age. Christ will return a second time as He promised, and He will raise up all the redeemed, both the dead and the living, to inaugurate His eternal kingdom. The key to entering that future kingdom is to repent of one's sins while there is still time, and receive Jesus as Savior and King today.

Implications for the Evangelical Apologetic to Islam

As already indicated, this understanding of the objective of mission to Islam is going to involve some adjustment in our apologetic approach to Muslims. We will need to make the kingdom of God a central part of our proclamation of the gospel. I believe that this will be helpful to enable us to better communicate the message to Muslims. It has become especially disconcerting to see radical Islam gaining strength and aggressively seeking to achieve the Islamic goal for the world through violence and terrorism. It is urgent that we address Muslim ideology in our apologetics and evangelism. In so doing, we have to be honest and acknowledge that, at times in the past, Christians *were* implicated in colonialism and territoriality, just as Islam has been. And yes, it was misguided and wrongheaded; it conflicts with Jesus' teaching that "My kingdom is not of this world" (John 18:36). We don't like to have to acknowledge that we were wrong, but doing so can be a starting point for correcting the Muslim view of the kingdom of God. Muslim territoriality and its vision of a political "kingdom of God" is also wrongheaded and misguided, as will be explained and demonstrated in what follows.

Just as preaching His gospel of the kingdom to the Jewish people was important in Jesus' day, I'm suggesting that it is equally important that Muslims hear this same gospel today in terms that address their misunderstandings. Why do I say that? Not only are Muslims separated from God without hope of salvation, but also Islam has misled them about what kind of kingdom to expect. They desperately need to have their false expectations for an Islamic "divine social order" corrected so that they have an opportunity to enter the true kingdom of God. Here again, to attempt a comprehensive exposition of the gospel of the kingdom for Muslims is beyond the scope of this chapter. Without entering the details, let me list several of its most important political implications for

Muslims, in terms of false Islamic teachings that need to be exposed and truths about the kingdom of God that Muslims especially need to hear. I recognize that for Muslims these are delicate matters that can only be addressed with care, so I am simply listing them without going into the details about how to do so.

A first fallacy that needs to be addressed is the positive view of human nature that they learn from the Qur'an. Human nature is not good, or "perfectible" through divine guidance, as Islam teaches. At this point, they need the biblical teaching on the sinfulness of human nature expounded to them in some detail.

A second fallacy, related to the first, concerns their view of Islamic law that they consider the very "Law of God." The truth is that no religious law, including the Shari'ah, is able to change human nature to render mankind submissive. The Bible teaches us that law is "powerless," because it is "weakened by the sinful nature" (Rom 8:3). Its true function is to make us "conscious of sin" in our lives (see Rom 3:20). This truth is especially important for Muslims to hear expounded.

A third fallacy to be addressed concerns Muslims' understanding of the kingdom of God that they identify with the Ummah of Islam. The truth to be communicated is that the kingdom of God exists only where God rules in person. The Bible teaches that the kingdom will exist on earth only at the end of the age when Christ returns a second time to establish His kingdom. How to communicate this is a delicate matter, but it must be done in such a way that the Muslim sees clearly that the Ummah of Islam could never be the kingdom of God; it still involves a human ruler. Unless and until God rules *in person*, you will only have corruption and injustice, for such is the nature of human political power.

The fourth thing that Muslims need to hear is that Jesus invites them to enter His kingdom now, before He returns and the door is shut. They need to "open the door" of their hearts and invite Him into their lives (Rev 3:20). The only way to enter the kingdom and experience the promised "restoration of all things" is to make Jesus king in their lives; they must "submit" to Him as King here and now. Only then can they experience the salvation promised of God and become citizens of God's eternal kingdom. And this implies an extensive discipleship training that again would take us beyond our subject.

Fifth, they need to hear that entering Christ's kingdom has nothing to do with changing political loyalties. The Bible says that when we "receive Christ" we become "children of God" (John 1:12) and "heirs of God and co-heirs with Christ" (Rom. 8:17); now, "our citizenship is in heaven"

(Phil. 3:20). In other words, they can become citizens of Christ's heavenly kingdom while they are still, at the same time, citizens of their own country on earth. Again, this truth will involve considerable exploration.

Muslims imagine that where the *Shari'ah*, that they consider to be "the Law of God," is the law, and a Muslim ruler (*khaliifa*) governs society, there you have the kingdom of God, a "divine social order." They need to see that their conclusion does not follow from the premise. An Islamic state with the best of rulers and the best of Shari'ah courts in place is still a human social order because it is still humans who have hands-on control, and not God. Muslims need to hear the truth about fallen human nature, and about the true nature of the kingdom of God according to Scripture, to be able to grasp the obvious disconnect that exists in Islamic ideology. Of course, it will take considerable effort on our part, beyond what is outlined here, to help them see all this.

To sum up, we urgently need to keep Jesus' kingdom focus in view as we define our mission and proclaim the gospel among Muslims. The kingdom of God will exist only when and where it is God who is exercising political rule in person, and this will happen *only* when Jesus Christ comes a second time in accordance with what the Scriptures teach. This means we must clearly differentiate Christian mission and its objective from that of Islam. The Christian church that we serve is not a political entity like the nations of the world. It has not received a political agenda from God. It is a spiritual kingdom, made up of all who acknowledge their sin before God and make Christ king in their hearts; they thereby receive His redemption and become children of God by faith and heirs of the kingdom. For the present, the kingdom is temporal and provisional, but at Christ's second coming He will raise from the dead the heirs of the kingdom and establish His eternal kingdom.

For us as evangelical Christians, then, mission is not political action with a view to taking political control of the world. Rather, it is spiritual action to deal with people's bondage to sin and to Satan and lead them into the kingdom. In the words of Christ, we are called to be His witnesses to the nations "to open their eyes and turn them from darkness to light, and from the power of Satan to God, so that they may receive forgiveness of sins and a place among those who are sanctified by faith in me [i.e., Christ]" (Acts 26:18). Could there be a more noble objective than that? And so we pray "Thy kingdom come" as our Lord Jesus Christ taught us to pray. Amen, come Lord Jesus!

9

The Theological Evaluation
of Religions

One thing that stands out from our study so far is that our contextual model is shaped to a large extent by our theology of religions, that is, the way one evaluates culture and religion theologically. Gerald Anderson has well said, "No issue in missiology is more important, more difficult, more controversial, or more divisive for the days ahead than the theology of religions. . . . This is *the* theological issue for mission in the 1990s and into the twenty-first century" (quoted in Rommen and Netland 1995:4). It must be emphasized that the theological evaluation of religions is not just an academic exercise that may be dispensed with; it is crucial to the way the missionary community, and the young church being raised up, relates to its culture of ministry. This observation leads to two questions: What then is the most appropriate standard that we should use in evaluation? And what does the Bible teach us about the evaluation of other religions and cultures?

Before examining these questions, let's take a brief look at how Christians have actually judged Islam. In a word, they have been "all over the map" (see, e.g., Bijlefeld 1959:319–24; Caspar 1978:1/45–63). Negatively, they have judged Islam to be of satanic origin, a product of the anti-Christ, a "manmade" or "natural" religion, or a "Christian heresy," and they have explained Muhammad's prophethood in terms of his being epileptic or a psychopath. On a more positive note, some have considered Islam to be heir of God's promises to Abraham concerning Ishmael, or in some vague sense a Christian sect. Still others have viewed the Qur'an to be partially inspired, *a* word of God among several, or "on the margins" of biblical tradition (Caspar 1978:1/56–63). Clearly, a sound biblical approach to evaluation is needed to give our contextual model a solid foundation.

The Search for a Sound Theology of Religions

When we examine past approaches to other religions, and especially Islam, we find considerable confusion on the subject, as one might expect from our studies in part one. For a number of years, there was considerable groping about for a criterion or standard to use in evaluating other religions.

Christianity as the Criterion

In the nineteenth century, the polemicists believed that, as the one true "revealed religion," Christianity itself is the standard. From Martyn to Tisdall, they breathed the rationalistic spirit so characteristic of the theology of the period. They assumed that all that was required was the "rational" comparison of other religions with Christianity (see H. D. McDonald 1959). In the *Mîzân ul-Haqq*, Pfander sets forth what he considers to be the "marks" of the "true" revelation and the "true" prophet (1867:vi-ix, 77), arguing that these prove Christianity to be the true revealed religion. He assumed that these "marks" can be discovered by looking within man and reflecting on nature, and that they are, therefore, universally valid. He writes, "If the cravings of the human soul, and the desire of the human conscience; and, yet again, the attributes with which the Unchangeable one has declared Himself in the universe, are scrutinized and pondered over, the desired characteristics will immediately appear" (v, vi).

Christians will find it helpful at some point to compare Islam with biblical Christianity, but what is the basis for such comparison? Pfander and the polemicists claimed to base their evaluation on reason. His marks, however, simply assume Christianity to be the true religion, while Muslims, for their part, use a completely different set of marks that assume Islam to be the true religion. In the last analysis, the marks used by each side represent presuppositions about man and his relation to the universe and to God that derive from their respective cultural traditions rather than from reason.

The "Essence of Religion" as Criterion

Early in the twentieth century, the Christian attitude toward other religions became the subject of intense debate. The "Layman's Foreign Missions Inquiry," *Re-Thinking Missions*, published in 1932, was especially controversial. It conceived the relationship of Christianity to other religions in terms of sharing, cooperation, and "a common search for truth" (1932:97–101), thereby calling into question the existence of a universally valid standard. Out of this debate emerged several conflicting approaches to evaluation.

Somewhat like Pfander, most looked within man for some universal or neutral principle by which to explain and evaluate the religions. This was the approach of the science of comparative religion that was later called the science of religion and eventually the history of religion. These scholars generally sought for the standard in terms of a general principle that they called the "essence of religion."

This approach came under vigorous criticism from Hendrik Kraemer (1956). Although acknowledging his indebtedness to their research, he was critical of their claim to be "scientific" and "empirical." The problem of starting with man, he argued, is that, however one defines the standard, every such approach "rests ultimately on an attitude and a decision as to what to think about man and his attitude in relation to the Beyond, which cannot be cogently and universally demonstrated" (1956:60). Such an approach, he argued, is "immanentistic" and can never lead to a universal standard.

Kraemer was especially critical of theologians and missionaries who follow the approach. In a paper prepared for the Tambaram Conference of the International Missionary Council, he wrote:

> How can I, and how can you, ignore the fact that our whole apprehension of religious life is molded and colored by our contact with and knowledge of Christ? How can we acknowledge Him as the ultimate authority and standard in all things religious, and then try to find a so-called wider and more inclusive standpoint from which to probe and determine the significance and meaning of the religious dream of mankind? This simply means that there is another ultimate standard than Christ, a so-called general religious *a priori* by which even Christ, who upsets all human

standards, is measured. At any rate for the Christian this standpoint leads to hopeless confusion. (1939:8)

The "Christian Revelation" as Criterion

Kraemer held that, for the Christian, the standard must be the "Christian Revelation" (or "Biblical Realism," 1956:66); this, he argued, is a reference that is truly "from above." One must not, however, suppose that by Christian revelation he means the Scripture or its teachings. On the contrary! His theology was dialectical and existential; in his view "Christianity" is just as relative and under the judgment of God as any religion and cannot therefore be the standard. Only the Christian revelation is "*sui generis*," absolute and final. He defined revelation, however, in terms of a synthesis of God's "objective" act of making Himself known and man's subjective experience of that revelation (1956:344–45).

While Kraemer's critique of the approach of scientists of religion has been salutary, his own approach is no less problematic. As E. C. Dewick has observed, Kraemer's standard "really implies that the theologian who applies this test possesses an infallible power of discernment" (1948:116).

The Person of Christ as Criterion

The majority of missionaries seem to have preferred a theological approach that holds that Jesus Christ Himself; as the sum and substance of the Christian message, is the standard. Close examination, however, reveals significant differences in how they understand this standard. Evangelicals like Samuel Zwemer and Robert E. Speer argued for "the finality (or absoluteness) of Jesus" (Vander Werff 1977:257–62; Speer 1933). By this, they meant that they evaluated other religions by the person of Jesus Christ as He is presented in the Scriptures.

Kenneth Cragg might seem also to take this approach when he speaks of Christ as the "measure" of other religions in *The Christian and Other Religion*. He writes:

> The criteria of our relationships [with "other religion"] must be 'the measure of Christ'. It is well to know where we are, with conviction and with humility, when we come to dialogue. Is it possible that our surest clue in that exacting role is to look to discover every 'in Christ' quality, or feature, or accent, that can be discerned in other religion, and to do this, not possessively, and certainly not patronizingly, as if we were proprietors, but with a lively and a generous hope? . . . What we

have called the Christic is not necessarily disqualified by recruiting the resources of the human manifold. What matters is which is determinative. (1977:63–64)

What he is saying here is clearly something quite different from what Zwemer and Speer had in mind. As with his "new hermeneutic," he approaches evaluation from inside Islam. He is not speaking in terms of the "absoluteness" of Christ but only of "Christ" as a symbol for what he calls "the Christ-event." In other words, by "Christ" he is referring to what might be called, using his terms, "Christic clues" within Islam.

Another Approach: Considering Culture and Religion to Be Neutral

Some scholars have approached our question from an entirely different angle. Rather than looking for a theological criterion by which to evaluate other cultures and religions, they have turned the idea of evaluation on its head and taken the position that other cultures and religions are neutral with respect to the relationship between God and man. In other words, they are not to be evaluated at all, whether negatively or positively.

Dutch Islamicist Willem Bijlefeld, for example, argues against theological evaluation in *De Islam Als Na-Christelijke Religie (Islam as a Post-Christian Religion*—see the English summary at the end of the book; 1959). He argues for the questionable position that Islam should be qualified simply as post-Christian.

The *post*-Christian character of Islam should not be qualified as either *anti*-Christian or *semi*-('potentially') Christian. Both qualifications are false anticipations. At the present time we have no way of knowing whether Islam has consciously repudiated or unintentionally misconceived the Biblical Message; whether it was scandalized by the Cross or by a caricature of Christianity. The actual confrontation of Islam with the Kerygma is still a matter of the future. (1959:323–24)

Missionary anthropologist Charles Kraft, in *Christianity in Culture*, argues for the theory that human cultures in general, including major religions such as Islam, should be considered essentially neutral with respect to the God-man relationship.

Culture is seen as a kind of road map made up of various forms designed to get people where they need to go. These forms and the functions they are intended to serve are seen, with few exceptions, as neutral with

respect to the interaction of God and man. Cultural patterning, organiz-
ing, and structuring of life, the functions they are intended to serve, and
the processes cultures make available to human beings are not seen as
inherently evil or good in themselves. (1979b:113)

Then, as we saw in chapter 7, on the basis of the theory above, a
further distinction between "faith-allegiance" to one's God and the supposed neutrality of the "religious structures" of one's faith, Kraft goes
on to argue that a movement of faith-allegiance to Christ that remains
attached to Islam could still be considered a "dynamic equivalence"
church. It is imperative that we examine this theory thoroughly because
so many in evangelical missionary circles have bought into it. Can it be
true that the cultures and religions of man are essentially neutral with
respect to the God-man relationship? What is the biblical view on this
question?

To begin, one must recognize that there is an element of truth to the
theory. From the anthropological point of view, all cultures are equal, and
in that sense neutral from the human standpoint; so the theory is valid
to a degree. But is the theory true from God's standpoint? Kraft qualifies
the theory somewhat by limiting the extent of the neutrality of culture
to its "forms" and "the functions they are intended to serve." But what
do the Scriptures say? I shall argue that at the least, the forms and functions of culture are ambivalent with respect to the interaction of God and
man, and are not neutral. Sometimes they are even in opposition to such
interaction. We shall return to this theory in later chapters. In any case,
we can say that the approaches to evaluating Islam examined so far are
woefully inadequate.

A Biblical Approach to the Theology of Religions

Let us now return to our original question: What does the Bible say
about God's approach to evaluating mankind and his religions? Several
missiologists have made useful contributions to the subject (e.g., Blauw
1961:31–41). The one who I believe goes to the heart of the matter is
Dutch missiologist J. H. Bavinck (see especially [1966]:117–27). The
Evangelical Missiological Society has also published a study in the "Biblical Theology of World Religions" (Rommen et al. 1995) that, while
it does not refer to Bavinck's work, is I believe compatible with his
approach. In the following exposition, I am for the most part indebted
to Bavinck.

The Two Universals of Romans

Bavinck takes us to the first two chapters of Romans, the biblical *locus classicus* on the evaluation of religions and cultures. According to Romans, God judges or evaluates man on the basis of two things that are universal to human nature.

The First Universal: Man's "Original" Knowledge of God

The first universal I shall call the "original" knowledge of God, of His requirements of man and His penalty for disobedience, and of man's failure to meet God's requirements. I use the term "knowledge" advisedly, because the terms "know," "knowledge," or their equivalent are the ones used in these two chapters. Let us examine the four passages where they occur.

Romans 1:21 says that man "knows" God. It is clear that the passage does not mean knowledge that man can acquire through the use of his rational powers; the apostle says elsewhere that "in the wisdom of God the world through its wisdom [Gr. *Sofia*, i.e., philosophy] did not know God" (1 Cor. 1:21). Nor is it the personal knowledge of God that the Bible says the believer obtains through his union with Christ (John 17:3). It means that man knows that behind the visible creation there exists its invisible Creator, the Eternal and Almighty God to whom he is accountable. It is a knowledge that man possesses immediately and intuitively by virtue of his creation "in the image of God" (Gen. 1:26–27). And this knowledge of God is "clearly seen" in his creation (Rom. 1:20), and in the "testimony" given by his provision for man's needs through rain and crops (Acts 14:17).

This knowledge has often been called general revelation, although the term is not completely satisfactory in view of unbiblical notions that have sometimes been identified with it in the past. The knowledge of general revelation is *not* mediated by reason, and it does not result in a body of natural theology, this being excluded by 1 Corinthians 1:21. I would, therefore, agree with those who reject the idea of natural theology and the *logos spermatikos* doctrine often associated with it (e.g., Bavinck 1960:223ff.; Kraemer 1956:340–65). As Bavinck insists, however, over against Karl Barth, the passage does teach that there *is* a general revelation (1960:135). Since the term has been misused, however, it would seem preferable to stick with biblical usage and call it original knowledge (see Bavinck [1966]:124).

In Romans 1:32 (actually, beginning with verse 29), a second aspect of man's original knowledge enters the picture. This is the knowledge of the moral requirements that God has placed upon man and the knowledge of his failure to meet those requirements and of the retribution merited by his disobedience. After listing "every kind of wickedness" in which mankind is involved, the passage concludes, "although they know God's righteous decree [cf. 2:15] that those who do such things deserve death, they not only continue to do these very things but also approve of those who practice them."

Romans 2 goes on to give two proofs that man does know God's requirements of him, quite apart from any special revelation. This is demonstrated by the faculty of judgment, what Jesus calls seeing "the speck in your brother's eye" (Matt. 7:3). Romans 2:1–3 argues that, when we scrutinize the behavior of others and "pass judgment" upon them, this proves that we have an immediate and intuitive knowledge of God's law. This is why God judges us by the standards with which we judge others (cf. Matt. 7:2). Romans 2:15 then goes on to show that our knowledge of God's law is likewise demonstrated by our conscience, which scrutinizes our own behavior. "They show that the requirements of the law are written on their hearts, their conscience also bearing witness, and their thoughts now accusing, now even defending them" (Rom. 2:15). This original knowledge is reflected in the values, mores, and legal systems, unwritten or codified, that govern all human societies. Even self-proclaimed atheists demonstrate such knowledge when they denounce the "injustices" of capitalistic societies.

Here once again, man's original knowledge of God's law must be distinguished from the philosophical concept of natural law, supposedly discoverable by reason. We are talking about a knowledge that man possesses immediately and intuitively, and is not the end product of the rational process, as would be the case with so-called natural law. If this were the case, ultimately it would make man the standard of right and wrong.

The Second Universal: The Repression and Suppression of the Truth, and Substitution of Untruth

The second universal that, according to Romans, is significant for the biblical approach to evaluation is man's repression and suppression of the original knowledge that he has by virtue of his creation in the image of God, and his substitution of untruth (Rom. 1:18, 23, 25). Bavinck contributes significantly to our understanding of the role of the universal religious consciousness at this point, and especially the dynamic of repression and substitution, in his exposition of Romans 1.

Repression is that process of the mind, brought to light by modern psychology that may be defined as "the process by which unacceptable desires or impulses are excluded from consciousness and thus being denied direct satisfaction are left to operate in the unconscious."[1] It represents an unconscious response to self-knowledge, impulses that are too painful for the conscious mind to accept. It is generally recognized that repression is a universal phenomenon, individuals differing mainly in the degree to which they repress. In the majority of individuals, repression is minimal because they have a more or less healthy ability to acknowledge reality, albeit with some difficulty at times. Relatively few people completely lose touch with reality; these represent the most severe cases of mental illness.

However, I would differ with Bavinck on one point; he seems to interpret Romans 1:28ff. only in terms of repression. Repression, however, is often accompanied and reinforced by a conscious suppression of truth, a willful and defiant effort to keep the truth from getting out. Because that which is repressed no longer operates in the conscious mind, false religious teachings take on an aura of plausibility that encourages suppression. This dynamic is very real in other religions. (It is noteworthy that Bavinck later switches to talk in terms of "suppression"—126.)

Thus, according to Romans 1:18, "the wrath of God is being revealed from heaven" because people "suppress the truth by their wickedness." (In the Greek, the verb is *katekho*—to "hold down" or "suppress.") Since it is a question here of truth about God that he has "made plain to them" (Rom. 1:19), it is clear that the passage is not referring to the suppression of scripturally revealed doctrine but rather the suppression of that original knowledge that all men have by virtue of their creation in the image of God.

This interpretation is reinforced by the fact that the passage goes on to speak of a threefold "exchange" or substitution taking place: the exchange of "the glory of the immortal God for images" (Rom. 1:23) and of "the truth of God for a lie" (Rom. 1:25), culminating in the exchange of "natural [sexual] relations for unnatural ones" (Rom. 1:26). Bavinck comments:

> Man has repressed the truth of the everlasting power and the divinity of God. It has been exiled to his unconscious, to the crypts of his existence. That does not mean, however, that it has vanished forever. Still active, it

1. Bavinck, 118, citing Webster's *New Collegiate Dictionary*.

reveals itself again and again. But it cannot become openly conscious; it appears in disguise, and it is exchanged for something different. Thus, all kinds of ideas of God are formed; the human mind as the *fabrica idolorum* (Calvin) makes its own ideas of God and its own myths. This is not intentional deceit—it happens without man's knowing it. He cannot get rid of them. So he has religion; he is busy with a god; he serves his god—but he does not see that the god he serves is not God himself. An exchange has taken place—a perilous exchange. An essential quality of God has been blurred because it did not fit in with the human pattern of life, and the image man has of God is no longer true. Divine revelation indeed lies at the root of it, but man's thoughts and aspirations cannot receive it and adapt themselves to it. In the image man has of God we can recognize the image of man himself. (122)

The mechanism of repression and substitution, and subsequent suppression, explains many of the phenomena of religion, most notably its ambivalence and contradictions. It explains how the religious man can be said to both respond to what he understands to be revelation, and, at the same time, to repress and reject that revelation. As Bavinck puts it:

The history of religions contains a dramatic element. It includes the divine approach and the human rejection. This rejection is hidden because man apparently is seeking God and serving Him, but the God he seeks is different from the true God because of the uncanny process of repression and exchange that enters in. (125)

Moreover, because the original knowledge of God and its repression are universal to man, there is no one, whether or not he has heard the biblical message, who can claim ignorance and escape responsibility. This is a fundamental presupposition of the biblical message.

When a missionary or some other person comes into contact with a non-Christian and speaks to him about the gospel, he can be sure that God has concerned Himself with this person long before. That person had dealings more than once with God before God touched him, and he himself experienced the two fatal reactions—suppression and substitution. (126)

To summarize biblical evaluation, let us turn to the central theme of Romans—righteousness. God's evaluation of man is based on the righteousness required by man's innate knowledge of God and of God's moral standards and on what he has done with that knowledge. Romans indicates that this knowledge requires man to acknowledge his responsibility to his Creator by glorifying him as God and giving him thanks (1:21), worshiping him alone (1:25), and living within the "natural" boundaries of intercreature relationships that God has built into his creation (1:24, 26–27). Anything that falls short of this requirement is "unrighteousness," from the repression of that original knowledge (1:18) to "every kind of wickedness" that men practice when they do not "think it worthwhile to retain the knowledge of God" (1:28–31). He who does such things "deserves death" (1:32), and when he judges others for doing those things he "condemns himself" (2:1).

Here we see a dynamic and creative alternative to the sterile approaches to evaluation that we have seen so far. We should not be under any illusions, however, that it will be universally acceptable. By the nature of the case, it is impossible for anyone, apart from the grace of God, to face the full truth of general revelation without repressing the most painful aspects of the truth. Indeed, we must not forget that we, as Christians, are not entirely free of repression and substitution ourselves. All this is to say that, although the standard may not be universally accepted, it *is* nevertheless truly universal to man and does not compromise the gospel. It, therefore, represents a neutral and just basis for evaluation that favors neither Christian nor non-Christian. Hence, we can with justification press its claim to be a universally valid standard.

A Biblical Perspective on Islam

We shall conclude our study of the theology of religions in chapter 12 with a theological evaluation of Islam in accordance with the above approach. Before going on to chapter 10, however, let us take a look at an interesting clue in the New Testament to the biblical perspective on Islam (adapted from Schlorff 1990).

Islam did not come along until some five centuries after the last book of the Bible was written, so the Bible does not give us any specific information about Islam. But might it give us some clues? To be sure, Muslims have long claimed to find prophecies of Muhammad in certain Bible passages. To the serious Bible student, it is abundantly clear that their interpretation of these passages is pure fantasy. They do not, therefore, concern us here.

Some Bible scholars interpret Genesis 17, where God promises Abraham that He will bless Ishmael and make him "the father of twelve rulers" and "a great nation" (v. 20), to point in some way to Islam; some even see in Islam the fulfillment of this promise. It seems clear, however, that the Bible considers Genesis 25:13–18 to be the fulfillment of this promise; Ishmael's twelve sons had by then become "tribal rulers" and a great nation, judging from the area where they settled.

The passage that I feel to be the most relevant to Islam is Galatians 4:21–31. Significantly, while it looks back to Ishmael, it ignores the promise of Genesis 17:20. Its approach, instead, is to take Ishmael and Isaac with their mothers as types of two opposing religious systems—law and grace. Observe what the passage says:

Hagar = Abraham's concubine, a slave | Sarah = Abraham's wife, a free woman

Ishmael = "born in the ordinary way" | Isaac = born supernaturally, "the result of a promise"

The Old Covenant = Mount Sinai, children are slaves = "the present city of Jerusalem" | The New Covenant = children are free = "the Jerusalem that is above"

Adherents of Judaism (and of Islam) = are slaves = not heirs | Followers of Christ = are freed from slavery = children of the promise and heirs

The correspondences between the Hagar column and Islamic origins are remarkable. Ishmael, Abraham's son by the slave woman, is claimed by Muslims to be the ancestor of Muhammad, although that is by no means proven. It is also noteworthy that the slave theme is central to Islam's ideal for the God-man relationship—God is "Lord" and man is His "slave." But what is most striking is the association of "the present city of Jerusalem and her children" with Hagar, instead of with Sarah. The context makes it clear that the religious system, Pharisaic legalism, is in view and not the Jewish people as an ethnic group. It is an established historical fact that Judaism is the main source of Islamic law! What the passage seems to be saying then is that Judaism has forsaken the heritage of Sarah (freedom through Messiah) for the heritage of Ishmael (slavery under religious law). Slavery under religious law (the *Shariah*) is the heritage of Islam. All things considered, then, this passage would appear to be basic to any Christian theological evaluation of Islam.

10

The Contextual/Theological[1] Starting Point

It would be helpful to begin by differentiating the contextual starting point from theological evaluation. The two are related but represent different functions. Theological evaluation defines the relationship of Christian faith to the receptor culture, both theologically and culturally. Building on that, the contextual starting point specifies the sources, whether theological or cultural, that will be used in the contextualization of the gospel and the church. The choice of starting point controls the hermeneutical method that will be used for interpreting the biblical message within the receptor culture.

Evangelical Christians take the Bible as the sole authority and source for the Christian faith and life; this is the principle of *sola scriptura*. Theoretically then, the Scriptures are, or at least should be, the contextual starting point for evangelicals. Actually, however, other starting points have been used, as we shall see.

1. I use the term "contextual starting point" and the term "theological starting point" of earlier theologians, as essentially equivalents.

The Qur'an and Islamic Culture as Starting Point

The main question to be considered at this point is this: May anything in the Qur'an or Islam be used as starting point for the contextualization of the gospel and the church? The question is important because, as we have seen, in the history of the Protestant approach to Islam, there have been many influential voices to answer in the affirmative. Those who do so may be identified, for the most part, with the positive uses of the Qur'an described in chapter 5.

Those who take this approach usually base it on the premise that all truth comes from God and that no person, people, race, or religion may claim, therefore, to have a monopoly on it. The Christian, it is said, is free to use truth wherever he may find it. Sometimes, Qur'anic elements that are used contextually are referred to as "moments of truth." Sometimes they are even attributed to the "working of the Holy Spirit," as we have already seen. Earlier, they were generally called "points of contact," but today, more often, they are called "bridges." Unfortunately, these terms mean different things to different people.

The objective is to "bridge" the semantic and cultural gap separating Christian and Muslim that is a major cause of the communication problem described in chapter 3. The problem, essentially, is how to communicate the gospel in such a way that genuinely biblical meanings are received, and not the caricatures that Muslims read into the Christian message. Proponents of the approach assume that to bridge the gap one must find allies within Islam—"gleams of truth" that are on our side—on which to build the truth of the gospel. This means that Islam is used as a contextual starting point. The objective is laudable, but is the assumption valid? Above all, does it accord with the biblical facts and with the principle of *sola scriptura*?

Before examining the case that proponents make for starting the contextual process within Islam, we would do well to remind ourselves that this approach has implications for our hermeneutical method. We shall examine that subject in the next chapter.

Rationales for the Use of the Qur'an and Islamic Culture

It is instructive to look at the various rationales that have been given to try to ground the practice in the Scriptures. It is noteworthy that the nineteenth-century polemicists did not seem to have felt a need, as did later writers, to justify their proof-texting by appeal to the Scriptures.

They do not, of course, tell us why. It is possible that it is related to the conviction, expressed by several writers, that the truth that Islam possesses was "borrowed from a purer faith" (e.g., Tisdall 1895:47). In any case, as they saw it, Islam is destined eventually to come crashing to the ground.

Since the early twentieth century, however, when the missionary approach to Islam underwent a paradigm shift, the proponents of using the Qur'an as starting point sought to ground the practice in biblical precedent. Here are the principal passages that were cited to justify the practice, and how those passages are interpreted:

> Matthew 5:17. Jesus' statement that "I have not come to abolish [the Law and the Prophets] but to fulfill them" is interpreted to mean that Jesus viewed Christianity in terms of the fulfillment of Judaism (Levonian 1931:123). This is taken as a precedent for viewing Christianity as the fulfillment of other religions as well (DeWolf 1961:199ff.; Cragg 1956:244).

> John 1:1, 14. John's use of the Greek term *logos* to express his Christology is taken to imply that he was thereby identifying Jesus of Nazareth with the cosmic "reason" (*logos*) of Greek philosophy, representing the principle of self-expression of transcendent Deity that gives order and intelligibility to the world (Bouquet 1961:183–98; Cragg 1979:200).

> Acts 17:23, 28. Paul's reference to an Athenian altar dedicated "to an unknown god," and his quotations from the Greek poets Epimenides ("For in him we live and move and have our being") and Aratus ("We are his offspring") are taken as precedents that justify using the Qur'an in support of Christian teaching, as described in chapter 5 ('Accad 1976:331; 1997:18ff.).

> 1 Corinthians 9:22. Paul's statement, "I have become all things to all men that by all means I might save some," is taken to mean that we should become as Muslims to win them to Christ. Some quote this verse to justify using the Qur'an in support of Christian teaching (Purdon 1924:140).

> In more general terms, Kenneth Cragg argues for the use of the Qur'an as theological starting point on the basis of the "Christian reception of the Old Testament" (1979:197; 1968b:40–63).

These arguments raise an important question: How exactly did the inspired writers use the receptor culture? I am not questioning here the fact of its use; the biblical evidence for this is too extensive to dismiss. The question I am raising concerns how it was used. Did the inspired writers find "glimmers of revealed truth" in Pharisaism and Hellenism, for example, or in Baalism and Canaanite culture? Did they use these religious systems as a starting point on which to build the gospel message and the life, worship and theology of the young church, or did they use them in some other way?

A Look at the Evidence

Within the limits of this chapter, it will not be possible to attempt anything like a complete study of this question. I will therefore limit myself to a brief look at the New Testament attitude toward Pharisaism and Hellenism as revealed in the above-mentioned passages. There are few theological studies on this question to help us (see, e.g., Von Allmen 1975:37–52). To this day, we still do not have anything like a thorough biblico-theological treatment of the subject. However, one often finds it assumed that interaction with one of these religious systems in the New Testament involves using it as theological starting point.

The Case of Judaism

Judaism, especially first-century Pharisaism, is an important case in point, in view of its historical relationship to biblical revelation. According to Harold DeWolf, "most Christian scholars would grant that their faith was a fulfilment rather than a radical displacement of Judaism" (DeWolf 1961:201). This would make Judaism a theological starting point for the gospel. Is this the position of the New Testament?

There can be no doubt but that the early Christian community was considerably influenced by Pharisaism in both its theological and insti-tutional expressions. To hold that it took Pharisaism as a theological starting point, however, flies in the face of a significant amount of New Testament data. In that case, how is one to explain Jesus' severe criticism of Pharisaic teaching and piety, beginning with the Sermon on the Mount? How does one explain the evidence for the Pharisees' mounting hostility toward Jesus, ending with His crucifixion, and all the passages dealing with the conflict between His teaching and theirs? Moreover, what is one to do with the teaching of the Pauline epistles on circumcision and on the function of the law of Moses in the divine economy?

Jesus gives us the answer in his reply to a questioner who asked why his disciples did not fast like the Pharisees. His reply shows that he considered Pharisaic teaching to be incompatible with his own.

> No one sews a patch of unshrunk cloth on an old garment, for the patch will pull away from the garment, making the tear worse. Neither do men pour new wine into old wineskins. If they do, the skins will burst, the wine will run out and the wineskins will be ruined. No, they pour new wine into new wineskins, and both are preserved. (Matt. 9:16–17)

What then did Jesus mean when He claimed to "fulfill the Law and the Prophets" (Matt. 5:17)? In the context of the Sermon on the Mount, where, again, Jesus' teaching is contrasted with that of the Pharisees, this verse is usually understood to mean that Jesus kept the Law and gave it its full meaning, sensitizing our conscience to sin. Later on, his fulfillment of the Law is understood to also include his fulfillment of Messianic prophecies and typology (Luke 24:44–46; cf. Hebrews). To interpret Christ to mean that he "fulfills" Pharisaic Judaism reads into Matthew 5:17 something that is contrary to his idea of fulfillment. Jesus claimed to fulfill the Old Testament Scriptures. Pharisaism is something else! It came into existence only during the intertestamental period and followed a hermeneutical tradition to which Christ and the apostles were opposed (Herford 1952:198ff.). I conclude, then, that however much the early church was influenced by Judaism contextually, it did not use Pharisaism as a theological starting point.

What then about Cragg's claim that the "Christian reception of the Old Testament" represents a precedent for taking the Qur'an as a theological starting point? He would have us maintain an "open attitude" toward the Qur'an's revelatory status. "A plea must be made immediately that we do not demand from ourselves a formal and prior verdict, in the abstract, about the ultimate status of the Quran. To do so would be to preclude the possibility of ever reaching one!" (1979:196).

It should be pointed out in reply that this is a circular argument, in that it assumes the conclusion it seeks to prove. An attitude of openness is no less "a formal and prior verdict, in the abstract" than any other attitude. All it means is that one has decided in the abstract to accept the Qur'an as being in some sense a revealed book. The Christian acceptance of the Old Testament can only be considered a "precedent" for an open attitude toward the Qur'an if one has assumed, *a priori*, that the Qur'an has the same revelatory status as the Old Testament!

The Case of Hellenism

Let us now examine the case for the theological use of Hellenistic Greek culture in the New Testament. Do the passages cited—John 1:1, Acts 17:23 and 28, and 1 Corinthians 9:22—prove such a use? Here once again, there can be no question but that the early church made considerable use of Hellenistic cultural forms since the New Testament is in Greek. As we shall see, however, the passages cited bear testimony to the fact that it is essentially Hebraic in its cultural background. One cannot assume that the New Testament's use of Greek involves the theological use of Hellenism.

A. C. Bouquet has written extensively on behalf of the theory that the Gospel of John identifies Christ with the mythological *logos* concept of Greek philosophy (1961:184–98). If he is correct, this would be a case in point. It is noteworthy, however, that he does not offer a single biblical example to prove his theory. He cites Philo, the Hellenized Jew, and Hellenistic Christianity subsequent to the New Testament, but neither the Hebrew cultural background of John nor the New Testament's overall attitude to Greek culture are brought into the picture.

In the end, Bouquet must confess that "when all is said and done, there seems always to be a gap between the sages [who symbolize the *logos* principle in history] and Jesus" (192). The former are always mythological beings while Jesus is not. "The essential point about Jesus of Nazareth is his contemporary historicity. He managed to replace all other cult personalities by being real instead of mythical" (196). This difference is crucial and decisive. It demonstrates that even if John were interacting with the Greek concept when he used the term *logos*, which is not at all certain, it does not follow, as Bouquet assumes, that he was using the concept as a theological starting point for his Christology.

What then of Paul's reference to an "unknown god" and his quotations from Greek poets in his Areopagus address in Athens (Acts 17:23, 28)? Do these represent, as is claimed, a theological use of Greek culture? Without presuming to treat the question exhaustively, there are several points to be made. I note, first of all, that neither in this passage nor elsewhere does the apostle quote a pagan Greek source that claims to be a revelation, such as one of the oracles. By contrast, the Qur'an claims to be the speech of God. Second, Paul likewise never quotes the pagan Greek poets in support of distinctive Christian teaching, such as the inspiration of the Old and New Testaments, the deity of Christ, the Trinity, or the substitutionary atonement. This, however, is what is involved in the theological use of the Qur'an, as we saw in chapter 5. The thrust of the apostle's argument is similar to that of Romans 1: the God whom you worship as "unknown" is really known, and this is proved by what your own poets have said.

New Testament scholar Ned Stonehouse examines Paul's argument at length in his monograph on the Areopagus address. Here is his conclusion:

> Thus, thoughts which in their pagan contexts were quite un-Christian and anti-Christian, could be acknowledged as up to a point involving an actual apprehension of revealed truth. As creatures of God, retaining a *sensus divinitatis* in spite of their sin, their ignorance of God and their suppression of the truth, they were not without a certain awareness of God and of their creaturehood. Their ignorance of, and hostility to, the truth was such that their awareness of God and of creaturehood could not come into its own to give direction to their thought and life or to serve as a principle of interpretation of the world of which they were a part. But the apostle Paul, reflecting upon their creaturehood, and upon their religious faith and practice, could discover within their pagan religiosity evidences that the pagan poets in the very act of suppressing and perverting the truth presupposed a measure of awareness of it. Thus while conceiving of his task as basically a proclamation of One of whom they were in ignorance, he could appeal even to the reflections of pagans as pointing to the true relation between the sovereign Creator and His creatures. (1957:30)

In other words, in quoting these poets Paul is appealing to truth that people ought to know, because mankind has received it via general revelation, but which they have repressed and suppressed. This is something quite different from using pagan Greek thought to prove doctrines that, according to the Bible, are given or understood only by means of special revelation.

We need not deal at length with 1 Corinthians 9:22, which states that the apostle Paul became "all things to all men," as this does not change the position expressed in Romans 1 and 2 and Acts 17. The verse is part of a lengthy passage dealing with a dispute in the church at Corinth over eating meat offered to idols (1 Cor. 8–10). It cites the apostle's example of voluntarily restricting his freedom so as to win the more to Christ as a model for the Corinthian Christians to follow. The larger passage enunciates several important contextual principles concerned with how to handle cultural practices (or forms) that have pagan ties or connotations (Clinton

1975; Parshall 1980:34–37). It does not, however, touch on the question of using the religious content of a culture as theological starting point.

Some Conclusions

To conclude, the supposed biblical precedents for the theological use of the Qur'an do not support this claim; the passages cited do not, as has been assumed, use the receptor culture as starting point for the contextualization either of theology or of the church. Indeed, I am convinced that a thorough biblical-theological study of both Testaments will show that the Bible as a whole rejects this approach to cross-cultural communication. Bavinck's critique of this approach is very much to the point here.

> All such endeavors mistakenly suppose that somewhere within non-Christian religions, perhaps in a hidden nook or cranny, there lie hidden moments of truth, and that it is to these that one should join his own argument. It is, of course, admitted that it is subsequently necessary to eliminate many errors, but it is still thought possible to find a point of contact from which one can climb up to the truth of Jesus Christ. . . . All such efforts and outlooks are to be rejected as improper and illegitimate. Such attitudes conflict with the unique character of the gospel. (1960:135)

In rejecting this approach, Bavinck is not saying, as does Barth, that cross-cultural evangelism occurs "in a void." "Nations do not dwell in a vacuum, but their abode is illuminated on every hand by the general revelation of God" (1960:135). All points of contact, such as the Athenian altar "to the unknown god," must be seen as "cries of distress of a heart torn loose from God" rather than as "pointing to the real Christ" (136).

The fundamental problem with using the religious thought of a culture as theological starting point is that it fails to take into account the devastating effects of repression and substitution on that culture.

> If we begin with the ideas of those we would convert, a point will be reached when the breach between our view and theirs is clearly evident. There is no direct uninterrupted path from the darkness of paganism to the light of the gospel. . . . Somewhere along the line, we must pause to point out our tremendous differences. Without that, our argument is not finished and it may even be dangerous and misleading. There is no detour that can bridge the gap; the transition from paganism to Christianity is not continuous and smooth, and it would be dishonest and

unfaithful to Christ if we were to try to camouflage the gulf separating the two. (136–37)[2]

[To conclude:] From a strictly theological point of view there is no point within pagan thought which offers an unripe truth that can be simply taken over and utilized as a basis for our Christian witness. If this is what is meant by a point of contact, then there just is none. (140)

All this does not mean that the receptor culture has no role to play in contextualization. On the contrary! "No one can be reached in a vacuum. A person can be reached only within a certain conceptual world. There is no other way" (139). There are still legitimate ways the Qur'an may be used effectively to communicate the gospel to Muslims. Unfortunately, these have been overshadowed by the attempt to find allies within Islam. To distinguish these from the theological uses I shall refer to them as communicational starting points.[3] Some of its linguistic and cultural forms may be usable as sign vehicles for the biblical message. This, however, raises the question of hermeneutical method, the third component of the contextual model, to which we now turn.

2. Note that Bavinck uses the terms "pagan" and "paganism" inclusively of all non-Christian religions, whereas in modern English usage the terms refer only to polytheism or the irreligious.

3. Bavinck calls these "points of attack" to distinguish them from "points of contact," understood to represent a theological starting point (1960:140).

11

The Cross-Cultural
Hermeneutical Method

The hermeneutical method is the central component of the contextual model. It determines exactly how the biblical message relates to the receptor culture and, consequently, how the young church in that culture understands and proclaims the message, lives the Christian life, and organizes itself. The importance of our theological evaluation and contextual starting point derive from their influence on the hermeneutical method.

The question that concerns us as evangelicals, then, is this: What hermeneutical method is most appropriate for interpreting the biblical message to Muslims? Since we need to relate to the Qur'an and Islamic culture one way or another, what method is most appropriate to our theology of religions and our contextual approach? We need a hermeneutic that is valid for both Qur'an and Bible, both Islam and Christianity.

The Method of Synthesis

Of the methodologies studied in part two, most of the uses of the Qur'an mentioned, especially those I called "positive" (chap. 5), represent a synthesizing approach to interpretation. And in chapter 10, the contextual approach that starts the process within Islam also represents a hermeneutic of synthesis. This method seeks to interpret the Bible and Christianity in relation to the Qur'an and Islam in such a way as to bring their perspectives close together into a kind of dialectical unity, a synthesis.

Does the Bible Sanction Synthesis?

To begin, we need first to examine the question as to whether the Bible itself sanctions synthesis, as the proponents of synthesis claim. We acknowledge that the Old Testament does make some use of forms from (pagan) Canaanite culture in Hebrew poetry, for example. But nowhere are forms used that give expression to a pagan worldview, as would be the case if this were synthesis. In this connection, it is noteworthy that Naaman, the Syrian leper, has sometimes been cited as a case where synthesis is approved. He vowed to sacrifice to Yahweh alone, expressing the hope that God would forgive him if he had to "bow down in the temple of Rimmon" out of political expediency (2 Kings 5:18). But Naaman is never heard from again. He can hardly be considered evidence that synthesis is valid.

The passage most often cited in support of synthesis is 1 Corinthians 9:19–23, interpreted to mean "become a Muslim to Muslims so that by all means you might save some." These verses occur in a section dealing with disputed practices—eating meat offered to idols (1 Cor. 8–10). In 1 Corinthians 9, the apostle explains that although he is not obligated to do so, he refrains from eating such meat to avoid causing fellow Jews to stumble (v. 13). So when he says, "I have become all things to all men" (v. 22), he means that he is sensitive to people's dietary scruples. Moreover, in 1 Corinthians 10, he goes on to say that while Christians are free to eat such meat in private without asking questions, they should not participate in feasts at idol temples: "You cannot drink the cup of the Lord and the cup of demons" (v. 21). One should not even eat a friend's meat if he says it was offered to idols (v. 28). In a word, these chapters oppose the method of synthesis!

As concerns the Qur'an, we have seen how Qur'anic passages that praise the "previous scriptures" are cited in support of the Bible. The argument is made that Muslims, therefore, should accept its divine authority. We have also seen how passages that call Jesus "Word of God" and attribute to Him other lofty titles, attributes, and deeds are interpreted in support of His deity. And we have heard it said that when the Qur'an is interpreted in its original historical context, unencumbered by assumptions that were imposed upon it by later theological controversies, its message is substantially closer to that of the Bible than Islam admits and should, therefore, be heeded by Christians as well as by Muslims. All these are synthesizing interpretations.

The Proof-Text Approach: One-Way Synthesis

There are significant methodological differences in the above examples. The first two, representing the proof-text method, envisage only a one-way synthesis. Christian meanings are read into selected passages from the Qur'an but not the other way around, and the approach uses synthesis selectively. However, at least one interpreter, Roman Catholic Islamicist Giulio Basetti-Sani, has attempted to "Christianize" essentially the whole of the Qur'an in this way. He has proposed, on the basis of the hermeneutical principle known as the *sensus plenior* ("full meaning"), to read the Qur'an with a "Christian Key" (1967:126–37, 186–96; see also 1977). Other Roman Catholics have been critical of his interpretation because of its highly speculative nature (Gaudeul 1979:286–89).

The New Hermeneutic: Two-Way Synthesis

The third example given above represents the New Hermeneutic of the Qur'an. It prefers a historical-critical methodology to the *sensus plenior* and envisages a two-way synthesis where both the Qur'an and the Bible are opened up to meanings from the other. The New Hermeneutic corresponds neither to the traditional Islamic interpretation of the Qur'an nor yet to biblical teaching. It is a "Christianization" that involves an interpretation of the Qur'an that is compatible with a more liberal Christianity.

The New Hermeneutic employs what Bruce Nicholls has called an "existential approach" to contextualization.

> Existential contextualization involves the interaction of two basic principles: the essential relativity of text and context, and the dialectical method of the search for truth. . . . This position usually rejects any understanding of propositional verbal revelation as objective and authoritative on the basis that knowledge is never free from subjectivity. (1979a: 24–25)

One popular theory holds that the Qur'an's attitude toward Christianity and Christ represents a criticism, not of orthodox Christianity and Christology, but rather, as Montgomery Watt puts it, of "Christian heresies which orthodox Christians would themselves criticize" (1967:197).

On this basis, some argue that the Qur'an is much closer to a Christian position than Muslims and Christians have previously thought. The argument is typical of the New Hermeneutic of the Qur'an[1] and is essentially the rationale Basetti-Sani gives for reading the Qur'an with a "Christian Key" (1967:188–90). Some evangelicals also hold the theory; Abdiyah Akbar 'Abdul-Haqq has espoused this view in *Sharing Your Faith with a Muslim* (1980: 67–73, 131–56, 173–89).

It should be noted that proponents of synthesis do not limit the method to Qur'an interpretation. As we have seen in chapter 7, some missionaries speak of the contextual process in terms of "filling non-Christian cultural forms with supracultural (i.e. Christian) meanings." This is a leading concept in Charles Kraft's approach that he calls "ethnolinguistic hermeneutics" (1979b: 116–46). A number of missionaries to Muslims have adopted the approach as well (e.g., Parshall 1980:55ff.). In expounding his hermeneutic, Kraft includes both "doctrines," "beliefs," and "practices" as well as linguistic forms (1979b:118–19). In a word, synthesis is extended to include both the contextualization of the gospel and the contextualization of the church.

Objections to the Method of Synthesis

A number of objections argue against the legitimacy of synthesis in cross-cultural hermeneutics and caution against quoting the Qur'an in support of Christian belief.

FIRST OBJECTION: SYNTHESIS CUTS THE TEXT OFF FROM ITS CONTEXT

One problem area is the understanding of language and of the culture that synthesis entails; it assumes that the Qur'an, in whole or in part, may carry meanings that are more or less Christian. This approach is to be rejected because it assumes that the meaning of a text is independent of its context. For example, take Sura 3:45: "O Mary, God giveth thee glad tidings of a Word from Him, Whose name is Messiah, Jesus, Son of Mary." Synthesis assumes that the meaning of "a Word from Him" does not depend on Qur'anic usage but rather on the Bible, where the identification of Christ as "Word of God" is found. Since this expression

---

1. In addition to the works cited in chapter 6 and the article of Watt, see, e.g., Nolin 1970:170–77.

in John 1 implies the deity of Christ, it is assumed that it means the same thing in the Qur'an.

Whether or not it can be established that some Qur'anic terms or concepts came from antecedent sources such as the Bible, a theory that is anathema to Muslims for theological reasons, the assumption that these terms carry meanings other than what they meant to their original hearers must be rejected on linguistic grounds. Modern studies in semantics have shown that the meaning of a text depends strictly on the relationship of its terms to each other in the language of which it is an expression. Ferdinand de Saussure, the founder of modern linguistics, puts it this way: "Language is a system of interdependent terms in which the value of each term results solely from the simultaneous presence of the others" (1966:114).

Space limitations do not permit examining the principle further. Its significance for cross-cultural hermeneutics is quite clear, however. It implies that the meaning of a term or proposition as used in one language or culture cannot be determined by the way that term or proposition, or its formal equivalent, may have been used in another language and culture. Its meaning is determined solely by the relationship of the various terms to each other within the culture itself. And that relationship in turn grows out of the worldview of the culture concerned. In the last analysis, it is the worldview and culture of those who use a language system that is the ultimate determinant of the meaning of its individual terms as used in a given text (see Kraft 1979b:53, 65).

Evangelical Bible scholars are increasingly cognizant of the influence of assumptions about language and culture on biblical interpretation. British New Testament scholar Anthony Thiselton, for example, who has written extensively on New Testament hermeneutics, writes this:

> Because biblical language *as language* can only be understood with reference to its context and extra-linguistic situation, attention to the kind of question raised in critical study of the text is seen to be necessary on purely *linguistic* grounds. To try to cut loose "propositions" in the New Testament from the specific situation in which they were uttered and to try thereby to treat them "timelessly" is not only bad theology; it is also bad linguistics. For it leads to a distortion of what the text *means*.(1977a:79)

The same is true for the interpretation of the Qur'an and Islamic cultural forms. If our use of such forms is to have a sound basis, linguistically and theologically, their meanings must be determined solely in reference to Qur'anic Arabic and the worldview that it expresses.

This is why "filling Muslim forms with Christian meanings" is to be rejected. It disregards the fact that such forms are already meaning-specific. As Thiselton puts it, "a word has meaning not autonomously or independently but 'only as part of a whole'. . . ; only within a field" (1977a:83). This is true for all cultural forms. If a form is to be used unambiguously, care is required to ensure that the way it is used corresponds in some way to its original semantic field. Forms from a given culture are meaning-specific and cannot be "filled" with other meanings. This holds not just for words and phrases but also for cultural forms such as the body movements in the ritual prayer.

SECOND OBJECTION: SYNTHESIS CUTS THE TEXT OFF FROM ITS ORIGINAL MEANING

The method of synthesis involves giving Qur'anic and Islamic forms meanings that are substantially different from what they meant to their original hearers and from what they mean to Muslims today. There is good reason for calling this approach, as I have done elsewhere, a "sectarian" hermeneutic of the Qur'an (1980:146). There is no essential difference between it and the sectarian biblical interpretations, for example, of the Mormons and the Jehovah's Witnesses.

The comments of Dutch Islamicist Willem Bijlefeld (the theory that the "Christianity" criticized in the Qur'an represents heretical, and not genuine, Christianity) are to the point here. He writes: "It may well be true—and personally I believe that it _is_ true that some passages in the Qur'an are less controversial and antagonistic with regard to Christianity than many people, Muslims _and_ Christians, have thought for centuries" (1967:175). Since so many have raised the issue, however, he goes on to suggest that a joint Muslim-Christian study of the matter would be "most desirable." "Such a joint endeavour is possible because theological presuppositions should not play a decisive role in the study of this historical issue" (176). What Bijlefeld finds questionable is that, on the basis of evidence that some passages may be less antagonistic to true Christianity than traditionally thought, some Christians have "rather uncritically" concluded that Islam and Christianity, therefore, "have much in common," that is, they are much closer than usually thought. Such a conclusion, he argues, cannot logically be deduced from the evidence.

In pointing out how much Muslims and Christians, Qur'an and Bible, have in common, some Christians 'fill' several Qur'anic passages with a biblical content and give the words and expressions used a meaning which is not only unfamiliar to contemporary Muslims, but which—as most of those who are opposed to such a 'Christian' interpretation believe and as some of those who are in favor of it themselves admit—is also different from the meaning which these words and passages had for those who recited and heard them in the seventh century. (1967:176)

Bijlefeld's objection is especially important in view of his commitment to the WCC program of dialogue with Islam. He opposes the approach on the ground that it impedes dialogue:

One of the basic principles of a dialogue remains the honest willingness to take 'the partner' seriously in what he says, and not because of what he *could* say or possibly in time *will* say. There is an imminent danger of degrading the Muslim-Christian dialogue once again to a Christian monologue by 'Christianizing' the Qur'anic message by which Muslims live, and by taking them seriously as partners in *that* 'Christian perspective' only. (177)

Bijlefeld certainly has a point. Surely, however, he is mistaken when he says that this is a purely "historical" question. On the contrary! It goes to the heart of the disagreement between Islam and Christianity. The theory points to the fundamental problem of the Qur'an—the "Christianity" it repudiates does not represent authentic Christianity. As a consequence, the Qur'anic view of Christianity functions like a filter through which the Muslim "hears" the Christian witness and that consistently distorts what he hears. To this day, Muslims, more than any other non-Christian peoples, have consistently twisted the Christian witness to make it mean something other than what it says. The reason for such consistent distortion is clear; if Muslims were to admit that the Qur'an does *not* give a true account of "Christian" teaching, they would have to admit that the Qur'an is in error. Muslims would hardly have adhered so tenaciously for fourteen centuries to such patent misinformation were not their faith at stake.

This exposes the fallacy of the claim that "the Qur'an is much closer to Christian teaching than usually thought," and indeed the fallacy of the synthesizing approach in general. Not only does it impede dialogue, but more importantly, it involves Christians in joining Muslims in distorting the truth. Muslims cannot help but perceive this to be anything less than what one of them has called "another attempt to change the Muslim view of Islam, and to render it as near as possible to Christianity" (Tibawi

1963:201). Unless Christians acknowledge this approach to be wrong, how can we expect Muslims to recognize that their distortions of Christianity and their attempts to Islamicise the Bible are wrong, and help them to find liberation from the vicious cycle of repression and substitution through the gospel?

Indeed, from an early date, Muslims have been interpreting the Bible from an Islamic perspective. Their claim to find prophecies of Muhammad in the Bible has always been part of their biblical hermeneutic (Cate 1974:78–86, 113–21). This claim derives in large measure from the fact that the Qur'an represents Jesus as "bringing good tidings of a Messenger who shall come after me, whose name shall be Ahmad" (61:6), interpreted by Muslims to mean Muhammad. In more recent years, a number of Muslims have gone even further and have attempted to develop a total Islamic approach to the Bible, including a defense of the Islamic view of Christ (Cate 1974:121–53; al-Faruqi 1963:283–93).

While we cannot prevent Muslims from interpreting the Bible Islamically (they have the right to try), we must, nevertheless, expose the fallacy and error in such an enterprise. If, however, we ourselves read Christian meanings into the Qur'an, we do not have a leg to stand on.

Third Objection: Synthesis Introduces an Authority Conflict into the Young Church

This approach introduces into the young church an authority conflict that creates theological ambiguity and invites syncretism (Schlorff 1980:147–49). One thing that stands out clearly from our discussion so far is that synthesis is characterized by an ambivalent, and in fact contradictory, attitude toward biblical authority. It involves what the prophet Elijah calls "wavering between two opinions" (1 Kings 18:21) in that it assumes that the Qur'an is in some sense inspired and authoritative.

Those who use the proof-text method usually deny that it implies accepting the Qur'an's authority. We only quote it, they say, as one would quote any text to prove a point, because it is authoritative for Muslims. The argument is fallacious, however. The doctrines that they attempt to prove from the Qur'an—the divine authority of the Bible, the deity of Christ, the Trinity—are truths that, according to the Bible, are available to man only by divine revelation (e.g., Matt. 16:16–17; Rom. 16:25–26; 1 Cor. 2:6–10; Eph. 3:2–11; Col. 1:26–27). These are not ideas that man can arrive at naturally. This means that if the Qur'an supports these Bible doctrines, then, on biblical grounds, it (or at least the passages quoted) comes from God. No wonder some have proposed that the Qur'an must somehow be a work of the Holy Spirit!

It is, thus, a contradiction in terms to quote the Qur'an in support of specifically biblical teachings and at the same time deny that this implies an acceptance of its divine authority. One could even go so far as to say that it is being dishonest, to oneself as well as to Muslims. While the New Hermeneutic of the Qur'an is no less ambivalent and contradictory than the proof-text method, it at least openly recognizes this assumption.

In either case, synthesis is unacceptable in that it introduces an authority conflict into the church. The problem is especially acute for the young church in Islamic society. If it is to be truly Christian, it must be solidly rooted in biblical teaching and under the sole authority of the Bible. Even when the new Christian's initial interest in Christ has been awakened by the Qur'an's cryptic witness, the choice is still clear-cut. He is unambiguously faced with a supernatural Christ and Savior only in the Bible. The Qur'anic "witness" is insufficient to lead him to saving faith. For that, he must go to the Bible. So then, if we implicitly recognize the Qur'an's authority in the way we use it, we introduce a second authority principle alongside the Bible and create a climate of theological ambiguity and inclusivism that invites syncretism. Well intentioned or not, such ambivalence creates a conflict in many a young Christian's mind that is difficult, if not impossible, satisfactorily to resolve.

I conclude, then, that synthesis in cross-cultural hermeneutics is counterproductive as far as the contextualization of the gospel and the church in Islamic society is concerned. Consciously or unconsciously, it is essentially syncretistic, tending toward a synthesis of Islamic and Christian teaching.

The Method of Analysis

If synthesis is inadequate, we are faced with the question: What kind of hermeneutic is left? What approach is consistent with the requirements of an evangelical contextual model? The same considerations that argue against synthesis would seem to require what I shall call an analytic approach to cross-cultural hermeneutics. The approach must be comprehensive, valid both for the interpretation of the Bible and the Qur'an. For far too long, Christian theologians, evangelicals included, have been using the Qur'an as if the way they interpret it makes no difference whatever for biblical interpretation and authority, as long as it favors a Christian view. Nothing could be further from the truth!

Several studies in cross-cultural hermeneutics representing what I have called an analytic approach have been produced by evangelicals in recent years (Nicholls 1979a:36–52; Padilla 1980:63–78). They have used other terms to describe their approach, however, such as "contextual" (Padilla) and "dogmatic" (Nicholls 1979a:24). I prefer the term "analysis" because the natural contrast with the term "synthesis" helps to clarify the distinction between the two methods. Traditional, historico-grammatical/critical methods still have an important place in analysis, but, as these writers acknowledge, the traditional methods alone are inadequate in the cross-cultural situation. While they are good at helping us understand what the text meant to its original readers, they are weak when it comes to interpreting what it means in the life of the modern reader of a different religious and cultural background (Padilla 1980:64ff.). Something more is needed to enable the interpreter to reckon with the pre-understandings that he or she brings to the biblical text, and in the cross-cultural situation with those of the receptor population. Let us, therefore, examine key principles of the analytic approach that have particular importance for the way we use the Qur'an.

First Principle: The Meaning of a Text is Determined by Analysis of the Original Language

Basic to the approach, as the term "analysis" suggests, is the principle that the "meaning" of a passage, in the Qur'an as in the Bible, can only be determined by analysis of the way its individual terms are used in relation to the Qur'an's original language system and cultural context. The focus is on what Muhammad understood the terms to mean and how his original hearers would have understood him. In practical terms, this means that Qur'anic language may not be interpreted in terms of what one might think similar biblical language might have meant. It cannot be filled with Christian content.

To illustrate the principle, let's take the well-known phrase in verse 5 of the first Surah, *al-fatiHa*, that is recited during every *Salaat* (ritual worship): "Show us the straight path" (*ihdina l-SiraaT al-mustaqiim*). Since the words are somewhat reminiscent of Christian prayer language, some Christians have thought that they too can pray this prayer alongside Muslims. But what do the words *mean*? The phrase "the straight path" is especially problematic. They do remind us of biblical language. In Psalm

27:11, for example, we read, "Teach me your way, O Lord; lead me in a straight path because of my oppressors" (cf. 5:8). And in the Sermon on the Mount, we read this famous passage (Matt. 7:13–14, especially in the KJV). "Enter ye in at the strait [narrow] gate; for wide is the gate and broad is the way that leadeth to destruction, and many there be which go in thereat. Because strait [small] is the gate, and narrow is the way which leadeth unto life, and few there be that find it." In other words, at first glance the phrase "the straight path" might appear to be speaking of living righteously as it does in these passages. But a study of Qur'anic language reveals otherwise. In Surah 6:161, we read, "Say: Lo! As for me, my Lord hath guided me unto a straight path, a right religion, the community of Abraham, the upright, who was no idolator" (see also 3:51). So then, in the Qur'an "the straight path" is a synonym for Islam. The bottom line, then, is that if I repeat this phrase during the *Salaat*, I am asking God to lead me to embrace Islam. Can a Christian in all sincerity ask God to do that?

To avoid the trap of synthesis, therefore, it must be recognized that, where the interpreter and his hearers are separated from the text to any extent by time, geography, language, and culture, there will be a distinct difference between the horizon or perspective of the text and that of the present-day interpreter in another culture. This means that, when we are interpreting both the Bible and the Qur'an, we must first interpret each book in terms of its original language, worldview, and culture before we try to interpret what each is saying to the receptor culture. This may sound complicated, but it is necessary to recognize such a distinction if we are to avoid semantic distortions and the resulting theological ambiguity and confusion. Nicholls, adapting the terms of Thiselton, calls the analytic method a "two-way process" that he defines as "the objective-subjective principle of distancing from and identification with the text" (1979a:49).

Second Principle: Interpretation Begins with the Believing Community's Presuppositions

This principle, also basic to the analytic approach and closely related to the first principle, concerns the presuppositions of Qur'anic interpretation. The influence of presuppositions on biblical interpretation is widely recognized today (Stanton 1977). Bruce Nicholls has written a helpful study of this question as it relates to the cross-cultural interpretation of the Bible (1979a:37–48). Likewise, presuppositions are important to Qur'anic interpretation (see Merad 1973). Unfortunately, however, both Christians and Muslims have tended to ignore the significance of presuppositions when citing each others' book for missionary purposes, and they often resort to the fiction of an objective, presuppositionless interpretation. Let us state the principle in relation to the Qur'an as follows: Our interpretation of the Qur'an as Christians must begin with the same presuppositions that the Muslim community uses to interpret the Qur'an. This should be considered the *sine qua non* of our use of the Qur'an in communicating the gospel to Muslims. It follows from the first principle enunciated above, and the illustration given is likewise relevant here. That "the straight path" refers to Islam is certainly the presupposition of Muslims.

This does not mean that we ultimately accept the presuppositions of the community as being true in themselves. Nor does it mean that we reject out of hand historico-critical methods for the study of the Qur'an, or historical findings such as the theory of the unorthodoxy of the "Christianity" rejected by the Qur'an. What it *does* mean is that we take the presuppositions of the Muslim community as the starting point to understanding the Qur'an's meaning, and, therefore, basic to our use of the Qur'an in presenting the gospel. Our interpretation of the Qur'an must begin with the frank recognition that the Qur'anic and biblical worldviews are fundamentally different and cannot be reconciled without doing violence to both. Sooner or later in our interaction with Muslims, we will no doubt begin to call into question their presuppositions; this is basic to our task as interpreters of the biblical message to Islam. We cannot, however, do so unless we have first recognized them to be the presuppositional basis of Qur'anic exegesis.

Third Principle: The Believing Community of the Book Is Central to Its Interpretation

Here again, this principle follows from the first two. It is, nevertheless, important enough to be treated separately. It can be stated as follows: In Qur'anic as in biblical interpretation, the believing community that lives by the book being interpreted and its hermeneutical tradition is central to the interpretive process. The believing community's hermeneutical tradition cannot be bypassed by outsiders if each side is accurately to understand the other.

In terms of biblical interpretation, Nicholls calls this "the bodylife principle of the believing community" and explains it as follows: "The hermeneutical task is not a private or purely individual one; it is the responsibility of the whole body of Christ and must be undertaken within the framework of the believing community" (1979a:51). He then goes on to spell out in some detail what this means for biblical interpretation.

Without entering into the details here, I would simply point out that, with all due allowance for the fact that the "Ummah" of Islam and the "Body of Christ" are quite different in nature, essentially the same principle holds for the interpretation of the Qur'an as for the interpretation of Scripture. Unfortunately, Christians have frequently violated this principle. One device they have often used is to try to put a wedge between the Qur'an and its classical Islamic interpretation by appealing to theological development that admittedly took place after the time of Muhammad. Muslims likewise have used this tactic to try to bypass the Christian hermeneutical tradition in their interpretation of the Bible (Schlorff 1980:146–47). It is therefore imperative, in our relationships with Muslims, that we as Christians respect the primacy of the Islamic tradition of Qur'anic interpretation and that we expect, and indeed require, Muslims to respect the primacy of the Christian tradition of biblical interpretation in their relationships with us. In the next chapter, I shall go into the application of this principle in some detail; we shall look at some of the tools and steps that can be taken on the practical level in interpreting the biblical message to the Muslim community.

In summary, then, I am suggesting that greater attention needs to be paid to the hermeneutic method implicit to the way we approach the Qur'an and Islamic culture as we carry out our mission. In particular, we need to avoid synthesizing approaches and focus on analytic methods of interpretation, including the traditional historico-grammatical methods of interpretation.[2] Before we go on to chapter 12, consider the following addendum that illustrates the analytic use of the Qur'an and Islamic culture in explaining the Trinity to Muslims.

Addendum Illustrating an Analytic Explanation of the Trinity

[The following is adapted from an article by the present author replying to a Muslim who wrote the Arab World Ministries web site to ask about the Trinity. It illustrates how a Qur'anic passage and an Islamic theological form may be used in witness by interpreting them analyti-

---

2. Let me suggest Marshall 1977, as well as Thiselton 1977b and Kaiser 1979.

cally—within their original semantic range and without doing violence to their original meaning.]

Unfortunately, many people have a lot of false ideas about the Trinity, so let me begin by examining a few. Many think, for example, that "Trinity" means that, despite all that we say, Christians really believe in three Gods, and what is worse, that these represent a father, a mother, and a son. I can assure you that no Christian, whatever his church, could think such a thing; the very idea is blasphemous and abhorrent to us. You may reply, "Is not the doctrine a contradiction in terms, however?" A fair question. But the answer is still no; we are not speaking of three gods, each with a different being and will, but of one essence with three persons, or three persons in one essence.

Our problem here is not the doctrine itself but the finiteness of our minds. God's nature surpasses the capacity of our minds to grasp. Does not the Bible declare? "Can you fathom the mysteries of God? Can you probe the limits of the Almighty? They are higher than the heavens— what can you do? They are deeper than the depths of the grave—what can you know?" (Job 11:7–9). And does not the Qur'an itself declare, "*laisa ka-mithli-hi shai'un*" ("There is nothing like unto Him"—Surah 42:11).* We Christians say that the Trinity is "*bi-la kaif wa-bi-la tashbih*" (without [asking] how and without anthropomorphism).** It can neither be proved nor disproved by reason; to argue that it is against "reason" is simply to make oneself the judge of what God can or cannot be, which is blasphemy. Quite simply, we will never be able fully to understand God's nature because it lies outside our experience and knowledge.

God revealed to us the Truth about the Trinity, *not so that we might fully understand His nature, or to satisfy our intellectual curiosity. He did it because we need to know what each one—Father, Son, and Holy Spirit—has done and is doing for our salvation. And we need to accept the ministry of each in our lives* before we will be able to experience their work of salvation on our behalf. In summary, here is what the Bible teaches on the subject:

The universal human experience: The Bible says that ever since the first man and woman, Adam and Eve, were expelled from the Garden, *all* of mankind have been "separated from the life of God" (Eph. 4:18) and "dead in your transgressions and sins" (Eph. 2:1). The Bible says moreover that "all have sinned and fall short of the glory of God" (Rom. 3:23). But it also says that God the Father was not content that we remain in that condition. He had a plan whereby we who were far from Him would be "brought near through the blood of Christ" (Eph. 2:13).

God the Son: Because we are not able to save ourselves from suffering the eternal death we deserve, God was not content to just "send down" laws and information about Himself while He remained aloof and unknown. He "came down" in the person of Jesus Christ, the Savior, to die on the cross and bring us salvation.

Jesus said, "I have come down from heaven not to do my will but to do the will of him who sent me" (John 6:38). "For God so loved the world that he gave his one and only Son, that whoever believes in him shall not perish but have eternal life. For God did not send his Son into the world to condemn the world, but to save the world through him. Whoever believes in him is not condemned, but whoever does not believe stands condemned already because he has not believed in the name of God's one and only Son." (John 3:16–18)

God the Holy Spirit: When we acknowledge our sin and ask God to save us through Jesus' blood, the Holy Spirit of God, also called the Counselor (Paraclete), comes to live in us and help us live for God.

Jesus said "I will ask the Father, and he will give you another Counselor to be with you forever—the Spirit of truth. The world cannot accept him, because it neither sees him nor knows him. But you know him, for he lives with you and will be in you" (John 14:16–17).

Again He says: "But the Counselor, the Holy Spirit, whom the Father will send in my name, will teach you all things, and will remind you of everything I have said to you" (John 14:26).

The Scriptures explain further: "You, however, are controlled not by the sinful nature but by the Spirit, if the Spirit of God lives in you. And if anyone does not have the Spirit of Christ, he does not belong to Christ" (Rom. 8:9).

God the Father: when someone has confessed his or her sin and has committed his or her life to Christ as Lord, and has received the Holy Spirit, the Father adopts him or her as His child.

"To all who received him, to those who believed in his name, he gave the right to become children of God—children born not of natural descent, nor of human decision or a husband's will, but born of God" (John 1:12–13).

"You did not receive a spirit that makes you a slave again to fear, but you received the Spirit of sonship. And by him we cry, 'Abba,

Father.' The Spirit himself testifies with our spirit that we are God's children. Now if we are children, then we are heirs—heirs of God and co-heirs with Christ, if indeed we share in his sufferings in order that we may also share in his glory" (Rom. 8:15–17).

We may not be able to explain the Trinity fully from the *metaphysical* standpoint, but we can certainly understand what the Father, Son, and Holy Spirit have done for our salvation, and that is all that matters. Praise the Lord!

* Muslims frequently quote this passage to affirm the absolute transcendence of God, but we use it here simply to affirm that God's nature surpasses the capacity of our minds to grasp the intricacies of His being.

** This phrase comes from Islamic theology. Muslim theologians struggle with anthropomorphisms in the Qur'an, for example, passages that speak of God "sitting" on the throne, "speaking," or "hearing," so they say that these phrases are "*bila kaif wa-bila tashbiih*" (without [explaining] how and without anthropomorphism).

12

The Church in Islamic Culture: A Biblical-Theological Model

I must confess that when the dynamic equivalence church model was first proposed, I was intrigued. One could hardly fault dynamic equivalence in Bible translation, even though one may on occasion criticize a particular translation choice. I was, therefore, interested in what the model could possibly offer, although I was concerned by ambiguities that I saw. It was not clear whether, in their enthusiasm for these new ideas, the theoreticians really intended what they appeared to be saying or whether their practice would turn out to be more balanced than their words. It has become increasingly clear, however, that my concerns were well founded. I am concerned for the future of evangelical mission work among Muslims if missionaries continue to follow this model in greater numbers.

In *The Theory and Practice of Translation* (1969), the classic work on dynamic equivalence Bible translation, Nida and Taber lay down rules designed to safeguard faithfulness to the intent of the original text as well as contextual equivalence. Unfortunately, the proponents of dynamic equivalence Muslim churches have not provided such safeguards in their adaptation of the model to contextualization.

I am proposing, therefore, another model based on different foundations and with theological safeguards that I shall call the betrothal model, a name inspired by the following passage in 2 Corinthians.

> I am jealous for you [i.e., the church in Corinth] with godly jealousy. *For I have betrothed you to one husband* [emphasis added], that I might present you as a chaste virgin to Christ. But I fear, lest somehow, as the serpent deceived Eve by his craftiness, so your minds may be corrupted from the simplicity that is in Christ. (2 Cor. 11:2–3 NKJV)

Note that the apostle compares the role of the church planter with that of the parents or legal guardians of the bride in Eastern Mediterranean societies. As it was in his day, so it is today; it is the parents who arrange the marriage, and the young couple is considered legally married at the betrothal, not at the wedding ceremony that comes later (see, e.g., Matt. 1:18–19). According to this model, then, the role of the church planter, much like that of the parents of the bride, is to "betroth" the young church to Christ, to bring it into a loving, healthy, lifetime, faith-commitment to Him. The betrothal concept is much more appropriate to the church's relationship to Christ in its cultural context than that of dynamic equivalence. In any case, it would be quite improper for the convert church, the "Bride of Christ," to flirt with its old religious system (Islam) by continuing to practice the ritual prayer and other Muslim "acts of worship," as the proponents of dynamic equivalence propose.

In setting forth the betrothal model, I shall challenge some of the principles of the dynamic equivalence model as described in chapter 7. Before entering into my critique, however, I want to make it quite clear that my purpose here is not simply to challenge, but to propose something better; hence, any critique given will be in the context of setting forth this alternative. Here, then, are the principles at the foundation of the betrothal model. You will note that they include the principles already enunciated in previous chapters but now expanded upon and formed into a model focused on mission in the Islamic context.

The Principal Cause of Muslim Resistance

Before expounding the model, I need to clear up a question left over from chapter 7. Is it true that "missionary extractionism" is the cause of Muslim resistance to the gospel? My own position is that, while this is indeed a problem in some areas, as it stands, the claim gives a one-sided view of extractionism in the Muslim world and is to be rejected. I must acknowledge, however, that an article I wrote some years ago could give the impression that I deny that missionary extractionsim even exists (2000:314–15). At the time, proponents of the dynamic equivalence model were claiming that missionary extractionsim is *the cause* of Muslim resistance. In hindsight, I must confess that my article came across too strongly, seeming to deny the reality of missionary extractionism instead of correcting the picture.

So let me be clear: Missionary extractionism *is* a problem, most notably in places where national churches continued to exist after Islam took control of the territory. One could hardly say otherwise, having seen repeatedly how "radical displacement" was the dominant model in the Muslim world well into the twentieth century; this certainly involved "extractionism." Nor do I deny that missionaries have often imported Western practices into the young churches and sometimes have encouraged converts to leave their culture. I would, moreover, wholeheartedly agree that we need to pay greater attention to the cultural dimension of the task and that contextualization is "a theological necessity demanded by the incarnational nature of the Word" (Nicholls 1979a:21). What I am calling into question is the claim that missionaries are the main perpetrators of extractionism and that this is the sole or even the principal cause of Muslim resistance.

First, the claim exaggerates the missionary role in extractionism. To say that missionaries have "demanded" that converts turn against their culture and have "isolated them from their culture" is to put it too strongly. Yes, missionaries have been extractionistic to a certain extent and have failed adequately to contextualize (they didn't know how), but that is not the main cause of extractionism. Where they have especially failed is to give converts adequate help in relating their new faith and life to their culture.

Furthermore, the claim does not explain the extractionism that does exist, or Muslim resistance itself. The missionary importation of Western culture is not unique to the Muslim world; for many years, much of missionary work has been more or less extractionistic, but that has not prevented the spread of the gospel elsewhere. Clearly, extractionism has not stirred up the kind of resistance elsewhere that we see in the Muslim world. There must be a better explanation for Muslim resistance.

The most serious problem with this claim is that it ignores what is obviously the main cause of extractionism in the Muslim world and adopts an explanation that leads young missionaries to try to counteract extractionism in ways that are counterproductive.

The Ideological Nature of Islamic Society

It is clear that Muslim resistance to the gospel is attributable mainly to the ideological nature of Islamic society. To adapt the famous phrase of Abraham Lincoln, Islam is a society dedicated to the proposition that all men are created to live in submission to God, as prescribed by "God's Law," the *Shariah* (Schlorff 1993:174ff.). Ensuring that all citizens conform to the *Shariah* is one of the main functions of the Islamic state. Given this ideal, the *Shariah* had to make allowances for non-Muslims in the body politic. The principal legal provisions to note are the *dhimmi* (or *zimmi*) system and the Law of Apostasy (Doi 1979; Gibb and Kramers 1953:75, 91, 245, 413, 570; Shahid 1992).

THE DHIMMI SYSTEM

The *dhimmi system* segregates "protected" non-Muslim communities from the majority community (the *Ummah*). *Dhimmis* (non-Muslims from one of the "protected" communities) are in reality second-class citizens. They are forced to live under certain legal disabilities, and male *dhimmis* must pay a special tribute (*djizya*), as well as a special land tax (*kharaj*) when they own land. A Muslim man may marry a *dhimmiya* (a female non-Muslim), but a Muslim woman may not marry a *dhimmi*. Muslims consider the system "tolerant," but the reality experienced by *dhimmis* is quite the opposite (see Betts 1978:10).

The effects of the *dhimmi* system on churches in the Muslim world are noteworthy. It has produced what has been called "Christian Ghetto" churches (Moffett 1987:481ff.; cf. Barkat 1978). Each church or denomination (called a *millet*) is, in effect, "a state within the state" that is ruled by its own leader in religious and civil matters but segregated from the Muslim majority and subject to the Muslim state in wider matters. The *dhimmi* church is thus subjugated and repressed, while overt evangelism among the majority is suppressed. It has also tended to respond defensively by using a distinctive religious language in Bible translation and Christian literature that Muslims find somewhat hard to understand (see chap. 3; Khair Ullah 1976:305–9; Abu Yaha 1986) and by raising social barriers such as anti-Muslim myths and polemic and distrust of converts from Islam. These barriers, intended to preserve the church's identity and prevent defections, are understandable in the circumstances, but they do hinder the evangelization of Muslims. Having said this, I hasten to add that these comments should not be taken as a criticism of those churches. They have my utmost sympathy. My purpose is simply to affirm as clearly as possible that the extractionism that we see in the Muslim world is mainly attributable to Islamic law.

THE LAW OF APOSTASY

The Law of Apostasy (*ridda*) is even more extractionist. In an ideological society where everyone must conform to the "Law of God," apostasy (defection from Islam) is seen as equivalent to sedition. What happens to the apostate is somewhat analogous to what we call "transplant rejection," where a transplanted organ triggers a rejection mechanism that must be treated medically or the patient will generally die. In ideological Islamic society, conversion to Christian faith triggers a rejection mechanism; according to the *Shariah*, an adult male apostate is to be given a short time to recant, failing which he will suffer the full severity of the Law. Upon being tried and convicted, he is stripped of all civil rights so that anyone is free to kill him, his marriage is declared null and void, his children are taken from him, and his property becomes spoil to the Muslim community. Since his family is thereby dishonored, it is often a family member who kills him. The female apostate, by contrast, is to be imprisoned until she recants, however long that may take. Sometimes, she too is killed by her family. Often, the convert's only recourse is to seek refuge abroad. Earlier in the twentieth century, Muslims who became Christians were at times treated somewhat leniently. But today, with the return of the fundamentalist spirit, we often seem to be witnessing a return to the full severity of the Law of Apostasy.

Some Conclusions

Clearly, then, it is the *Shari'ah*, especially the *dhimmi* system and the Law of Apostasy, that is the primary cause of extractionism. These two provisions are in effect in most Muslim countries, even where they are not explicitly written into the constitution. And where extractionism can be attributed to missionaries, or to the *dhimmi* type national church's inhospitality to converts, it is still Islamic law that has created the conditions that brought about such extractionism and inhospitality to converts.

I agree, however, that we have failed, as missionaries, to respond adequately to the pressures of Islamic ideology, and that this failure is a significant component of the extractionism that exists. It is something we must work on. We must adopt a sound approach to contextualization and make a much greater effort to contextualize. We need to do a much better job of helping converts relate their new faith and life to their culture. One cannot expect a Muslim-background believer (MBB) to integrate painlessly and without help into one of the "Christian Ghetto" churches in the Middle East. It is only natural that such churches look at MBBs with some suspicion. One solution might be some kind of halfway-house, MBB fellowship, to ease their integration into the churches. Other solutions may come to light as we pray about it.

To return to my main point, instead of blaming missionaries for extractionism, church planters in the Muslim world should familiarize themselves with the ideological nature of Islamic society and be prepared realistically to work at counteracting its effect on the convert and the young church. The widespread attempt to blame Muslim resistance on missionary extractionism has encouraged younger missionaries to experiment in ways that can only be described as extreme. I am thinking of those who have felt that they should identify themselves as Muslim (i.e., "Muslims who follow *'Isa"*) rather than as Christian and who perform the *Salaat* and other Muslim practices, in more or less the prescribed Muslim manner (see Racey 1996:304). Having been told that missionaries are the cause of extractionism that must be avoided at all costs, they have concluded that, to be successful in church planting, they must become as Muslim as possible and must encourage converts to remain within Islam. All indications are that not just a few of the younger missionaries have been involved in these practices.

It would seem that Asian religions, including Asian Islam and Asian Christianity, may have a syncretistic bent. If that is the case, one can understand how Christian workers in such areas might be favorably disposed to "Islamicized contextualization." But such efforts are mostly counterproductive in the long run. I would agree with Phil Parshall when he says they represent a "dangerous slide" toward syncretism (*EMQ* 1998:405ff.). They are comparable to what the Qur'an calls "hypocrisy" (*nifâq*)—pretending to be Muslim but secretly working against Islam (Sherif 1985:87–89). I believe David Shenk is correct when he offers the following recommendation:

> It is wise for the church in mission in Muslim settings to function unobtrusively. It is important to attempt to function with a low profile and to work in convergence with the local culture as much as possible. But my judgment is that little is gained and perhaps much is lost when

Christians identify with the Muslim community in ways that can easily be interpreted as undermining the internal integrity of the Muslim community. My judgment is that it is much easier for Muslims to tolerate the presence of Christians among them when the definitions of that Christian community are quite clear. This does not mean that the definitions of the community shall be obnoxious or noncontextual. But the Muslims must be able to know who the followers of Jesus are in distinction to those who seek to walk in the *sunnah* (customary practice) of Mohammed. (1994:16)

Which is to say that, if we are to solve the problem of Muslim resistance to the gospel, we have to begin with a correct understanding of its cause and its effect on the church and on missionary work in Muslim lands. In later sections of this chapter, we shall examine measures that may be taken and approaches to contextualization that endeavor to contextualize effectively and without synthesis.

The Objective of Mission to Muslims as Concerns the Church

As we saw in chapter 8, the objective of mission to Muslims may be expressed in broad, general terms as the coming and extension of the kingdom of God in Islamic society. Here, we shall focus more specifically on the objective as concerns the church. Having thoroughly examined the issues in the preceding chapters, we can now affirm conclusively that the emergence of "a people movement to Christ that remains within Islam" is not a legitimate objective from the biblical standpoint. Unorthodox movements with Muslim trappings may well emerge now and then, as they have in the past, but missionaries should not be encouraging such movements or telling converts to stay in Islam. Sooner or later, Muslim leaders will confront such "Muslim Christians" and pressure them to return to Islam; such a "halfway" position makes them vulnerable to pressure both from without and from within. Likewise, if *we* should meet such "halfway" Christians, would it not be our duty to urge them, in the words of Elijah (1 Kings 18:21), to stop "wavering between two opinions"?

I believe that the future of evangelical missions to Muslims lies with that approach that views the objective in terms of bringing Muslims into the kingdom of God as Jesus preached it; including leading them to faith in Christ, training and mentoring them in Christian discipleship and leadership, and gathering them into distinctly Christian flocks that retain social and cultural ties with Muslim society as much as possible, but without outwardly remaining Muslim. With the many aspects of Islamic life that are tied to culture, Muslim-background believers may be considered Muslim by those around them, unless their lifestyle and their words reveal otherwise. There is a vast difference between this view of the objective and that which views the objective in terms of planting Islamicized churches in Islamic culture (chap. 7). As we have seen, a kingdom of God focus is especially important in the Islamic context with its vision of a political, this-worldly, kingdom of God. In any case, if the kingdom approach is to have any practical value, parameters are needed such as exist for Bible translation, especially biblical approaches to the evaluation of Islam and other religions, to contextualization, and to cross-cultural hermeneutics.

A Biblical-Theological Evaluation of Islam

In chapter 9, we saw that from the biblical perspective, the forms and religious structures of Islam cannot be considered "a neutral vehicle" in the contextual process, as the proponents of dynamic equivalence would have us believe. We proposed instead an approach to evaluation based on Romans 1 and 2 that I shall apply to Islam in what follows.

As bearers of the image of God (Gen. 1:26–28), all human beings possesses an intuitive knowledge of God and of His requirements of them (Rom. 1:18–2:16) that has been called general revelation. Herein lies the origin of human culture. All cultures have an essentially religious nature and reflect the *imago dei* to a certain extent. But, apart from Christ, human beings are cut off from the life of God and are spiritually dead (Gen. 3:17–24; Eph. 4:17–19). As a consequence of this and of Satan's influence, all people, to a greater or lesser extent, repress and suppress general revelation and exchange it for untruth (Rom. 1:18, 22–23, 25, 28). We see a kind of dialectic at work in human cultures; they reflect the fact that all humans possess a genuine, albeit intuitive, knowledge of God and of his requirements, but they also repress and suppress that knowledge and rebel against God. Christians are not exempt from this dialectic, but they have Christ within to help break the vicious circle of repression, suppression, substitution, and rebellion. The power of the gospel is absolutely unique in this respect. When the truth of Christ's death for my sin sinks into my heart, it liberates me from the vicious circle of repression and suppression and frees me to confess my sin and to ask God for salvation through Christ. It is "the power of God for the salvation of everyone who believes" (Rom. 1:16).

Islam provides a perfect illustration of the cycle of sin, repression and suppression, substitution, and more sin. One can see this clearly when reading the Qur'an, especially in Arabic. Space limitations allow only a few highlights drawn mainly from a previously published study (Schlorff 1981).

- The Qur'anic view of God, especially its doctrine of absolute transcendence, cuts the Muslim off from the knowledge of God that he or she has by means of general revelation and from a "saving knowledge" of Christ. God appears to be so distant, essentially unknown and unknowable, and the Trinity in Unity appears so impossible, because Islam has repressed the truth about God and substituted for it untruth.

- Islam has also repressed and suppressed the knowledge of the truth about ourselves and our guilt before God, and of His requirements of us, that we have received through general revelation. Islam categorically rejects the biblical doctrine of a moral fall; it attributes our separation from God and our sinful human condition to God's transcendence and not our sin, thus considering our present condition to be normal rather than abnormal. The Qur'an teaches that we are intrinsically good, and indeed we are "born Muslim" and able to do the good. We are just "weak," so that all we need is divine "guidance" (i.e., the Qur'an) to be able to attain the "submission" required by God.

- Along with cutting the Muslim off from the knowledge of God, Islam interposes a religious law between man and God that further reinforces that separation. According to Dutch missiologist J. H. Bavinck, "In Islam, the danger of a legalistic religion has been extreme from the very beginning. The *fikh*, the doctrine of duties, has for centuries constituted the very heart of Moslem theological thought. Islam is characterized by a theocratic awareness, and this theocratic idea is accompanied by a strong emphasis upon the obligations of the believer. Anyone who has experienced this piety in practice knows how easily Allah is reduced to a distant, unapproachable concept, to something really unimportant. . . . Allah remains only as the lawgiver and the final rewarder" (1960:264).

- An important consequence of Islam's suppression of the truth of general revelation is the long-standing Muslim practice of

denying or distorting Christian teachings. Why, despite everything that has been done over the centuries to disabuse them of
these false ideas, would Muslims still hold so tenaciously to the
notion that Christians are tritheists who believe the polytheistic
idea of a carnal union between a god and a woman and who
have corrupted the text of the "former Scriptures," were it not
that the Qur'an teaches such falsehoods? (Might not one do
well to ask them: "How can you say the Qur'an is the Word
of God when it teaches you such demonstrable falsehoods?")

In spite of this repression and suppression of truth, one can still affirm
that there is no culture so alienated from God as to be devoid of all traces of
the divine image and no culture that cannot be sanctified and transformed
into a channel for communicating God's grace to people. This holds for
Muslim cultures as well. But because of the dialectic of sin and suppression of truth and its consequences, one must also say that the forms and
functions of Islamic culture are far from neutral as concerns the relationship between man and God. At the very least they are ambivalent, but
more often they are antithetical. Some forms may legitimately be used as
vehicles for the gospel of God's grace to Muslims (keeping also in mind
that some forms thought to be Muslim may be generically Middle Eastern
and not particularly Muslim). Some Islamic forms give clear expression to
man's rebellion against God and cannot transmit the gospel. If the Christian mission to Muslims is to be adequate to the task, therefore, it must
be based on an approach that is realistic and biblical.

The Contextual/Theological Starting Point

As we saw in chapter 10, it would be improper to begin the contextual process from within Islam on the assumption that Islam contains
"moments" of truth. One cannot use the Qur'an as a source of truth for
proclaiming the gospel or try to fill Muslim forms with Christian meanings.
One may sometimes refer to something in the Qur'an or Islamic culture
to get an idea across to Muslims, but that is not the same thing. And one
may do so only under certain conditions. As it stands, the proposal to fill
old forms with new meanings is too sweeping, and grossly simplistic and
misleading. What is worse, it encourages ill-advised adventurism and the
misuse of Muslim forms. The proposal to exploit the distinction between
faith-allegiance and religious structures is a good example of misuse.

Even if one were to grant this distinction, it does not mean that the two may be totally separated, and the faith-allegiance of one religion joined to the religious structures of another, like so many Lego blocks, without semantic distortion and theological confusion.

The problem with this approach is that it assumes that form may be divorced from meaning. Paul Hiebert has written a helpful article that clarifies the relationship of form to meaning in contextualization, and he points out the dangers inherent in the attempt to separate the two (1989:101–20). I hasten to add that one should read the entire article because it contains much more of value than could be summarized here.

> First, the separation of form and meaning is based on a too simple view of culture. In this view, language is the basis of culture, and all other areas of culture can be understood by analogy to linguistics. But culture is more than language. It is made up of many symbol systems, such as rituals, gestures, life styles and technology. In these, . . . the relationships between form and meaning are often complex. . . . People in other cultures will interpret what we say in terms of their own cultural categories, and there is no way to test whether their ideas correspond with ours or not. (105)

> In the second place, a total separation of meaning and form tends to be asocial. It does not take seriously enough the fact that symbols are created and controlled by social groups and whole societies. As individuals and minority groups, we may create our own symbols and words to express our faith in our own circles. When we try to reinterpret symbols used by the dominant society, however, we are in danger of being misunderstood and ultimately of being captured by its definitions of reality.
>
> [He cites the church of South India that uses the Hindu term for God as an example of this problem.] The Hindus who dominate the culture and make up over 75 percent of the people also use the word but with Hindu connotations. In such a setting it is difficult for the Christian community to maintain a biblical understanding of God. In the long run the church is in danger of accepting the Hindu worldview of the dominant society around it. (106)

> Third, to separate meaning and form is to ignore history. Words and other symbols have histories of previously established linkages between form and meaning. Without such historical continuity, it would be impossible for people to pass on their culture from one generation to the next or to preserve the gospel over time. We are not free to arbitrarily link meanings and forms. To do so is to destroy people's history and

culture. Moreover, it is to forget that people who become Christians gain a second history—the history of *Christianity*. Among their new spiritual ancestors are Abraham, Moses, Jesus, Paul, Aquinas, Calvin, Luther, and many others. (107)

[He concludes:] The greatest danger in separating meaning from form is the relativism and pragmatism this introduces. Relativism undermines our concern for the truth of the gospel. Pragmatism turns our attention from the cosmic history of creation-fall-redemption to solving the immediate problems of our everyday life. (108)

I couldn't agree more! The following word illustration may be over-simplified, but it illustrates the point. When a word stands alone (a simple form), it may take any one of several possible meanings, the tie between form and meaning is loose, and the word alone usually does not convey a message. Thus, the word fast has several meanings. Used in a sentence (a complex form), however, its meaning becomes definite and fixed, and the sentence conveys a message: the boat stuck fast on the sandbar; the fast was now already past; he was fast asleep in the stern. As far as the sentence is concerned, then, form cannot be divorced from meaning.

The same rule holds for religious ritual, such as the Muslim ritual prayer or the Christian sacraments. Composed of several body movements (simple forms) performed in a certain order in a religious setting such as worship, religious rituals are complex forms that communicate visually in a way similar to words in a sentence. They convey a message visually rather than verbally. For example, the *Salaat* (ritual prayer) visually expresses the Muslim's submission to God and to the Prophet, even though most of the components of the ritual (standing, bowing, prostrating, kneeling, and chanting religious texts) may have originated in Christianity, where they conveyed a different message (cf. Woodberry 1989b:285–303).

This demonstrates why the Qur'an and Islamic culture cannot be considered neutral vehicles that may be given Christian meanings. According to Bavinck, "From a strictly theological point of view there is no point within [Islam] which offers an unripe truth that can be simply taken over and utilized as a basis for Christian witness" (1960:140). By the same token, there are no neutral "religious structures" (such as the ritual prayer) that may be joined to Christian faith-allegiance without creating serious semantic distortion and theological confusion.

This is one reason I reject the intuitive approach suggested by some—contextualization by experimentation. One may sometimes need to experiment, but not as a primary means of determining what to contextualize. We don't determine truth or morality by experimentation, do we? Why then promote experimentation as the way to contextualize? Such contextualization is based on wishful intuition rather than sound theological reflection. Search where you will in the literature, you will not find any solid theological discussion of what makes a form "biblically permissible."

The betrothal model, by contrast, takes the Scriptures as its contextual and theological starting point. "Points of contact" within Islam may be used to point the receptor audience to the biblical message. But, as with Bible translation, procedural rules must be in place to ensure that the message being communicated is faithful to the Scriptures and relevant to the context. This brings us to the question of hermeneutical method.

Cross-Cultural Hermeneutics

We have said that the approach used to interpret Scripture across cultures is the central component of the contextual model. In Muslim society, cross-cultural hermeneutics includes not just the way we interpret the Bible and the Christian faith and life but also the way we use the Qur'an and Islamic culture in communicating the gospel to Muslims. This complicates the interpretive process considerably, for the way we interpret the Qur'an cross-culturally has implications for the authority of the Scriptures.

In chapter 11, we saw that cross-cultural hermeneutical approaches divide naturally into two types, synthesis and analysis. Synthesizing approaches start the contextual process from within the Qur'an and Islamic culture, and analytic approaches start the contextual process from within the Scriptures. We examined the method of synthesis at some length, concluding that it is essentially syncretistic and to be avoided. We concluded that only a hermeneutic of analysis is adequate to the task of communicating the gospel cross-culturally. As a matter of principle, avoid trying to merge the biblical and Qur'anic perspectives. Show respect to the Qur'an, but let there be no ambiguity as to which book is the Word of God. This approach to contextualization may seem like walking a tightrope, but it is the only way one can relate to the Qur'an and Islamic culture without doing violence to the gospel.

We looked at three key principles of the analytic method. Since we have already explained them in some detail, our focus here will be on illustrating the principles and especially in laying down procedural rules, where appropriate, that will help to ensure faithfulness to the Scriptures and relevance to the context. Here are the three principles in summary form. Analysis seeks to understand each book in terms of its own categories of thought and the cultural context of that book's believing community.

1. The meaning of a passage, in the Qur'an as in the Bible, can be correctly understood only by an analysis of the way its original terms are used in relation to that book's original language system and cultural context.
2. Our interpretation of the Qur'an and Islamic forms must begin with, and relate to, the presuppositions the Muslim community uses in interpreting the Qur'an, just as our interpretation of the Bible begins with the presuppositions of the Christian community. The same principle should hold when Muslims interpret the Bible. One may later question the validity of the Islamic presuppositions, but only after first relating to them as foundational to an understanding of the Muslim understanding of the Qur'an.
3. The believing community that lives by the book being interpreted and its hermeneutical tradition is central to the interpretive process. (See chapter 11 for the exposition of the three principles.)

To illustrate the first principle, let's look at the first Surah of the Qur'an (*al-fâtiha*) that Muslims repeat in Arabic at the beginning of every *Salaat* (ritual prayer). Ask yourself: Is it a prayer that Christians too may pray? To view it that way is to take the approach of synthesis and read Christian meanings into the passage. Since the words appear at first glance to be somewhat similar to Christian prayers, Christians often assume that they mean what *we* take them to mean, without consideration for what they mean in the Islamic context. The analytic approach, by contrast, looks at the Surah in terms of the Qur'an's categories of thought and finds that it means something quite Islamic. For example, the phrase "Show us the straight path" (v. 5), may remind us of language in the Psalms (e.g., 5:8; 27:11) that refer to living righteously. When we compare the phrase with Qur'anic usage elsewhere, however, we discover that it refers to Islam itself. For example, Surah 6:161 reads: "Say: Lo! As for me, my Lord hath guided me unto a straight path, a right religion, the community of Abraham, the upright, who was no idolater" (see also 3:51). So then, if

I recite the Surah during a ritual prayer, praying "Show me the straight path," in Islamic usage I am asking God to lead me to adopt the way of Islam! Can a Christian in all sincerity ask God to do that?

In sum, the same cross-cultural approach must be used with both books. Appropriate linguistic and cultural forms from Islamic culture may be used as a cultural vehicle for communicating the biblical message, but only when doing so does not do violence to the original meanings of those forms.

As for the second principle, let me suggest several related rules. First, when we do use Islamic terms or cultural forms, *we should be careful to remain within the semantic range that they have historically had in their Islamic context*, rather than trying to reinterpret them or read into them some Christian meaning (the sample text in the addendum to chapter 11 gives us a good illustration of this). Otherwise the Muslim will misinterpret what we are trying to say, as Hiebert has wisely warned (see also Carson 1985:203–6 for helpful ideas on the limits of dynamic equivalence translation). As recommended in chapter 3, studies in the semantics of Qur'anic language (or the comparative semantics of biblical and Qur'anic language) comparable to what has been done for biblical language (see Thiselton 1977a), would be helpful at this point.

Second rule: When citing one of the many qur'anic points of contact with Scripture in witness to Muslims, it has been advised that *it is important to make a clear distinction between the biblical and the Qur'anic understandings of the event, term, or phrase in question.* David Shenk has given us a helpful procedure to follow on this point; he advises that we invite the Muslims to interpret for us what the Qur'an has to say on the subject, and when they have replied, invite them to listen to what the Bible has to say on the same subject (Shenk 1993:44–45). This helps keep the distinction between the two clear. For example, the Qur'an refers to Jesus a number of times by the title *kalimatullah* ("Word of God"). One may ask them, therefore, to explain what the Qur'an means by this term. You will get only speculative answers, because the Qur'an never explains the term's meaning. When they are finished, you can then say, that's interesting, because the *Injil* (gospel) also calls Jesus *kalimatullah*, but it gives the term a very specific meaning. Then take them to John 1:14 and other such passages to show them that the term refers to His deity and incarnation. This illustrates the truth that the Qur'an does not give witness to the gospel. Keep in mind, also, that the rule works both ways; when Muslims try to read a prophecy of Muhammad into the *paraclete* passages of John, we must remind them of this rule and insist that these passages in John can refer only to the Holy Spirit!

Similarly, applying what Hiebert has called the social and historical dimensions of symbols, one should be very careful about using religious and theological forms that have a close association with the Islamic worldview and worship. In an article on the use of Arabic terms in Bible translations for Muslims, Kenneth Thomas of the United Bible Societies lays down the rule that *one should avoid Arabic religious and theological terms that both Christians and Muslims recognize to be exclusively Islamic in usage and significance* (1989:104). I would suggest that the principle applies not just to Bible translation but also to the way we do theology in context and use Muslim forms in general. The Qur'anic name for Jesus, *'iisa*, is a good case in point. As indicated in Chapter 3, it has the same referential meaning as Jesus or *yasuu'* but a different connotative meaning. The critical factor is that it is exclusively Islamic in usage and significance, and is distasteful to Arab Christians. Hence, it would be unwise to make a general practice of using it, except to identify Jesus with the Arab Christian form *yasuu'* in conversations with Muslims who may not be familiar with that term.

The third principle requires that we respect the central role of the believing community and its hermeneutical tradition in the contextual process (see Nicholls 1979a:51). In "Critical Contextualization," Hiebert outlines a promising four-step procedure for helping the young church through the contextual process (1987:109–10). Here are the basic four steps, but again I recommend reading the whole article to get the complete picture.

> **Exegesis of the Culture:** The first step . . . is to study the local culture phenomenologically. Here the local church leaders and the missionary lead the congregation in *uncritically* gathering and analyzing the traditional beliefs and customs associated with some question at hand. For example, in asking how Christians should bury their dead, the people begin by analyzing their traditional rites: first by describing each song, dance, recitation and rite that makes up their ceremony; and then by discussing its meaning and function within the overall ritual. The purpose here is to understand the old ways, not to judge them. If at this point the missionary shows any criticism of the customary beliefs and practices, the people will not talk about them for fear of being condemned. We shall only drive the old ways underground.

> **Exegesis of the Scripture and the Hermeneutical Bridge:** In the second step, the pastor or missionary leads the church in a study of the Scriptures related to the question at hand. In the example we are considering, the leader uses the occasion to teach the Christian beliefs about death and

resurrection. Here the pastor or missionary plays a major role, for this is the area of his or her expertise.

The leader must also have a metacultural framework that enables him or her to translate the biblical message into the cognitive, affective, and evaluative dimensions of another culture. This step is crucial, for if the people do not clearly grasp the biblical message as originally intended, they will have a distorted view of the gospel. This is where the pastor or missionary, along with theology, anthropology, and linguistics, has the most to offer in an understanding of biblical truth and in making it known in other cultures. While the people must be involved in the study of Scripture so that they grow in their own abilities to discern truth, the leader must have the metacultural grids that enable him or her to move between cultures. Without this, biblical meanings will often be forced to fit the local cultural categories. The result is a distortion of the message.

Critical Response: The third step is for the people corporately to evaluate critically their own past customs in the light of their new biblical understandings, and to make decisions regarding their response to their new-found truths. The gospel is not simply information to be communicated. It is a message to which people must respond. Moreover it is not enough that the leaders be convinced about changes that may be needed. Leaders may share their personal convictions and point out the consequences of various decisions, but they must allow the people to make the final decision in evaluating their past customs. If the leaders make the decisions, they must enforce these decisions. In the end, the people themselves will enforce decisions arrived at corporately, and there will be little likelihood that the customs they reject will go underground. [Here he goes into the various ways they may respond to old beliefs and practices: keep them when they are not unbiblical, reject them when they are, modify them so they can carry Christian meanings, adapt or adopt forms from another culture or from Christianity, or create new forms]. . . .

New Contextualized Practices: Having led the people to analyze their old customs in the light of biblical teaching, the pastor or missionary must help them to arrange the practices they have chosen into a new ritual that expresses the Christian meaning of the event. Such a ritual will be Christian, for it explicitly seeks to express biblical teaching. It will also be contextual, for the church has created it, using forms the people understand within their own culture. (109–10)

To summarize, we who are outsiders to the culture have no business pontificating about how the young church should contextualize in language and cultural forms. We simply do not have the intimate knowledge of the different forms that is needed, or of the meanings associated with them, to make such a call. Our role is to ground the national Christians in the Word of God sufficiently that they will recognize what should be contextualized and how. It seems to me that Hiebert's approach is exactly what is needed to help the young church avoid the pitfalls associated with the uncritical adoption of Muslim forms.

To illustrate how Hiebert's procedure might work in a Muslim context, let us say that an MBB group is seeking God's will concerning the forms of worship and prayer to use in public worship. They study Muslim prayer and its significance to Muslims, and, among other things, note, as we saw earlier in the chapter, that in the prayer ritual (standing, bowing, prostrating) the main thing that is visually expressed is the worshiper's submission to God and to the Prophet. In this connection, they find that Muslims believe that an act performed as prescribed in "God's Law" is somehow magically transformed into the ideal that is symbolized, i.e. performing the prayer turns one into a person who is in submission to God—and thus pleasing to him. (As one Muslim put it, "It is man's works, his actualization of divine will on earth as it is in heaven, that constitutes redemption"; al-Faruqi 1968:69). When one compares this with the Christian view of worship, including the sacraments and prayer, it is abundantly clear that there is nothing in common between the two. There can be no question but that the main focus of Christian worship in its various forms is the celebration, with praise and thanksgiving to God, of the redemption that He has given us freely in Christ Jesus. The works ethos of the *Salaat* (ritual prayer) is incompatible with the celebration ethos of Christian worship, with its thanksgiving and praise to God for His salvation and grace. It is unrealistic to think that one can make the *Salaat* mean anything but what it has always meant to Muslims.

As for how the young church might decide the forms its worship should take to express its faith when this procedure is followed, one cannot of course foresee. Its worship may resemble Muslim worship in some respects, for example, if it uses a liturgy, and retains forms such as bowing and kneeling. But if faithfully taught what the Word says about Christian worship, its worship cannot help but be quite distinct from the Muslim ritual prayer. I believe Parshall is right when he says there could not be "continued involvement in prayers at the mosque" (1985:184). I am convinced that, if it is taught well, the young church will find itself unable to perform the ritual prayer, even in modified form, both collectively and individually, because it is intrinsically incompatible with

Christian worship. This will be clearly seen by everyone. May the Lord help us who are teachers of the Word and examples to the flock to do our part well, so that the young church becomes a tribute in every way to the Lord who bought her!

Summary of the Betrothal Model

Let us now sum up the betrothal model for the church in Islamic culture as we did for the other models. While input from social sciences has provided useful insights, concepts, and understandings of culture that help us understand the contextual process, the theological parameters gleaned from Scripture are primary for determining the ultimate shape of the model. As we saw, there are four key elements in the contextual model, as follows:

The Objective of Mission in Islamic Culture: to bring Muslims into the kingdom of God through a faith commitment to Christ and train them in discipleship, with a view to forming communities of the kingdom that are looking forward to the return of Christ and the inauguration of His eternal kingdom.

The Theological Evaluation of Islam: When we evaluate according to Romans 1 and 2, we recognize that, as creatures made in the image of God, Muslims have an intuitive knowledge of God, of His requirements, and of their guilt before Him for failing to meet those requirements, but that Islam leads them to repress and suppress this knowledge and replace it with a false religious system that deceives them and keeps them from the truth.

The Cultural/Theological Starting Point: Since Islam is not a neutral vehicle for communicating the gospel, we cannot use it as a contextual/theological starting point. We do not try to read Christian meanings into Qur'anic passages or Islamic cultural forms, as that tends only to a synthesis of things Islamic and Christian. The only legitimate contextual/theological starting point for contextualization is the Scriptures.

The Cross-Cultural Hermeneutical Method: We, therefore, do not try to merge the horizons of the Qur'an and the Scriptures into a synthesis. We take the analytic approach, interpreting each book on its own terms.

We use the Qur'an and Islamic cultural forms in contextualization only when we can do so while remaining in the same semantic range that these have in their Islamic context.

The Church Strategy: As "workers together with Christ," we seek to "betroth" the young church to Christ, so that each believer lives in faith commitment to Him but also relates to the culture in a manner faithful to the gospel.

Concluding Comments

What does all this mean in the complex situation of mission in the Muslim world? For one thing, it means that Christian workers need to do their homework well and especially learn as much as they can about the society where they serve, and about Islamic law and its impact on that society and on the churches of Muslim background believers in particular. Some years ago, fellow workers in North Africa often talked as if worshiping groups could not be considered "churches" as long they do not have "government recognition." But worshiping groups *are* churches, whether or not they have government recognition! Such an attitude is not only unrealistic, it may very well have a negative impact on national Christians. In any case, as I understand it, applying for government recognition would likely mean applying for *dhimmi* status for the church, with all that this implies. This is something only the national church should attempt to do, and even then only after due consideration of the risks involved. One must especially consider whether or not the government would likely refuse, for then the church would probably be worse off than before! In any case, without government recognition, worshiping groups may not have legal status, but they are still churches before God. Of course, North African Christians would have the civil status of Muslims, which may not be the best situation, but neither is it the worst possible situation to be in.

Is the solution to push Muslim countries to accept democracy and religious pluralism? Certainly we should do all in our power to work for greater justice and religious liberty in the Muslim world. It is a fact, however, that democracy and religious pluralism are incompatible with Muslim ideology that takes the Prophet's religious state at Medina as the model to be followed. It would be most unrealistic, then, to assume that a given Muslim country would be able to make a transition to a more democratic model any time soon—if ever. I am reminded of the lively discussion that took place at the Christian-Muslim dialogue organized by the WCC at Chambesy, Switzerland (1976:427–52). The Christians pleaded cautiously for pluralism, but the idea was rejected by the Muslims. They expressed outrage that, although Muslims were a majority in Indonesia, their attempts to install a Muslim state had hitherto been thwarted.

One conclusion that seems reasonably safe is that the traditional *dhimmi* church (C1 or C2 in Travis's spectrum) is still a viable option in areas where the church has not died out, such as the Middle East. Measures should be taken, however, to counteract the adverse effects of the *dhimmi* system as much as possible, and efforts made to contextualize in a sound manner. However, I think that we also need seriously to consider the possibilities of the underground house church/cell church model, especially in areas where Christianity died out after the rise of Islam. There is no tradition of *dhimmi* churches in such areas to which one can relate.

As concerns the model that I have proposed for churches in Islamic culture, the betrothal model, someone might well ask, "Can you cite cases where it has been tried and proven viable?" To begin, let me point out that, while I may have coined the term, the model is not really new. There are those who have more or less based their ministry on the model for some time; in any case, they have not followed either the ecumenical or dynamic equivalence models. In terms of the C1 to C6 spectrum, it might be loosely identified with the C3 model (defined as "contextualized Christ-centered communities using insider, i.e., Muslim, language and religiously neutral insider cultural forms") or the C4 model (defined similarly as using insider language, but with "biblically permissible Cultural and Islamic forms") (*EMQ* 1998:407–8). To cite a case that I believe fits within the biblical parameters, Christianity took root in a certain non-Arabic tribal area in North Africa over the past thirty years or so, and since then the church has grown remarkably. I cannot give all the known facts for security reasons, but, significantly, it has been an entirely indigenous Christian effort from the start; the only significant help these Christians have received has been training in technical areas, such as radio broadcasting, publishing Christian literature, including the Scriptures, in their own language, and Bible training. They have done remarkable things to spread the gospel, and I understand that some villages in the area are now more or less half Christian. And this in a country where the church died out after the Muslim conquest!

My experience with the model began around 1970, when I was appointed to lead in the development of discipleship materials for preparing North African believers of Muslim background to take part in local church fellowships (Schlorff 1981:1–3). Several colleagues assisted in various capacities, most notably the late Wendell Evans. The resulting *Guide to the Christian Faith and Life*, published in French in 1972 and in Arabic in 1973, has been in use ever since. Although, to my knowledge, no research has been done on its impact on church life and growth in North Africa, it is nevertheless clear that it has had a positive influence on the church.

Having said all that, I wish to express the conviction that "there is no key that will unlock the door to the Muslim mind and heart," apart from giving faithful attention to fulfilling the foundational tasks our Lord gave us at the beginning: proclaiming the Good News, making disciples of the new believers, gathering them into churches, and training leaders who will pass on to others what they have learned (Matt. 28:18–20; cf. 2 Tim. 2:2). Bible translation and distribution is an integral part of this task. The Scriptures have an important role to play in helping us carry out each of the above responsibilities, so having a good translation on hand to assist in the ministry is essential.

In that connection, let me briefly complete our discussion of Arabic translations in chapter 3 by giving a few guidelines as to the choice of a translation for ministry (mostly suggested by various consultants).

1. Consider using different versions for different audiences (e.g., a contemporary version for young people).

2. Sometimes a Bible with introductions and notes can be an advantage—but scrutinize their contents.

3. The variety of tastes and perceptions about versions often has to do more with regional factors related to the history of a translation than to its quality. Acceptance is as much a problem as intelligibility.

4. Accuracy is important for a translation, but this needs to be balanced against intelligibility. A version can be "accurate" in terms of matching the terms and constructions of the original, but parts of it (e.g., the Epistles) can be unintelligible to many readers. Intelligibility is as important as accuracy.

5. One must consider the possibility, and the possible consequences, of needing to change versions (e.g., when one needs a complete Bible for discipling believers, Bible study, or worship).

As I said, the fulfillment of the foundational tasks mentioned above is the real key to success in church planting among Muslims, as elsewhere. As necessary as it may be, contextualization is not the key, whatever the model that is followed. May the Lord find us to be "good and faithful servants."

In closing, I want to say that although I have been critical of the dynamic equivalence model and the like and have radically disagreed with the theoreticians and architects of the approach, I still respect them and in no way want to communicate a spirit of condemnation and rejection. Indeed, I have learned very much by interacting with the ideas of Charles Kraft, Phil Parshall, and Don McCurry of the dynamic equivalence school, as well as from men like Kenneth Cragg and many others, and the present work shows my indebtedness to them. They have done the hard part, and I have benefited from their labors.

Appendix

Church Without Walls, and Its *Meetings for Better Understanding* Model

In part three of this book, we discussed in four chapters the requirements of a biblical contextual model for the church in Islamic culture. Then, in chapter 12, we joined the different principles thus elucidated, along with their methodologies of application, into the model that I feel best meets those requirements—the betrothal model.

Now, in this appendix, we shall leave all that behind. Allow me to direct your attention here to a model of ministry to Muslims, developed quite independently of the preceding, that illustrates in many respects the principles of the betrothal model. I'm speaking of that ministry, known as Church Without Walls (CWW), founded by my good friend Dr. Anees Zaka; and, in particular, his *Meetings for Better Understanding (MBU)* model for ministry. Later, we will examine whether and how this model fits within the parameters of the betrothal model as described in the previous chapter. However, Dr. Zaka and his colleagues discuss the subject of the model in very different terms from those I have used; so, for now, I shall simply quote them in their own terms.

What Is Church Without Walls?

Church Without Walls was founded by Dr. Zaka, with his wife, Fareda, in November 1982, during his years as a student at Westminster Theological Seminary (WTS) in Philadelphia. Dr. Zaka had been a pastor in the Middle East prior to coming to this country. Iain Coulter, a colleague in the Houston section of CWW, briefly relates its origins: "Drawn by the freedom of religion and growing Muslim presence in North America, Dr Zaka came here with the specific purpose of reaching Muslims for Christ" (2002:14).[1] It was during his time at Westminster Seminary that the concept of Church Without Walls and the strategy of Meetings for Better Understanding were conceived. In October 1985, CWW became a ministry of the Presbyterian Church of America (PCA), specifically of the Philadelphia Presbytery of the PCA. It functions under the auspices of the Mission to North America of the PCA (2002:14–17).

The basic idea behind Church Without Walls is that the "walls" of misunderstanding and distortion between Christians and Muslims are so high and massive that the church must take deliberate action to break down those walls and create conditions where genuine communication can take place. CWW seeks to do this by encouraging Christians in cooperating churches, who have a heart for reaching their Muslim neighbors, to participate through their church in "Bridge Teams" that interact with Muslims in local mosque communities. *Meetings for Better Understanding* (MBUs) are at the heart of this strategy.

It was during those early years that I met Dr. Zaka while I was completing graduate studies in missions at Westminster. Interested in observing his approach in action, I attended many of the early meetings that were organized over a period of several years with several mosques in the Philadelphia area.

As I recall, often the mosque leadership would back out after three years or so. But by the time that happened, Muslims in the mosque had been systematically taught many biblical topics—as if they had accumulated two hundred hours or more of Systematic Theology 101. After awhile, six months or more later, some of them asked CWW to meet with them for Bible study in their homes. As a result, some of these people left their mosque and joined Bible-believing churches in their area. CWW elders

---

1. Much of my information comes from Coulter's book, besides that gained from Dr. Zaka and his books.

witnessed their water baptism in different churches, and they became active members in those churches.

Since those early years, Dr. Zaka has traveled to various cities around the country and overseas to give training in the approach and demonstrate the MBU model. Over the years, CWW sections have been established in churches in twelve cities across the United States, as well as in the United Kingdom and in three other countries in Africa and the Middle East. And the number is growing. Reports from the sections clearly indicate that Muslims are quite open to meeting with Christians and are generally positive about such meetings, especially when it involves promoting a "better understanding" of the Qur'an and Islam, not to mention the Bible and Christianity.

In 1994, Dr. Zaka and some colleagues founded the Biblical Institute for Islamic Studies (BIIS) in Philadelphia. It is a program for training Christians in Islamics and ministry to Muslims (*BIIS Handbook* n.d.:2–3). Some of those former Muslims, who had left their mosque and joined local churches, enrolled in the BIIS classes to study Islamics in order to witness to Muslim family members. These are men and women who by the power of the gospel came out of Islam and are associated with CWW and BIIS even today. And the Lord is still adding the lost to His fold, as He promised in John 10:14–16.

Since BIIS came into being, ties have been established with several graduate-level programs so that, at present, good students may go on to obtain an advanced degree, up to the Ph.D. (*BIIS Handbook* n.d.: 3, 11–13). And one may now take a course on the CWW/MBU model in four theological schools in the United States, including WTS and BIIS. Meanwhile, the MBU model is being put to use now, even outside a missionary context. Dr. Zaka tells me that the Jimmy Carter Center in Atlanta has adopted the model for their efforts to get opposing political groups in African countries, such as Ethiopia and the Sudan, to sit down together and try to understand one another and resolve their problems peacefully. Carter Center leadership has told CWW that the model is ideal for improving understanding between different political or cultural groups and promoting peace.

Theological Foundations

Let us now explore the theological foundations of Church Without Walls. We have already said that it is associated with the Presbyterian Church of America, so it is not surprising to find it evangelical and Reformed theologically. It adheres to the theological basis of the PCA—the Westminster Confession of Faith—and was greatly influenced in its origins by such reformed thinkers as James M. Boice, Harvie Conn, and Cornelius Van Til (Coulter 2002:18–23).

The small book entitled *Explaining the Biblical Faith*, by Dr. Zaka and his son Alfred (Zaka 2004), is a good example of the Reformed connection. It represents an adaptation of the Westminster Shorter Catechism for Muslims, with scriptural passages added to support each answer. Dr. Zaka writes in the introduction to the book:

> This modern edition of the Catechism is written specifically for conversations with Muslims about the Biblical Faith, with the hope of providing accurate and incisive instruction. While the quantity and order of questions have been retained, the wording of the questions and answers and the depth of the Biblical proofs have been adjusted to meet the needs of our Muslim friends in understanding the Biblical Faith. (n.p.)

Its Reformed connection does not, however, mean that Church Without Walls is narrowly denominational. It opens the door to Christians of other denominational backgrounds to take part in its Bridge Team ministries among Muslims. Moreover, some CWW sections are not connected organizationally with the PCA. When I asked Dr. Zaka about this, he stated that CWW works with all Bible-believing Christians, "whether Reformed, less Reformed, or non-Reformed." The main point is that they agree on the "foundational points of our biblical faith." CWW people have agreed not to let their theological differences interfere with God's ministry among Muslims. He says the approach has worked very well and that many non-Reformed missionaries are using the approach in the United States, Great Britain, the Middle East, and Africa. Iain Coulter highlights this characteristic of the ministry as well:

> The CWW ministry provides an opportunity for Bible-believing Christians from many different denominations and theological backgrounds to work together in common mission as a true communion of saints. This communion can only come about if we agree to subject our differences to the far greater reality of our union with Christ as essential to all our fellowship with Him and with each other. . . . This implies that we will keep to the essentials of our faith and do and say those things that promote the peace and purity of our fellowship at all times. (2002:48)

Coulter goes on to recommend ways in which Bridge Team leaders can promote the "peace and purity" of the fellowship of their team when it is a mixed group of Christians. For example, one CWW section "decided to limit team participation to communicant members of the evangelical or Bible-believing churches in which they are in good and regular standing" (2002:49).

Meetings for Better Understanding

We now come to the heart of the Church Without Walls model of mission—Meetings for Better Understanding, or MBUs. To give you a more complete understanding of the MBU concept, I could do no better than quote an article that appeared in a British online journal, *Evangelicals Now*, in January 2005. The author, Mike Taylor, a pastor who has participated in some of Church Without Walls' MBU meetings in the United Kingdom, writes about it as follows.[2]

> Recently I had an opportunity to put a question to Imam Mumtaz, the Imam of Streatham mosque, regarding the Muslim view of the sinlessness of the prophets. The Imam seemed to admit that, from an absolute standpoint, everyone is a sinner. This was the first time I had had an opportunity to speak face-to-face with a South London Imam.
>
> Unfortunately, confrontation is a frequent feature of Christian-Muslim encounter. Therefore, opportunities for such discussion in a friendly atmosphere are rare. Real communication often just does not happen.
>
> Both Islam and Christianity are missionary religions. Christians are obligated by the Great Commission to share the gospel with the unsaved. Muslims are compelled by the responsibilities of *da'wah* (Islamic mission) to seek the conversion of non-Muslims. This is especially true in the West, since Islamic law forbids long-term residence outside the Muslim world unless those Muslims living in a non-Muslim state engage in *da'wah*. Younger Muslims in Britain are particularly eager to share their faith.
>
> *Middle way*
>
> Large meetings have the advantage of allowing people who might be interested in the 'other side' to hear the facts without being concerned what others might say if they saw a Christian entering a Muslim house, or a Muslim turning up at a church. Accordingly, Muslims and Christians do have organised debates about issues such as the true divine revelation, the deity of Christ, or even whether Britain should be an Islamic state. But,

2. http://www.e-n.org.uk/2005–01/2914-Meetings-for-better-understanding.htm.

while in many ways such events have their uses, the problem nearly always attached to them is the degree of heated controversy they frequently engender. On the other hand, inter-faith dialogue always runs the risk of obscuring the differences between the religions, and implying that all roads lead to God. Clearly, then, there is a need for a forum where Christians and Muslims can meet in large numbers to hear what the other community believes without succumbing on the one hand to liberal ecumenism or on the other deteriorating to a shouting match. A middle way has long been needed to facilitate more intelligent discussions and understanding of the very real differences between Islam and Christianity.

That middle way is attempted by those organising forums called Meetings for Better Understanding (MBUs). MBUs have been successful in North America, and more recently here in Britain. These are not debates. Any public criticism of either the Muslim or Christian religion is not encouraged since that would lead to unproductive arguments. Neither are they ecumenical dialogues, in that the aim is not for either side to compromise its message or mix the two faiths. Rather, MBUs promote a mutual comprehension of what Muslims and Christians believe. These meetings enable the two communities to encounter one another in a relaxed context of friendship and learning. They acknowledge the missionary nature of both Christianity and Islam, but see that as no bar to dialogue leading to enhanced mutual understanding.

How it works

Speakers from both communities address the meeting for about 30 minutes on the same, agreed-upon topic. A 30-minute question-and-answer period is held after both speakers have presented their messages. Questions, which may be directed to one or both of the speakers, are to be kept on the topic and are not to be statements of the views of the questioners. Each speaker may follow up on the answer of the other speaker once. Other questions that are of personal interest, but are not related to the topic, may be discussed in individual conversations after the formal sessions. For each meeting the host group selects a moderator whose role is to ensure that the above guidelines are followed. There is ample time after the formal meeting for people attending the meeting to meet personally with members of the other faith. Meetings can vary in frequency, but once a month is suggested. Topics are classified as 'theological' or 'social', so a topic like, 'Who is Jesus Christ?' would be 'theological', whereas 'Marriage, divorce, and remarriage' would be 'social'. The areas for discussion can be alternated for maximum breadth of interest.[3]

3. For more details on how MBUs are organized, see Coulter 2002:48–67, 110ff.

Council attention

ABC (Association for Biblical Christianity)[4] has been utilising this method for some years. For example, in Slough, these meetings have been held for three years and have seen great numbers attending, including local councillors and an MP. The meetings have caught the attention of the local council to the extent that they provide funding each year to help defray the costs of the food served after each meeting!

In Tooting, meetings have also been fruitful. Comparing different types of 'outreach methods' such as debate, dialogue, door-to-door visitations among London Muslims, MBUs have proved far better and encouraging, because they involve a non-threatening environment. Participants have expressed their appreciation for meeting one another. Unlike other public religious assemblies of members belonging to the two faiths, there has always been a friendly ambience. Many misunderstandings have been removed on both sides. This has resulted in more openness for relationships. Perhaps the best thing is that Muslims willingly come to listen to what the Bible has to say on chosen topics. After all, the Imam, their local leader, has given his approval to the gatherings. Numerous times, team members have gone away with several addresses to follow up.

More Christians needed

The practical outworking of the MBUs suggests that it is a major way forward. It does not preclude other methods of outreach, but so often house-to-house knocking is met with a quickly-shut door, whereas MBUs allow one to get over the threshold. Debates enable Christian doctrines to be presented, but MBUs guarantee them a better (and a quieter) hearing. The elements of fear and defensiveness are dispelled by this kind of Muslim-Christian encounter. Initially the meetings require a church to contact a local mosque to suggest the meetings and explain the motivation behind them—that is, to encourage 'community cohesion' (an 'in' phrase in contemporary community relations) and better relations at the local level between evangelical Christians and Muslims through a more adequate understanding of what the other believes.

So far, Christians attending these meetings have nearly always been outnumbered by Muslims, and Muslims are reluctant to have more meetings with so few Christians in attendance. Therefore, it is important for Christians to get involved to make MBUs work. I certainly found my visit to Streatham very stimulating, very broadening and very worthwhile.

4. The Association for Biblical Christianity is an informal association geared toward reaching Muslims in the United Kingdom.

A Closer Look at the Missiology of Church Without Walls

To get a good idea of how the missiological model of Church Without Walls compares with that advocated in the present work, let us now take a closer look at how it is described in CWW literature. As noted earlier, Dr. Zaka approaches the subject in different terms from those I have used, but are they conflicting terms? In what follows, I shall quote a number of passages from the literature that I believe give us an inside look at his missiological model. To facilitate comparison with the betrothal model at the end of this appendix, I shall put an asterisk by those statements that compare directly with that model.

Let's begin with a small work entitled *It Is Written! The Use of Cornelius Van Til's Biblical Apologetics for Doing Mission among Muslims* (2005), by Dr. Zaka and his son. This small work is a good introduction to his missiology.

> Since their beginning, CWW and the Biblical Institute for Islamic Studies (BIIS) have been using Cornelius Van Til's apologetics in their proclamation of the Gospel to Muslims and training future missionaries in North America and around the globe. The Lord has been pleased to richly bless our human efforts in using Van Til's presuppositional approach. As a result, we have seen many converts among Muslims, whom Christ brought to Himself, through the proclamation of the Gospel. Also, many Bible-believing Christians were trained under this system—now working among Muslims all over the world. (2005:1)

On page 8, they begin a fairly detailed exposition of "selected ideas and quotations from Van Til, applicable for doing missions among Muslims." In what follows, I have extracted the main ideas relevant to our subject.

Biblical Revelation

- *The theology of doing missions among Muslims must be biblical, historical, and Reformed. Van Til built his apologetics on Reformed doctrine.
- *Christ of the Scriptures should be presented to Muslims as a challenge to their thinking and living. Christ must be offered to them without compromise. (Do not confuse Christ of the Bible with Christ of the Qur'an.)
- *Start with God's revelation, the sixty-six books of the Bible, in your conversations with Muslims. Van Til said, "The basic structure of

Christian Theology is simple. Its every teaching should be taken from the Scriptures of the Old and New Testament as being the words of prophets and apostles spoken on the authority of Jesus Christ, the Son of God and the Son of Man, the Savior of sinners. We must begin by asking what it is we believe" (*The Defense of the Faith*, 7).

- *We must teach Muslims that the Bible is authoritative on everything of which it speaks. And it speaks of everything, either directly or indirectly. It gives us a philosophy of history as well as history (ibid., 8).
- *Therefore, we must present to Muslims the system of truth as contained in Scripture in our witnessing. (2005:8, 9).

[There follows brief sections on biblical doctrines that I shall omit here—the doctrine of God, the personality of God, the Trinity, the doctrine of man, man's relation to the universe, the fall of man, the doctrine of Christ, the doctrine of salvation, the doctrine of the church, and the doctrine of the last things.]

The Christian Philosophy of Knowledge

- *The source of Christian belief is the Holy Bible, which is the infallible and inspired word of God. From the Bible, we have taken our doctrines of God, man, Christ, salvation, and the last things.
- *When seeking to persuade Muslims to accept doctrine revealed in Scripture, we speak of our Christian view of life. . . .
- *Speaking to Muslims, we must make a distinction between the Christian view of life and the Muslim view of life.
- *The difference between these two is that Christians worship and serve Yahweh the true Creator, while Muslims worship and serve Allah.
- *Because of the fall of Adam, the representative of all men, we all became creature worshipers.
- *Through the redemption of Christ—applied to us by the Holy Spirit— the elect have learned to worship and serve the Creator more than the creature.
- *As a result, the elect believe the theory of reality offered in Scripture, and they now believe in God as self-sufficient and as Creator of all things in this universe.
- *Also, they believe in the fall of man at the beginning of history and in the "regeneration of all things" through Christ. (2005:15–16)

The Christian Philosophy of Behavior

- *The Christian view of ethics is that good works are to be done to the glory of God.
- *The redeemed must live to the glory of God.
- *This is done be seeking to establish the kingdom of God.
- *Man cannot set his own standard by which he will seek to realize the Kingdom of God.
- *His standard must be the revealed will of God in Scripture.
- *As a sinner, man has no power to establish the Kingdom of God.
- *Without faith it is impossible to please God.
- *Faith comes from God through regeneration by the Holy Spirit.

The Point of Contact with Muslims

How can we defend and propagate what we believe?
- *To defend the Christian faith is to take Muslims to the Scriptures to see its truth, consistency and absolute authority.
- According to Calvin and Van Til, the point of contact for the presentation of the gospel to non-Christians is the fact that they are made in the image of God and therefore have the ineradicable sense of deity within them.
- *We must tell Muslims that because of the fall, the image of God was broken.
- *The restoration of it only takes place through Christ Jesus and His redemption. (2005:17)

The Defense of Biblical Christianity

To defend biblical Christianity, the following facts must be considered:
- *Truth must be set over falsehood.
- There is a global war between Christ and Satan.
- All men are participants in this war. All of them are either for or against God.
- There are two principles opposed to one another.
- Those who fight for the truth must fight with spiritual weapons only.
- Their opposition to Satan is intended to win converts to the love of God in Christ.
- *Christians interpret every fact in the light of the story of God, the Holy Bible.
- *Christians must be consistent in their witnessing to Muslims through the knowledge of the Scriptures and their living.
- *The argument for Christianity and its truth must be that of presupposition (that the Bible is the Word of God, and every truth derives

from it). Augustine put it this way: "It must be maintained that God's revelation is the sun from which all other light derives." The best, the only, the absolutely certain proof of the truth of Christianity is that unless its truth be presupposed, there is no proof of anything.

- *Christianity is proved as being the very foundation of the concept of proof itself. Therefore, Christians must challenge Muslims by what "**IS WRITTEN**." (2005:15–18)

A Presuppositional Model

For a summary of Dr. Zaka's missiology, let me now quote several passages from *The Truth About Islam: The Noble Qur'an's Teachings in Light of the Holy Bible* (2004), by Zaka and Diane Coleman.

*This book is written on the presuppositional conviction that the One True God reveals Himself and his Truth in the Holy Bible. We are certain, based on many convincing proofs, that the text of the Holy Bible has not been corrupted but is a document we can trust to define biblical Christianity. We therefore rely on it as our standard for evaluating all other philosophical and religious positions so that every thought is made obedient to the Lord Jesus Christ (2 Cor. 10:5), who is Lord of all. (2004:4)

On the next page the authors state: * ". . . we are not seeking to conduct a comparative study between the two faiths. Biblical Christianity and Qur'anic Islam are not equal in terms of doctrine or behavior and are therefore not in that sense comparable." (5)

Further on in the book, the authors add that this model, presuppositional in nature, includes other "common characteristics" as follows:

- Fostering mutual respect between Christian and non-Christian, including careful and attentive listening to one another, taking the initiative to reach out in compassion, and taking the time to form relationships.
- Allowing biblical spiritual insight to anoint the relationship, balancing boldness and sensitivity through the leading of the Holy Spirit.
- *Using the Holy Scriptures as the primary source of gentle instruction and humble appeal, without compromising Truth in order to build bridges, but instead using Truth as the bridge.
- *Presenting Jesus Christ to others in both word and deed and praying continually that his voice and Person may be recognized.
- *Boldly proclaiming him and inviting repentance in his name. (2004:166ff.)

Several pages later, the authors take note of six "barriers to free communication" that must be broken down in order that Christ may be presented to Muslims effectively. I shall simply list them here.

- The Wall of Hatred [hatred of Muslims for Christians and vice versa, harsh treatment and rhetoric]
- The Wall of Distrust [false accusations, fiery debates, uncivilized behavior]
- The Wall of Isolation [not associating with one another]
- The Wall of Misunderstanding [ignorance, rumors about each other]
- The Wall of Miscommunication [false charges and misinformation about each other's book, etc.]
- The Wall of Conversion [entering relationship with each other solely to convert the other] (2004:168ff.)

"To remove these barriers to communication, CWW recommends the following principles."

- Learn to listen to one another and listen to learn about one another.
- Overcome stereotypes and see people clearly.
- Understand and clarify that Western culture is *not* biblical Christianity! [very important]
- Contextualize the message.
- Adapt cross-culturally when biblically permissible.
- Plow and sow for the kingdom.
- Be prepared to discuss the Holy Trinity. It is a main source of misunderstanding and error for Muslims.
- Practice Christian community and genuine brotherly love. (2004:169.)

Next Steps with Interested Contacts

The MBU is the evangelistic tool of choice because of its effectiveness in opening the lines of communication with Muslim affinity groups, but it is just one of several tools. Church Without Walls also uses a variety of traditional methods to minister to Muslims. These include one-on-one conversations, both during the MBU and at other times as well. These often open the door to befriending the Muslim and to helping with his or her needs and cultural adjustments, in the case of immigrants. Such acts of friendship and kindness often lead to opportunities to witness and to one-on-one Bible studies and Qur'an studies, or even small group Bible and Qur'an studies in the home. Coulter has helpful chapters on how these tools may be used effectively to follow up on those contacted through the MBUs (2002:71–100). Also, Dr. Zaka has produced a helpful resource guide for Bible and Qur'an studies concerning three crucial doctrinal subjects.[5] It is through the more intimate contact afforded one on one and in the small group, and the opportunities they provide to demonstrate the love of Christ, that the ministry of the Holy Spirit bears fruit in the heart of Muslims unto salvation.

Muslim-Background Believers—The Discipling Process

Discipling Muslim-Background Believers (MBBs)

Bringing Muslim contacts to a point of faith in Christ is just the first objective. Their faith needs to be strengthened, and they need help in developing an ongoing daily walk with God; this involves a discipling, mentoring process. The work, *Muslims and Christians at the Table*, by McDowell and Zaka (1999), shows how Church Without Walls goes about accomplishing this task. I can only quote parts of it here.

> For most Muslims, coming to faith in Christ is a process. Therefore, it may not always be clear at what point they have made a commitment to following Christ. They will continue to have many questions that need answered about the faith. Don't be quick to tell others about their conversion. Allow new believers to tell their friends when they are ready to do so. A lot of time will need to be invested in discipling new believers. For the most part this should initially be done one-on-one.

> Muslims who make a commitment to Christ need to be discipled in four key areas: doctrine, devotion, ministry and character. Although new converts will have learned some doctrine during the evangelism process, it is important that they become well grounded in the biblical doctrine of God, Christ, the Holy Spirit, man, grace, and the Scriptures. They will still have many Islamic ideas in these areas that need correction. Muslims come from a belief system of good works, which gives them no assurance of salvation. At the beginning of the discipling process, they need to have assurance of their salvation, such as is taught in 1 John. (1999:245f)

The authors then briefly discuss areas where the MBB needs to be discipled. These include "the basic devotional practices of Bible reading,

5. Anees Zaka, *Moslems and Christians: Witnessing without Compromising, A Practical Guide with Qur'anic and Biblical Texts* (Philadelphia: CWW, 2001).

Bible study, Bible memorization, prayer, fellowship," and the like. This leads to matters related to bringing them into the fellowship of a church, equipping them for ministry, and preparing them for spiritual warfare.

*Bringing new Muslim background believers into fellowship with a local church is a key issue in any model. Church Without Walls materials reveal two basic lines of approach for integrating them into the church. These are the integration of the MBB into an existing church (i.e., C1 or C2) or the establishment of an MBB house church (i.e., C3 or C4). I find no evidence, and this is a critical point, that Church Without Walls has ever entertained any thought of raising up C5 churches, that is, "Messianic Muslim" churches, or "Jesus mosques."[6]

*Integration Into Existing Churches

Sometimes, when the MBB has come to the Lord through the ministry of a particular church, or a Christian in that church, after having already been in the country awhile and adapted well to the culture, he or she may decide to become a member of that church. Several such cases are related in *Muslims and Christians at the Table*, including this story of a Muslim lady who was won to Christ by Christian love.

> Amina came to America as an immigrant. A religious lady by nature and family background, she was looking to go to the mosque as usual. She asked one of her countrymen and his wife to give her a ride to the mosque. . . . The husband said he would do so, but he did not do it. Amina felt very strongly that the man and his wife were not true Muslims because they did not keep their word. Since Amina did not drive she went for a walk. The sovereign Lord led her by a church building. Out of curiosity, she knocked on the church door. A Christian woman was in the building and opened the door for her with a big smile. Amina was amazed at that. After she was invited in and befriended, she was invited to attend a Bible study and the Sunday service. She attended both consistently. Then she was put in contact with me [one of the authors]. As I was talking with her on the phone, I introduced her to Christ. She gave her life to the Lord Jesus right then. Later I preached at the service in which I witnessed her water baptism. She is now a member of that church and is trying to reach her sons for Jesus. I asked her why she

6. For clarification on the meaning of these terms, see chapter 7, especially "The EMQ Debate over Islamicized Contextualization."

became a Christian. She responded, "I was touched by the love of the lady who opened the church door for me." (1999:214ff.)

*The Establishment of MBB House Churches

Often, however, integrating new believers of Muslim background into the fellowship of an existing local church is unrealizable. This is because churches in North America are often so Western in culture and insensitive to foreigners that someone newly arrived from the Middle East, Africa, or Asia would not feel at home or comfortable there; likewise, the church members would not know how to relate to them. The warm fellowship that is so important for the spiritual growth of the new believer and the spiritual health of the church does not readily develop and grow in such a situation. It is, no doubt, for this reason that CWW seems to have put more stress on the house church model. McDowell and Zaka conclude their book with a section on house churches. In their last chapter they explain in detail why "house churches need to be planted among Muslim converts."

This would fit the needs and cultural context for most of them. We have discovered eight reasons why house churches are effective among Muslim converts:

1. Before their conversion, the Muslim converts may have belonged to a mosque that met in a home. Therefore, they are familiar with using the home for the worship of God.

2. House churches help new converts feel more comfortable and secure in coming out of Islam. Traditional churches have many things that are foreign to them: pews, art with pictures of people, wearing shoes, crossing one's legs, men and women sitting together, Western dress, organizational structure, and the like. Additionally, many church members may be insensitive to the culture and background of converts from Islam.

3. House churches encourage warm fellowship. This creates a sense of community among new converts that makes up for the loss of the Islamic community and Muslim family members, from whom they are now separated. House churches help new converts to develop new friendships and communities. House churches also provide them with the most encouraging setting for establishing true Christian community. Such community does not exist in Islam.

4. House churches make ideal centers from which converts can reach out to their Muslim friends. A Muslim will be more likely to visit a home than a church building.

5. House churches may be used as centers for training in ministry. They can become a school, a hospital, a factory to train its people to become more educated, healthy and productive.

6. In house churches, new converts discover and practice their gifts as they participate in ministry and a variety of activities, since worship in house churches is led by lay people (i.e. the converts from Islam).

7. A house church made up of former Muslims would probably be quicker to meet members' felt needs than if the new believers were incorporated into existing churches.

8. The house church is the ideal place for the children of converts to grow up in the fear and admonition of the Lord as covenant children.

[The authors then go on to give this remarkable personal testimony of how the CWW ministry led to a house church.] "Our ministry of having Meetings for Better Understanding over a three-year period in a major African-American mosque in a large American city led to thirty-four families leaving the mosque and forming house churches in their homes. It fits the urban setting" (1999:258–60).

The Testimony of CWW Associates from Across the Country

We close with several testimonials from two who have participated in CWW and its MBU ministry for some time. By all accounts, those who have had considerable experience in the MBUs see them as an effective way to reach Muslims. MBUs provide a natural setting for establishing friendly relationships with Muslim communities where they live and work, and facilitate sharing the love of Christ and explaining the gospel in depth.

A leader in a CWW branch in California expresses his appreciation for the approach in the following terms.[7]

In 1993, the Bridge Team and MBU approach was taught to several of us by the CWW. It was an eye opening experience for us. Most of us had studied the more confrontational approaches to reaching people of other religions.

The MBUs lead to discussions privately and in small groups. By respectfully listening to Muslims, we "earned" their trust and their friendship. This gave us a valuable opening to explain how God's word provided the Christian with answers for life. It similarly gave our Muslim friends,

---

7. Extract from an e-mail report sent to Dr. Zaka and forwarded to me. Names and identifying characteristics are omitted.

who came from various countries, an opportunity to answer questions we had about their understanding of Islam. Every opportunity we had with our Muslim friends opened a door for us to know their hearts, ways of thinking and concerns they had in life! Sometimes they asked us to pray for them and their problems involving health, marriage, and employment or immigration paperwork. God gave many gracious answers and blessings. We learned to mourn with those who mourn and to rejoice with those who rejoice.

Personal and family friendships developed, many of them have continued, especially among the women. During Ramadan, the Muslims invited us to the evening breaking of their fast. We were able to have very wonderful spiritual discussions with them during these times. On one of these evenings the Muslim leader read about Paradise from the Qur'an. In response, one of the Christians in our group asked permission to read the last two chapters from the book of Revelation in the Bible about Heaven. The eyes of the Muslims were bright with amazement when they heard about this beautiful and holy place described in the Bible! Often when the Muslims hear the Bible, they are amazed.

We were also invited to sit in and listen to the Friday (Juma) noon sermons that were given in English. These gave good insights as to what Muslims were being taught in their mosques and again provided valuable interaction time. One large mosque had a special time when people from other religions could attend and ask questions about Islam. One of the men in our group has continued to attend these meetings for almost nine years. This provided him with valuable information that he used in writing numerous papers and articles. These writings provided answers to questions that many Christians were looking for in order to especially explain the Bible to Muslims. These papers were also given directly to Muslims. After reading the material, several Muslims were motivated to carefully study the teachings of Jesus in the Gospels. They also encouraged other Muslims to pray the Lord's Prayer, know the commandments of Jesus and study His Sermon on the Mount. The work continues with some drawing closer to Jesus as some others reject and go away. The LORD gives us patience and wisdom to have the privilege to work with Him in this gradual harvest. The CWW and MBU methods were what opened the doors of our hearts and these opened the doors of various mosques to us.

A church in Virginia has formed a CWW section and has been holding MBUs with a number of mosque ommunities. A Bridge Team member from that church writes the following.[8]

> In contrast to the conventional methodology of evangelism, I experienced that more people were transformed outside the customary door-to-door evangelism agenda. Relationships in the normal course of life, such as work associates, friendships, over-the-fence neighbors, or familial relationships all fared better at communicating Jesus Christ with constructive results. . . . Our particular Church perseveringly channels time, energy, and funds to the good work of presenting Christ in word and deed to all that God leads us.

> MBUs are the vehicle we have participated in with Muslims. Muslims we have endeavored to understand during the meetings give us warm feedback ranging from polite smiles and a robust embrace to repressed tears with expressed words of gratitude.

> The meetings provide a quality of freedom to speak what each group deems as truth, no matter what disagreeable or agreeable content may be presented. Debate and dialogue are deemed as ineffectual forms of rationale for our meetings. Interrogation and manipulative questions are unwelcome. Grace and understanding are gratifying and appreciated.

> Our respective groups do have much in common when it comes to moral desires. Condemnation of mutual foes and subjects such as the sensationally motivated news media or the senseless terrorist find an easy path to agreement. Subject matter clarification is a natural exercise and is always on the agenda from both groups.

> Our Christian group does not compromise the commission to share true-truth as revealed in the 66 books of the canon of Scripture. The discussions course the theologically crucial and eternal purposes of the God of the Bible. We are also desirous to understand the specific belief system of the Muslim person that we speak to face-to-face.

> Ultimately, God and His perfect sovereignty has provided us opportunities for those in our Church to believe that He can open doors that once looked impossible to knock on. We go with no other agenda than to be open, honest, and to understand the Muslim person who we speak

8. Extract from another e-mail report sent to Dr. Zaka and forwarded to me. The web site is http://Mbu.faithweb.com.

to corporally or personally. We are open to listen. We are honest and will not detract from the truth we hold so precious. Seeking to understand has opened the door wide for communicating the true-Gospel and opportunities for the Christian to collapse the paradigms of century old stereotypes that have infected the Church and Islam.

The theological topics have guided our efforts to share Biblical doctrine. The social topics have helped clarify how we are living Biblically in this present world-view. The two arenas of topics have helped balance out declaration and deed when it comes to understanding and communicating the belief system of each other. We do not spread seed on rocky soil . . . we go to pluck rocks from the soil so that one day the soil may be prepared for the seed.

As already indicated, even Muslims participants have expressed appreciation for the MBUs. A non-American Muslim at a mosque in the South wrote the following (edited and corrected slightly for publication).[9]

The MBU is an effective method to develop Muslim/Christian relations as well as contribute [to the] common social life of the participants. There are Muslims who want to open up themselves, and deserve understanding. There are Muslims who think that Islam is misunderstood by most Christians. The MBU is a good place for them to express themselves and teach themselves. There are Christians who want to get to know Muslims better, or who [only] knows them second hand. . . . The MBU is a perfect place for them.

The MBU is important . . . also for social interactions between different cultures. Therefore, it contributes [to the] overall health of the society by providing an environment for people to express themselves freely. Free self-expression is a need for individuals as well as for groups. The MBU provides this opportunity in both levels at the same time.

Remember that this was written by a Muslim, and from a Muslim perspective. Of course, at least initially, Muslims are looking for opportunities for *da'wa* ("calling" Christians to embrace Islam), but, at the same time, MBUs offer Christians an excellent opening to communicate the gospel over a period of time.

9. Extracted from an e-mail report of a Bridge Team leader to Dr. Zaka.

Summary and Conclusion

To sum up the CWW/MBU model for Muslim ministry, let me quote two paragraphs found at the close of Dr. Zaka's booklet, *Ten Steps in Witnessing to Muslims*.

> The main idea behind the concept of Meetings for Better Understanding is to encourage face-to-face contact between groups of Muslims and Christians that they may learn from each other. North America affords a tremendous amount of freedom compared to most Muslim countries. May this fact bring us to our knees, to plead with God to preserve our liberty and empower us to obediently proclaim the gospel before that liberty is taken from us.
>
> Church Without Walls has seen God work *mightily* through Meetings for Better Understanding. Through them, Christians and Muslims have built friendships, shared needs and family problems, shared meals, cried together, loaned money to each other, and been drawn close. Through God's grace, the ice has been broken and melted as our relationships with Muslims have become warm and personal. (1998:69)

Let us now return to the question with which I began this appendix: Does Church Without Walls, with its model of Meetings for Better Understanding, fit within the parameters of the betrothal model for the church in Islamic culture, as set forth in part three? In our study of the missiological model of Church Without Walls earlier in this appendix, we quoted Dr. Zaka's writings extensively, marking with an asterix those statements that compare directly with the betrothal model. So let me summarize here in abbreviated form the five basic principles of the betrothal model.

1. The object of mission: to bring Muslims into the kingdom of God through a faith commitment to Christ and train them to be disciples totally committed to Christ who do not remain outwardly Muslim.
2. The theological evaluation of Islam: that Muslims, like all humans, have a knowledge of God intuitively, but Islam leads them to repress and suppress that knowledge, and substitute untruths (Rom. 1 and 2).
3. The cultural/theological starting point: that the Scriptures are the *only* legitimate starting point for contextualization; Islam is *not* a "neutral vehicle," as some suppose.

4. Cross-cultural hermeneutic: that a hermeneutic of analysis is the only valid hermeneutic in the cross-cultural situation; it is not legitimate to "read Christian meanings" into the Qur'an or Islamic cultural forms.
5. The church in Islamic culture: to "betroth" the young church to Christ so that each believer lives in total faith commitment to Christ, relating to Islamic culture in a manner faithful to the gospel.

I think it is clear from all that has preceded that the Church Without Walls/MBU approach described above fits well within the parameters of the betrothal model as described here. Indeed, the missiological model of CWW, as quoted above, covers these principles in much greater detail than I have done, even though in different terms as already noted. I believe it is an excellent example of a betrothal-type application. It is, moreover, interesting to note that it is a Middle Eastern model, not North American model (although it was first used in North America), because its originator is a Middle Easterner.

Having said that, I must immediately add that there are other fine ministries, both in North America and overseas, that fit well within the parameters of the betrothal model, but space and time limitations do not allow me to include them here. In any case, I did not have detailed information about any of them ready at hand. This appendix was added at the request of my friend Anees Zaka, and I already knew Church Without Walls to be an outstanding work.

References Cited (Annotated)

*= pseudonym

'Abboud, Maroun. 1950. *Saqru Lubnaan* ["The Falcon of Lebanon," a biography of Shidyaq qv]. Beirut: Manshuraat Dar al-Makshuf.

'Abdul-Haqq, Abdiyah Akbar. 1980. *Sharing Your Faith with a Muslim*. Minneapolis: Bethany Fellowship.

Abu Yahya.* 1986/1987. "Christian Arabic in Bible Translation: A Problem for Muslim Evangelization." *Seedbed* 1/4 (1986):50–56. See also the "Summary of Responses." *Seedbed* 2/2 (1987):18–23.

'Accad, Fu'ad. 1976. "The Qur'an: A Bridge to Faith." *Missiology* 4/3 (July): 331–42.

_____.[1978]. *Have You Ever Read the Seven Muslim-Christian Principles?* Limassol, Cyprus: Ar-Rabitah.

_____. 1997. *Building Bridges: Christianity and Islam*. Colorado Springs, CO: NavPress.

'Ali, A. Yusuf. 1977. *The Holy Qur'an: Translation and Commentary*. 2nd ed. Indianapolis: American Trust Publications.

Anderson, Gerald H., ed. 1961. *The Theology of the Christian Mission*. New York: McGraw-Hill.

Anderson, John D. C. 1976. "The Missionary Approach to Islam: Christian or 'Cultic'?" *Missiology* 4/3 (July):285–300.

Arberry, Arthur J. 1964. *The Koran Interpreted*. Oxford: Oxford University Press. The only English translation of the Qur'an in rhymed prose.

['Atiyah, Pastor.] 1893. *Sweet First-Fruits*. Translated by Sir William Muir. London: Religious Tract Society.

_____. 1894. *The Beacon of Truth*. Translated by Sir William Muir. London: Religious Tract Society.

_____. 1900. *The Torch of Guidance to the Mystery of Redemption*. Translated by Sir William Muir. London: Religious Tract Society.

Bailey, Kenneth E., and Harvey Staal. 1982. "The Arabic Versions of the Bible: Reflections on Their History and Significance." *Reformed Review* 36:3–11. One of the most complete listings of Arabic versions.

Barkat, Anwar N. 1978. "Church-State Relationships in an Ideological Islamic State," in *Church and State: Opening a New Ecumenical Discussion*, 43–61. Geneva: WCC.

Basetti-Sani, G. 1967. "For a Dialogue Between Muslims and Christians." *MW* 57 (April and July):126–37, 186–96.

_____. 1977. *The Koran in the Light of Christ*. Translated by W. R. Carroll and B. Dauphinee. Chicago: Franciscan Herald Press.

Bavinck, J. H. 1960. *Introduction to the Science of Missions*. Translated by David H. Freeman. Grand Rapids: Baker.

_____. [1966.] *The Church Between Temple and Mosque*. Grand Rapids: Eerdmans.

Benz, Ernest. 1961. "Ideas for a Theology of the History of Religion," in *The Theology of the Christian Mission*, 135–47. Edited by G. H. Anderson. New York: McGraw-Hill.

Betts, Robert B. 1978. *Christians in the Arab East*. Atlanta: John Knox Press.

Bijlefeld, Willem A. 1959. *De Islam Als Na-Christelijke Religie [Islam As A Post-Christian Religion]*. The Hague: Uitjeverij Van Keulen.

_____. 1966. "Recent Theological Evaluation of the Christian-Muslim Encounter: Part II." *IRM* 55 (October):430–41.

_____. 1967. "The Danger of 'Christianizing' Our Partners in Dialogue." *MW* 57 (July):171–77.

Bishop, Eric F. F. 1936. "Do We Want a New Version of the Arabic New Testament?" *MW* 26 (April):153–60.

Blauw, Johannes. 1961. "The Biblical View of Man in His Religion," in *The Theology of the Christian Mission*, 31–41. Edited by G. H. Anderson. New York: McGraw-Hill.

Board of Missionary Preparation. 1916. *The Presentation of Christianity to Muslims*. New York: Foreign Missions Conference of North America.

Boormans, Maurice. 1978. "The Muslim-Christian Dialogue of the Last Ten Years." *Pro Mundi Vita Bulletin* 74 (September-October):1–52.

Booth, Newell S. 1970. "The Historical and the Non-Historical in Islam." *MW* 60 (April):109–22.

Bosch, David J. 1980. *Witness to the World: The Christian Mission in Theological Perspective*. Atlanta: John Knox Press.

Bouquet, A. C. 1961. "Revelation and the Divine Logos," in *The Theology of the Christian Mission*, 183–98. Edited by G. H. Anderson. New York: McGraw-Hill.

Bradnock, Wilfred J. 1953. "On the Use of the Name 'Isa." *BT* 4 (July):102–6.

Brislen, Mike. 1996. "A Model for a Muslim-Culture Church." *Missiology* 24/3 (July):355–67.

B.T. 1967. "Trends in Bible Translation." *The Bible Translator* 18 (October):153.

Buhl, F. 1953. "Muhammad," in *Shorter Encyclopedia of Islam*, 390–405. Edited by H. A. R. Gibb and J. H. Kramers. Ithaca, NY: Cornell University Press.

Campbell, William F. 1986. *The Qur'an and the Bible in the Light of History and Science*. Upper Darby, PA: Middle East Resources.

Carson, D. A. 1985. "The Limits of Dynamic Equivalence in Bible Translation." *Evangelical Review of Theology* 9/3 (July):200–212.

Caspar, Robert. 1978. *Cours de Théologie Musulmane*. 2 vols. Rome: Institut Pontifical d'Etudes Arabes.

Cate, Patrick O. 1974. "Each Other's Scripture: The Muslims' Views of the Bible and the Christians' Views of the Qur'an." Ph.D. dissertation, The Hartford Seminary Foundation.

Christensen, Jens. 1952–1953. *A Practical Approach to Muslims*. Lahore: West Pakistan Christian Council, Committee on Islamics. Reprint ed., Marseille: North Africa Mission, 1977.

Clinton, Bobby. 1975. *Disputed Practices*. Coral Gables, FL: West Indies Mission.

Clowney, Edmund P. 1976. *The Doctrine of the Church*. Biblical and Theological Studies. Edited by Robert L. Reymond. Philadelphia: P&R.

Conn, Harvie. 1977. "Missionary Myths about Islam." *Muslim World Pulse* 6 (September):1–13.

Coulter, Iain T. 2002. *Meetings for Better Understanding: Reaching Muslims for Christ, A Church Without Walls Model*. Philadelphia: Church Without Walls, Inc.

Cragg, Kenneth. 1956. *The Call of the Minaret*. New York: Oxford University Press.

_____. 1957. "Hearing by the Word of God." *IRM* 46 (July):241–51.

_____. 1959. *Sandals at the Mosque*. London: Oxford University Press.

_____. 1964. *The Dome and the Rock*. London: SPCK.

_____. 1968a. *The Privilege of Man*. London: Athlone Press.

_____. 1968b. *Christianity in World Perspective*. London: Lutterworth Press.

_____. 1971. *The Event of the Qur'an*. London: George Allen & Unwin.

_____. 1973. *The Mind of the Qur'an*. London: George Allen & Unwin.

_____. 1977. *The Christian and Other Religion: The Measure of Christ*. London: A. R. Mowbray.

_____. 1979. "Islamic Theology: Limits and Bridges," in *The Gospel and Islam: A 1978 Compendium*, 196–207. Edited by Don M. McCurry. Monrovia, CA: MARC.

Darlow T. H., and H. F. Moule. 1963. *Historical Catalogue of the Printed Editions of Holy Scripture in the Library of the British and Foreign Bible Society*. Reprint ed. 2 vols. New York: Kraus Reprint Corp. Originally published 1903 in London by the BFBS.

de Saussure, Ferdinand. 1966. *Course in General Linguistics*. Edited by C. Bally, A. Sechehaye, and A. Reidlinger. Translated by Wade Baskin. New York: McGraw-Hill. First published in 1959.

Dewick, E. C. 1948. *The Gospel and Other Faiths*. London: Canterbury Press.

_____. 1953. *The Christian Attitude to Other Religions*. Cambridge: Cambridge University Press.

DeWolf, L. Harold. 1961. "The Interpenetration of Christianity and the Non-Christian Religions," in *The Theology of the Christian Mission*, 199–212. Edited by G. H. Anderson. New York: McGraw-Hill.

D. O. 1991. "A Jesus Movement Within Islam." In *Interconnect 5* (January): 12–27.

Doi, Abdur-Rahman. 1979. *Non-Muslims Under Shari'ah [Islamic law]*. Brentwood, MD: International Graphics.

Dorman, Harry G. 1948. *Toward Understanding Islam. Contemporary Apologetic of Islam and Missionary Policy*. New York: Teachers College, Columbia University.

Dretke, James P. 1979. *A Christian Approach to Muslims: Reflections from West Africa*. Pasadena, CA: William Carey Library.

Evangelical Alliance. 1976. *Report of the Conference on Christianity and the World of Islam Today: 6–9 January 1976*. London: The Evangelical Alliance. The papers presented were published in *Missiology* 4/ 3 (July).

Eenigenburg, Don. 1997. "The Pros and Cons of Islamicized Contextualization." *EMQ* 33/3 (July):310–15.

Eerdman, Paul. 1937. "The Arabic Version of the Bible." *MW* 27 (July):218–36. A useful documentation of the debate about the need for a new translation of the Bible in Arabic.

EMQ Debate. *Evangelical Missions Quarterly* 1998, 1999, 2003, 2004.

_____. 1998: 34/4 (October). "Danger: New Directions in Contextualization," Phil Parshall, 404–10.

"The C2 to C6 Spectrum," John Travis,* 407–8.

"Must All Muslims Leave 'Islam' to Follow Jesus?" John Travis,* 411–15.

"Context Is Critical in 'Islampur' Case," Dean Gilliland, 415–17.

_____. 1999: 35/2 (April). "His Ways Are Not Our Ways," Joshua Massey,* 186–97.

"Letters to the Editor," Sam Schlorff and J. Romaine, 394–99.

_____. 2003: 39/2 (April). "A Biblical Look at C5 Muslim Evangelism," Scott Woods, 188–95.

_____. 2004: 40/3 (July). "Lifting the *Fatwa*," Phil Parshall, 288–93.

"Misunderstanding C5: His Ways Are Not Our Orthodoxy," Joshua Massey,* 296–304.

Evangelical Alliance, The. 1976. *Report of the Conference on Christianity and the World of Islam Today: 6–9 January 1976.* London: The Evangelical Alliance. A summary of the conference. The papers presented were published in *Missiology* 4/3 (July).

Fairman, Walter T. 1926. "The Approach to Moslems." *MW* 16 (July):272–76.

Faruqi, Al-, Ismail. 1963. "A Comparison of the Islamic and Christian Approaches to Hebrew Scripture." *Journal of Bible and Religion* 31 (October):283–93.

_____. 1968. "Islam and Christianity: Dialogue or Diatribe?" *Journal of Ecumenical Studies* 5:45–77.

_____. 1976. "On the Nature of Islamic Da'wah." *IRM* 65 (October):391–400.

Fisk, Eric G. n.d. *On the Use of the Name 'Isa.* Beech Grove, England: Author. Privately printed tract.

Foerster, Werner. 1964. "Iésous," in *Theological Dictionary of the New Testament*, 3:284–93. Edited by Gerhard Kittel. Translated by G. W. Bromiley. 10 vols. Grand Rapids: Eerdmans.

Gabriel, Mark.* 2002. *Islam and Terrorism.* Lake Mary, FL: Charisma House.

Gairdner, William H. T. 1915. "Moslem Tradition and the Gospel Record: The Hadith and the Injil." *MW* 5 (October):349–79.

_____. 1919. "Mohammed Without Camouflage: Ecce Homo Arabicus." *MW* 9 (January):25–57.

_____ , and W. A. Eddy. 1928. "Christianity and Islam." In *The Jerusalem Meeting of the International Missionary Council, 1928.* Vol. 1: *The Christian Life and Message in Relation to the Non-Christian Systems*, 191–229. New York: The International Missionary Council.

Gaudeul, Jean-Marie. 1979. "Review of *The Koran in the Light of Christ*, by G. Basetti-Sani." *Islamochristiana* 5:286–89.

Gibb, Hamilton A. R. 1962. *Studies on the Civilization of Islam.* Edited by S. J. Shaw and W. R. Polk. Boston: Beacon.

_____ , and J. H. Kramers, eds. 1953. *Shorter Encyclopedia of Islam*. Ithaca, NY: Cornell University Press. Articles: "*Dhimma*," "*Djizya*," "*Kharadj*," "*Murtadd*," and "*Talak*," 75–76, 91–100, 245, 413, 570 (#7).

Goble, Phil, and Salim Munayer. 1989. *New Creation Book for Muslims*. Pasadena, CA: Mandate Press.

Haddad, Yvonne Y. 1982. *Contemporary Islam and the Challenge of History*. Albany: SUNY Press.

Haleblian, Krikor. 1983. "The Problem of Contextualization." *Missiology* 11/1 (January):95–111.

Hallencreutz, Carl F. 1970. *New Approaches to Men of Other Faiths*. Research Pamphlet no. 18. Geneva: WCC.

Harrison, Paul W. 1934. "The Arabs of Oman." *MW* 24 (July):262ff.

Hayek, Michel. 1962. "L'Origine des Termes 'Isâ-al-Masîh (Jésus Christ) dans le Coran." *Orient Syrien* 7:223–54.

Hesselgrave, David J. and Edward Rommen. 1989. *Contextualization: Meanings, Methods, and Models*. Grand Rapids: Baker.

Hiebert, Paul G. 1987. "Critical Contextualization." *IBMR* 11/1 (January): 104–12.

————. 1989. "Form and Meaning in the Contextualization of the Gospel," in *The Word Among Us: Contextualizing Theology for Mission Today*, 101–20. Edited by Dean S. Gilliland. Dallas: Word.

Horowitz, Joseph. 1925.dd "Jewish Proper Names and Derivatives in the Koran." *Hebrew Union College Annual* 2:145–227.

Hughes, Thomas P. 1979. *Dictionary of Islam*. Reprint ed. Safat, Kuweit: Islamic Book Publishers. Originally published 1885 in London by W. H. Allen & Co.

Ibn Khaldun. 1958. *The Muqaddimah: An Introduction to History*. Bollingen Series no. 43. 3 vols. Translated by Franz Rosenthall. New York: Pantheon.

Imad-ud-din. [1893]. *Mohammedan Converts to Christianity in India*. London: Church Missionary Society.

IRM. 1976. "Consultation on Christian Mission and Islamic Da'wah." *IRM* 65 (October):365–460. Besides the papers presented, it includes the discussion on the papers.

Jadid, Iskander. n.d. *The Infallibility of the Torah and the Gospel*. Basel: Markaz Ash-Shabiba.

Jeffery, Arthur. 1977. *The Foreign Vocabulary of the Qur'an*. Reprint ed. Lahore: Al-Biruni. Originally published 1938.

————. 1952. *The Qur'an as Scripture*. New York: Russell F. Moore Co.

————. 1958. *Islam: Muhammad and His Religion*. New York: Liberal Arts Press.

Jeremias, Joachim. 1967. *Jesus' Promise to the Nations*. Philadelphia: Fortress.

Jessup, H. H. 1910. *Fifty Three Years in Syria*. 2 vols. New York: Fleming H. Revell.

John of Damascus. See John W. Voorhis, 1934 and 1935.

Johnston, Arthur. 1978. *The Battle for World Evangelization*. Wheaton, IL: Tyndale House.

Jones, L. Bevan. 1940. "How Not to Use the Qur'an: An Urdu Tract Examined." *MW* 30 (April):280–91.

————. 1953. "On the Use of the Name 'Isa." *BT* 4 (April):83–86. A summary of the arguments of Isidor Loewenthal (see below).

————. 1932. *The People of the Mosque*. London: SCM Press. Third rev. ed., Calcutta: Baptist Mission Press, 1959.

————. 1964. *Christianity Explained to Muslims*. Calcutta: Baptist Mission Press. Rev. ed. First published in 1937.

Kaiser, Walter C., Jr. 1979. "Legitimate Hermeneutics," in *Inerrancy*, 117–47. Edited by Norman L. Geisler. Grand Rapids: Zondervan.

Kateregga, Badru D., and David Shenk. 1980. *Islam and Christianity: A Muslim and a Christian in Dialogue*. Nairobi: Uzima Press.

Khair Ullah, Frank S. 1976. "Linguistic Hang-Ups in Communicating with Muslims." *Missiology* 4/3 (July):301–16.

Koelle, Sigismund W. 1889. *Mohammed and Mohammedanism Critically Considered*. London: Rivingtons.

Kraemer, Hendrik. 1956. *The Christian Message in a Non-Christian World*. Third ed. Grand Rapids: Kregel. First published in 1938.

————. 1939. "Continuity or Discontinuity." *The Madras Series*. Vol. 1: *The Authority of the Faith*, 1–21. New York: IMC.

————. 1956. *Religion and the Christian Faith*. London: Lutterworth Press.

————. 1960. *World Cultures and World Religions: The Coming Dialogue*. London: Lutterworth Press.

Kraft, Charles. 1974a. "Guidelines for Developing a Message Geared to the Horizon of Receptivity," in *Conference on Media in Islamic Culture*, 17–33. Edited by C. Richard Shumaker. Clearwater, FL: International Christian Broadcasters; Wheaton, IL: Evangelical Literature Overseas.

————. 1974b. "Distinctive Religious Barriers to Outside Penetration," in *Conference on Media in Islamic Culture*, 65–76.

————. 1974c. "Psychological Stress Factors Among Muslims," in *Conference on Media in Islamic Culture*, 137–44.

————. 1979a. "Dynamic Equivalence Churches in Muslim Society," in *The Gospel and Islam: A 1978 Compendium*, 114–28. Edited by Don M. McCurry. Monrovia, CA: MARC.

————. 1979b. *Christianity in Culture*. Maryknoll, NY: Orbis.

Lausanne Committee on World Evangelization. 1978. *The Willowbank Report—Gospel and Culture*. Lausanne Occasional Papers, no. 2. Wheaton, IL: LCWE. Also published as a conclusion in John R. Stott and Robert T. Coote, eds. *Gospel and Culture*. Pasadena, CA: William Carey Library, 1979.

_____. 1980. *Thailand Report—Christian Witness to Muslims*. Lausanne Occasional Papers, no. 13. Wheaton, IL: LCWE.

Layman's Foreign Missions Inquiry. 1932. *Re-Thinking Missions: A Layman's Inquiry after One Hundred Years*. New York: Harper and Brothers.

Lee, Samuel. 1824. *Controversial Tracts on Christianity and Mohammedanism*. Cambridge: J. Smith. Contains a translation of tracts of Henry Martyn and others, and Lee's own approach to Islam.

Levonian, Lootfy. 1928. *Moslem Mentality: A Discussion of the Presentation of Christianity to Moslems*. London: George Allen & Unwin.

_____. 1931. "Fulfilment Not Destruction." *MW* 21 (January):122–25.

Loewenthal, Isidor. 1911. "The Name 'Isa." *MW* 1 (July):267–82.

Madany, Bassam M. 1981. *Sharing God's Word with a Muslim*. Palos Heights, IL: The Back to God Hour.

Marraccio, Ludovico. 1698. *Alcorani Textus Universus*. Patavii: Ex. Typographia Seminarii.

Marsh, Charles R. 1975. *Share Your Faith with a Muslim*. Chicago: Moody Press.

Marshall, I. Howard, ed. 1977. *New Testament Interpretation*. Grand Rapids: Eerdmans.

Massey, Joshua.* 1999. "His Ways Are Not Our Ways." *EMQ* 35/2 (April):188–97.

McCallum, F. W., comp. 1923. *Christian Literature in Moslem Lands*. New York: George H. Doran Co.

McCurry, Don M., ed. 1979. *The Gospel and Islam: A 1978 Compendium*. Monrovia, CA: MARC.

_____, and Carole Glasser. 1980. *Muslim Awareness Seminar* (Looseleaf notebook of printed materials). Pasadena, CA: The Zwemer Institute. (The sections "Things to Know" and "The Relation of Form and Structure to Spirit" are what interest us here.)

McDonald, Duncan B. 1916. "What Christianity May Add to Islam," in *The Presentation of Christianity to Moslems*, 77–89. New York: Board of Missionary Preparation. Reprinted in *MW* 8 (July 1918):340–51.

McDonald, H. D. 1959. *Ideas of Revelation: An Historical Study 1700–1860*. London: Macmillan.

McDowell, Bruce A., and Anees Zaka. 1999. *Muslims and Christians at the Table*. Phillipsburg, NJ: P&R.

Merad, Ali. 1973. "Revelation, Truth, and Obedience," in *Christian-Muslim Dialogue: Papers from Broumana 1972*, 58–72. Edited by S. J. Samartha and J. B. Taylor. Geneva: WCC.

_____. 1975. "Dialogue islamo-chrétien: pour la recherche d'un language commun." *Islamochristiana* 1:2–10.

_____. 1980. "Christ According to the Qur'an." *Encounter* 69 (November): 1–17.

Mingana, A. 1927. "Syriac Influence on the Style of the Kur'an." *Bulletin of the John Rylands Library* 11 (January):77–98.

Moffett, Samuel H. 1987. "Early Asian Christian Approaches to Non-Christian Cultures." *Missiology* 15/4 (October):473–86.

Morey, Robert A. 1994. *The Moon-God Allah in the Archeology of the Middle East*. Newport, PA: Research & Education Foundation.

Muir, Sir William. 1878. *The Coran: Its Composition and Teaching, and the Testimony It Bears to the Holy Scriptures*. London: SPCK.

_____. [1883]. *The Rise and Decline of Islam*. Present Day Tracts no. 14. London: Religious Tract Society.

_____. 1887. *Mahomet and Islam*. London: Religious Tract Society.

_____. 1897. *The Mohammedan Controversy and Other Indian Articles*. Edinburgh: T&T Clark.

_____. 1899. *The Old and New Testaments, Tourat, Zubur, and Gospel; Moslems Invited to See and Read Them*. Edinburgh: T&T Clark. See 'Atiyah and Tisdall for other books translated by Muir.

Mylrea, C. Stanley G. 1913. "Points of Contact or of Contrast." *MW* 3 (October):401–6.

Nicholls, Bruce. 1979a. *Contextualization: A Theology of the Gospel and Culture*. WEF Theological Commission: Outreach and Identity Monograph no. 3. Downers Grove, IL: InterVarsity Press; Exeter: Paternoster.

_____. 1979b. "New Approaches to Muslim Evangelism," in *The Gospel and Islam: A 1978 Compendium*, 155–62. Edited by Don McCurry. Monrovia, CA: MARC.

Nida, Eugene A., and Charles R. Taber. 1969. *The Theory and Practice of Translation*. Leiden: The United Bible Societies and E. J. Brill.

Niebuhr, H. Richard. 1951. *Christ and Culture*. New York: Harper and Row.

Nolin, Kenneth. 1970. "Al-Ustadh al-Haddad: A Review Article." *MW* 60 (April):170–77.

Nowaihi, Al-, Mohamed. 1976. "The Religion of Islam: A Presentation to Christians." *IRM* 55 (April):216–25.

Owen, David. 1987. "Project Sunrise: Principles, Description and Terminology." *Seedbed* 2/4 (1987):50–59.

Padilla, Rene. 1979. "Hermeneutics and Culture: A Theological Perspective," in *Down to Earth*, 63–78. Edited by John R. Stott and Robert T. Coote. Grand Rapids: Eerdmans, 1980.

Parrinder, Geoffrey. 1965. *Jesus in the Qur'an*. London: Faber and Faber.

Parshall, Phil. 1980. *New Paths in Muslim Evangelism: Evangelical Approaches to Contextualization*. Grand Rapids: Baker.

————. 1985. *Beyond the Mosque: Christians Within Muslim Community*. Grand Rapids: Baker.

Pfander, Carl G. 1867. *The Mizan Ul-Haqq: or Balance of Truth*. Translated by R. H. Weakley. London: Church Missionary House.

————. 1910. *The Mizanu'l Haqq (Balance of Truth)*. Translated and revised by William St. Clair Tisdall. London: Religious Tract Society. Reprint ed., Basel: Markaz Ash-Shabiba, n.d.

————. 1912a. *Miftahu'l Asrar (The Key of Mysteries)*. Translated and revised by William St. Clair Tisdall. London: Christian Literature Society for India.

————. 1912b. *Tariqu'l-Hyat (The Path of Life)*. Translated and revised by William St. Clair Tisdall. London: Christian Literature Society for India.

Pickthall, Mohammed Marmaduke. 1953. *The Meaning of the Glorious Koran*. New York: Mentor Books.

Prideaux, Humphrey. 1697. *The True Nature of Imposture Fully Displayed in the Life of Mahomet*. London: William Rogers.

Purdon J. H. 1924. "Our Angle of Approach." *MW* 14 (April):140–42.

Racey, David.* 1996. "Contextualization: How Far Is Too Far?" *EMQ* 32/3 (July):304–9.

Rice, Walter A. 1910. *Crusaders of the Twentieth Century*. London: The Author.

Ridderbos, Herman. 1962. *The Coming of the Kingdom*. Philadelphia: P&R.

Riggs, Henry H., ed. 1938. *Near East Christian Council Inquiry on the Evangelization of Moslems*. Beirut: American Mission Press.

Rommen, Edward, and Harold Netland. 1995. *Christianity and the Religions: A Biblical Theology of World Religions*. Evangelical Missiological Society Series no. 2. Pasadena, CA: William Carey Library.

Rouse, G. H. n.d. *Tracts for Muhammedans*. London: Christian Literature Society.

Rudvin, Arne. 1979. *The Gospel and Islam: What Sort of Dialogue Is Possible?* Rawalpindi: Christian Study Centre. Reprinted from *Almushir* 21/3 and 4.

Saal, William J. 1991. *Reaching Muslims for Christ*. Chicago: Moody Press.

Said, Edward. 1978. *Orientalism*. New York: Pantheon.

Sale, George, trans. 1850. *The Koran: Commonly Called the Alcoran of Mohammed; Translated into English Immediately from the Original Arabic; with*

Explanatory Notes, Taken from the Most Approved Commentators, to Which Is Prefixed a Preliminary Discourse. London: William Tegg & Co.

_____. 1925. *maqaala fi l-islaam* [*Essay on Islam*]. Translated by Hashim al-Araby. Cairo: Nile Mission Press. A translation of the "Preliminary Discourse."

Saliba, Issa A. 1975. "The Bible in Arabic: The Nineteenth-Century Protestant Translation." *MW* 65 (October):254–63.

Samartha, S. J., ed. 1977. *Faith in the Midst of Faiths: Reflections on Dialogue in Community.* Geneva: WCC.

_____, and J. B. Taylor, eds. 1973. *Christian-Muslim Dialogue. Papers Presented at the Broumana Consultation, 12–18 July 1972.* Geneva: WCC.

Schlorff, Sam. 1980. "The Hermeneutical Crisis in Muslim Evangelization." *EMQ* 16 (July):143–51.

_____. 1980. "Theological and Apologetical Dimensions of Muslim Evangelization." *Westminster Theological Journal* 42/2 (Spring):335–66.

_____. 1983. "The Catholic Program for Dialogue with Islam: An Evangelical Evaluation with Special Reference to Contextualization." *Missiology* 11/2 (April):131–48.

_____. 1990. "What Clues Do We Find in the Bible as to God's Perspective on Islam." *Update* 3.

_____. 1993. "Muslim Ideology and Christian Apologetics." *Missiology* 21/2 (April):173–85.

_____. 2000. "The Translational Model for Mission in Resistant Muslim Society." *Missiology* 28/3 (July):305–28.

Scudder, Lewis R., Jr. 1982. " 'We Wish to See Jesus'—Christianity Through Muslim Eyes." *Reformed Review* 36 (Autumn):12–24.

Shahid, Samuel. 1992. *The Right of Non-Muslims in an Islamic State.* Colorado Springs, CO: Al-Nour, n.d. Reprinted from *Reach Out* 5/3 (1992):5–11.

Sharpe, Eric J. 1965. *Not to Destroy but to Fulfill: The Contribution of J. N. Farquhar to Protestant Missionary Thought in India Before 1914.* Uppsala: Swedish Institute of Missionary Research.

Shenk, David. 1993. "Some Thoughts on the Use of the Qur'an in Christian Witness to Muslims." *Seedbed* 8/3 (Third Quarter):43–45.

———. 1994. "Hypocrites Are Dangerous." *Seedbed* 9/1 (First Quarter):16.

Sherif, Faruq. 1985. *A Guide to the Contents of the Qur'an.* London: Ithaca Press.

al-Shidyaq, Faris. *kashfu l-makhba'*, quoted in Maroun 'Abboud, 1950. *Saqru Lubnaan* ["The Falcon of Lebanon," a biography of Shidyaq]. Beirut: Manshuraat Dar al-Makshuf.

Shumaker, C. Richard, ed. 1974. *Conference on Media in Islamic Culture*. Clearwater, FL: International Christian Broadcasters; Wheaton, IL: Evangelical Literature Overseas.

Sidersky, D. 1933. *Les origines des legendes musulmanes dans le Coran et dans les vies des prophetes*. Paris: Librairie Paul Geuthner.

siirat-ul-masiiH bi-lisaan 'araby faSiiH. [*The Life of the Messiah in a Classical Arabic Tongue*.] 1987. Larnaca, Cyprus: Abdo.

Smith, Jay. 1998a. "Courage in Our Convictions," with "Two Other Views," Anonymous and Phil Parshall. *EMQ* 34 (January):28–43.

_____. 1998b. "Reaching Muslims in London: Is It Time to Confront?" *Urban Mission* (March):37–46.

Smith, Wilfred Cantwell. 1957. *Islam in Modern History*. New York: Mentor Books.

Speer, Robert E. 1933. *The Finality of Jesus*. New York: Fleming H. Revell Co.

Spencer, H. 1956. *Islam and the Gospel of God*. Delhi: SPCK.

Stanton, Graham N. 1977. "Presuppositions in New Testament Criticism," in *New Testament Interpretation*, 60–71. Edited by I. Howard Marshall. Grand Rapids: Eerdmans.

Stonehouse, Ned. 1957. *Paul Before the Areopagus, and Other New Testament Studies*. Grand Rapids: Eerdmans.

Stott, John R., and Robert T. Coote, eds. 1979. *Gospel and Culture*. Pasadena, CA: William Carey Library. Abridged and published as *Down to Earth: Studies in Christianity and Culture*. Grand Rapids: Eerdmans, 1980.

Taylor, Mike. 2005. "Meetings for Better Understanding." *Evangelicals Now* (an online journal), January: http://www.e-n.org.uk/2005–01/2914-Meetings-for-better-understanding.htm.

Thiselton, Anthony C. 1977a. "Semantics and New Testament Interpretation," in *New Testament Interpretation*, 75–104. Edited by I. Howard Marshall. Grand Rapids: Eerdmans.

_____. 1977b. "Understanding God's Word Today," in *Obeying Christ in a Changing World*. Vol. 1: *The Lord Christ*, 90–122. Edited by John Stott. Cleveland: Fountain Books.

Thomas, Kenneth J. 1989. "The Use of Arabic Terminology in Biblical Translation." *The Bible Translator* 40/1 (January):101–8.

Thompson, John A. 1956. *The Major Arabic Bibles: Their Origin and Nature*. New York: American Bible Society. Reprinted from *BT* 6 (January, April, July, October 1955):2–12, 51–55, 98–106, 146–50.

Tibawi, A. L. 1963. "English-Speaking Orientalists: A Critique of Their Approach to Islam and Arab Nationalism." *MW* 53 (July and October):185–204, 299–313.

_____. 1966. *American Interests in Syria—1800–1901*. Oxford: Clarendon Press.

Tisdall, William St. Clair. 1895. *The Religion of the Crescent*. London: SPCK.

_____. 1904. *A Manual of the Leading Muhammedan Objections to Christianity*. London: SPCK. Reprint ed., *Christian Reply to Muslim Objections*, Villach, Austria: Light of Life, 1980.

_____. 1905. *The Original Sources of the Qur'an*. London: SPCK. A scholarly study of the question. The following title is a polemical work on the question, addressed to Muslims.

_____. 1910. *The Sources of Islam: A Persian Treatise*. Translated by Sir William Muir. Edinburgh: T&T Clark. Reprint ed., Birmingham: Birmingham Bible Institute Press, n.d. See Pfander for other works translated and revised by Tisdall.

Uddin, Rafique. 1989. "Contextualized Worship and Witness," in *Muslims and Christians on the Emmaus Road*, 267–72. Edited by J. Dudley Woodberry. Monrovia, CA: MARC.

Upson, A. T. 1913. "Arabic Christian Literature Since the Lucknow Conference." *MW* 3 (October):416–20.

_____ n.d. [as Abd Al-Fadi]. *Sin and Atonement in Islam and Christianity*. Beirut: Markaz Ash-Shabiba.

_____. n.d. *The Person of Christ in the Gospel and the Qur'an*. Reprint ed., Basel: Markaz Ash-Shabiba.

_____. n.d. *majmuu'ah 'ashri khuTab: al-majmuu'atu l 'uula wal-thaaniyah* [*Collection of Ten Sermons: Collections 1 and 2*]. Cairo: Nile Mission Press.

Van Dyck, Cornelius V. A. 1891. "Arabic Versions," in *The Encyclopedia of Missions*, 1:91–93. Edited by Edwin M. Bliss. 2 vols. New York: Funk & Wagnalls.

Vander Werff, Lyle. 1977. *Christian Mission to Muslims: The Record*. Pasadena, CA: William Carey Library.

Verkuyl, J. 1978. *Contemporary Missiology: An Introduction*. Translated by Dale Cooper. Grand Rapids: Eerdmans.

The Vital Forces of Islam and Christianity. 1915. Edinburgh: Oliphant, Anderson & Ferrier.

Von Allmen, Daniel. 1975. "The Birth of Theology." *IRM* 64 (January):37–52.

Voorhis, John W. 1934. "John of Damascus on the Moslem Heresy." *MW* 24 (October):391–98.

_____. 1935. "The Discussion of a Christian and a Saracen, by John of Damascus." *MW* 25 (July):266–73.

Watt, W. Montgomery. 1967. "The Christianity Criticized in the Qur'an." *MW* 57 (July):197–201.

_____. 1970. *Bell's Introduction to the Qur'an: Revised and Enlarged.* Islamic Series no 8. Edinburgh: Edinburgh University Press.

Weil, Gustav. 1878. *Historische-Kritische Einleitung in Den Koran.* Beilefeld and Leipzig: Zweite verbesserte Auflage.

Wherry, Elwood M. 1905. *The Muslim Controversy.* London: Christian Literature Society.

_____. 1907. *Islam and Christianity in India and the Far East.* New York: Fleming H. Revell.

_____. 1910. *Islam Refuted on its Own Ground.* London, Madras, and Colombo: Christian Literature Society for India.

Wilder, John W. 1977. "Some Reflections on Possibilities for People Movements among Muslims." *Missiology* 5/3 (July):301–20.

Wilson, J. Christy, Sr. 1950. *The Christian Message to Islam.* New York: Fleming H. Revell.

Woodberry, J. Dudley, ed. 1989a. *Muslims and Christians on the Emmaus Road.* Monrovia, CA: MARC. A compendium of papers from the Zeist conference, sponsored by the LCWE, in July 1987.

_____. 1989b. "Contextualization Among Muslims: Reusing Common Pillars," in *The Word Among Us: Contextualizing Theology for Mission Today,* 282–312. Edited by Dean S. Gilliland. Dallas: Word.

WCC. 1976. "Christian Mission and Islamic Da'wah." *IRM* 65 (October). Special issue containing the papers, edited discussion, and final statement of the Chambesy Conference, June 1976.

_____. 1977. *Christians Meeting Muslims: WCC Papers on Ten Years of Christian-Muslim Dialogue.* Geneva: WCC.

_____. 1979. *Guidelines on Dialogue with People of Living Faiths and Ideologies.* Geneva: WCC.

_____. 1981. *Christian Presence and Witness in Relation to Muslim Neighbors.* A Conference, Mombasa, Kenya, 1979. Geneva: WCC.

WMC. 1910. *The World Missionary Conference, 1910.* Vol. 4: *Report of Commission IV: The Missionary Message In Relation to the Non-Christian Religions.* Edinburgh and London: Oliphant, Anderson & Ferrier; New York: Fleming H. Revell.

Youssef, Michael. 1980. *Making Christ Known to Muslims.* Atlanta: Haggai Institute.

Zaka, Anees. 1998. *Ten Steps in Witnessing to Muslims.* Philadelphia: Church Without Walls.

_____. 2001. *Moslems and Christians: A Practical Guide with Qur'anic and Biblical Texts.* 2nd ed. Philadelphia: CWW/BIIS.

_____. n.d. *Biblical Institute for Islamic Studies (BIIS) Handbook*. Philadelphia: CWW.

_____ , and Bruce A. McDowell. 1999. *Muslims and Christians at the Table: Promoting Biblical Understanding among North American Muslims*. Phillipsburg, NJ: P&R.

_____ , and Diane Coleman. 2004. *The Noble Qur'an's Teachings in Light of the Holy Bible*. Phillipsburg, NJ: P&R.

_____ , and Alfred A. Z. Siha. 2004. *Explaining the Biblical Faith: The Westminster Shorter Catechism Written for Muslims with Scripture Proofs*. Philadelphia: CWW.

_____ , and Alfred A. Z. Siha. 2005. *It Is Written! The Use of Cornelius Van Til's Biblical Apologetics for Doing Missions among Muslims*. Philadelphia: CWW.

Zwemer, Samuel M. 1905. *The Moslem Doctrine of God*. New York: American Tract Society. Reprint ed., Gerrards Cross, England: WEC Press, n.d.

_____. 1911. Preface to "The Name 'Isa."_*MW* 1 (July):265.

_____. 1912. *The Moslem Christ*. London: Oliphants.

_____. 1916. *The Disintegration of Islam*. New York: Fleming H. Revell.

_____. 1941. *The Cross above the Crescent*. Grand Rapids: Zondervan.

Index

Index

"Mohammedan Controversy", 4
Moslem World / Muslim World (Journal), 8-10
Muir, Sir William, 4-6, 51, 52, 55, 66-67
The Testimony Borne by the Coran to the Jewish and Christian Scriptures, 66-67

Near East Christian Council, *Inquiry on the Evangelization of Moslems*, 79-80
Newcastle Bible of 1811, 42
New Hermeneutic, 72-78
  Comparison with proof-text method, 76-78
  Development of, 74-78
  Two-Way Synthesis, 126-27
Nicholls, Bruce, 126, 134, 135
Nida, Eugene & Taber, Charles, *The Theory and Practice of Translation*, 140
North American Conference on Muslim Evangelization, 24, 81, 84

Paradigm shifts, xix
Parrinder, Geoffrey, 74-75
  Jesus in the Qur'an, 74
Parshall, Phil, 57, 82-83, 84, 86, 88, 122, 145, 157
  Beyond the Mosque, 84
  "Danger: New directions in contextualization", 86
  "Lifting the Fatwa", 87
  New Paths in Muslim Evangelism, 84
Persian language, 32
Pfander, Karl Gottlieb, 50, 51, 57, 67, 104, 105
Pickthall, 34
Prideaux, Humphrey, 4

Proof-texts interpreted to support Christianity, 61-66
  compared to new hermeneutic, 76-78
  crucifixion of Christ, 64-65
  deity of Christ, 63-64
  divine authority of Scripture, 61-63
  historical development of, 66-71
  rejection and return of, 70-71
  truths of sin and salvation, 65-66

Rice, Walter A., 69-70
  Crusaders of the Twentieth Century, 69
Rouse, G. H., 51, 52
Rudvin, Arne, 52

Sabat, Nathaniel, 42
Sale, George, 3-6
Schlorff, Samuel P., 148
Shahid, Samuel, 45
Shari'ah (Law of God), 102, 114, 143, 144
Shenk, David, 145-46, 154
Shorrosh, Anis, 57
Siirat-ul-MasiiH, 45-46, 47, 48
Smith, Eli, 42
Smith, Jay, 57, 60
Smith-Van Dyck Version, 42-44, 48
  Revised Smith-Van Dyck Version, 44
Society for Promoting Christian Knowledge, 42
Speer, Robert E., 106, 107
Stonehouse, Ned, 121

Tambaram Conference, 8, 17, 105
Taylor, Mike, 167
Theology of religions, 104-14
  biblical approach, 108-13

biblical perspective on Islam, 113-14
  search for a criterion, 104-08
  "Christian revelation" as criterion, 106
  Christianity as criterion, 104-05
  "essence of religion" as criterion, 105-06
  Person of Christ as criterion, 106-07
Thiselton, Anthony, 128
Thomas, Kenneth, 155
Thompson, John A., 42
Tisdall, William St. Clair, 6-7, 40, 51, 56, 68-69, 72, 104
  Manual of the Leading Muhammedan Objections to Christianity, 68
Today's Arabic Version / Good News Arabic Version (TAV/GNA), 47
Travis, John, 87
  "The C1 to C6 Sprectrum", 87

Ud-din, Imad, 6
Ud-din, Rafique, 88
Ummah (idealized Muslim community), 97
Upson, A. T., ('Abd al-Fadi), 73
Urdu language 32

Vander Werff, Lyle, 74
Van Dyck, Cornelius, 42
Van Til, Cornelius, 166
Verkuyl, Johannes, 98

Watt, Montgomery, 126
Weil, Gustav, 4-6, 70
Wilder, John, 80-81, 88
  "Some Reflections on Possibilities for People Movements Among Muslims", 80-81
Wilson, Christy Sr., 13, 70
Woods, Scott, 87

Index

"A Biblical Look at C5 Evangelism", 87
World Evangelical Fellowship, 24
World Missionary Conference—Edinburgh 1910, 7-8, 94
Report of Commission IV, 8
Youssef, Michael, 26

Zaka, Anees, 163-166, 170, 173, 175, 177, 178, 180, 181, 182, 183
It is Written! The Use of Cornelius Van Til's Bibilical Apologetics for Doing Mission among Muslims, 170ff
Muslims and Christians at the Table, 175ff

Ten Steps in Witnessing to Muslims, 182
The Truth about Islam: The Noble Qur'an's Teachings in Light of the Holy Bible, 173
Zeist conference, 88
Zwemer, Samuel, 6-7, 8, 36n, 73, 74, 106, 107

Sam Schlorff (B.A., Wheaton College; M.Div., Fuller Theological Seminary; Th.M., Westminster Theological Seminary) is a retired missionary of Arab World Ministries (formerly North Africa Mission) with 36 years of active service in North Africa, France, and the U.S.—from 1959 to1995. He is married to the former Frederica Hauner, and has two adult children. He served as AWM Missiologist from 1978 to 1995.

Sam also served in the U.S. Army during the Korean conflict and also earned two Arabic certificates from the University of Paris, France. His published works include: *Discipleship in Islamic Society* (NAM 1981); and *Understanding the Muslim Mindset: Questions About Islam* (AWM 1995—a collection of articles originally published in AWM's Quarterly *Update),* as well as articles, mainly on contextualization, published in *Evangelical Missions Quarterly* and *Missiology.* He has also written some unpublished works for the use of AWM.